Getting It Done

Getting It Done
A Memoir

DEREK H. BURNEY

Derek Burney

McGILL-QUEEN'S UNIVERSITY PRESS   Montreal & Kingston · London · Ithaca

ISBN 0-7735-2926-8

Legal deposit second quarter 2005
Bibliothèque nationale du Québec

Printed in Canada on acid-free paper.

McGill-Queen's University Press acknowledges the support of the
Canada Council for the Arts for our publishing program. We also
acknowledge the financial support of the Government of Canada
through the Book Publishing Industry Development Program
(BPIDP) for our publishing activities.

Library and Archives Canada Cataloguing in Publication

Burney, Derek H. (Derek Hudson), 1939–
Getting it done : a memoir / Derek H. Burney.

Includes index.
ISBN 0-7735-2926-8

1. Burney, Derek H. (Derek Hudson), 1939– 2. Ambassadors–
Canada–Biography. 3. Diplomats–Canada–Biography. 4. Canada–
Foreign relations–20th century. I. Title.

FC631.B87A3 2005   327.71'0092   C2005-900659-5

Design and typesetting by studio oneonone in Adobe Garamond 11/13

Contents

Foreword
The Honourable John Crosbie

At a time when pundits lament the declining role and growing irrelevance of Canada in world affairs, this memoir from the inside by Derek H. Burney, which runs from the end of the Pearson "golden era" in Canadian diplomacy through the Mulroney decade, offers particularly valuable, timely, and useful insights. *Getting It Done* describes Burney's experiences and impressions from a colourful thirty-year career in Canada's foreign service, a career that began with his appointment in 1965 as third secretary at one of the country's smallest overseas missions, New Zealand, and culminated in the ambassadorship in Washington between 1989 and 1993, a posting he describes as "the best job in the Canadian foreign service." Along the way, Burney served in Tokyo, held various positions at External Affairs in Ottawa, was ambassador to Korea, and acted as chief of staff to Prime Minister Brian Mulroney in 1987–88, including the "free trade election" of 1988. In the course of his career with External Affairs, he also served as personal representative of the prime minister at the G7 Summits of 1990, 1991, and 1992. Burney was awarded the Public Service of Canada's Outstanding Achievement Award in 1992 and named an officer of the Order of Canada the following year. He is currently an adjunct professor and senior distinguished fellow at Carleton University.

Derek Burney was not only one of our most effective trade negotiators and ambassadors but a brilliant chief of staff in the Mulroney PMO, which under his leadership functioned in a well-organized, disciplined, and creative way, with the staff and ministers and their staffs all working together toward common objectives. He was a no-nonsense type who knew how to delegate authority and how to respond when people did not measure up. Burney did not play power games or flatter. His role in the successful conclusion of the US-Canada free trade negotiations, on behalf of the prime minister and in support of ministers Michael Wilson and Pat Carney and chief negotiator Simon Riesman, was vital when all seemed lost. He was also invaluable during the 1988 election campaign in briefing the prime minister and the campaign managers about the FTA.

Burney's experiences as chief of staff to Brian Mulroney and subsequently as ambassador in Washington are at the heart of this memoir, as are his observations about the free trade negotiations and management of Canada's relations with the United States. He gives particular emphasis to the choices Canada faces in dealing with this often vexing but most important relationship, which range from complacency to engagement, from annoyance to influence. Certainly, Burney made a difference in both Ottawa and Washington and was one of Canada's most influential ambassadors to the United States since the end of World War II. If lessons are to be drawn from experience, then his should be relevant to those facing similar challenges today.

Burney points out that our proximity to the United States gives us both a huge market for our goods and services and a security blanket. We have thus achieved two fundamental goals of foreign policy without much effort or direction from our own government in the last decade. He argues that we have to engage the Americans systematically and at times forcibly to ensure that our vital interests are not adversely affected and that our views are known. If we do not manage our most important relationship properly, we are unlikely to gain much respect or influence in the world at large. On the issue of ballistic missiles, Burney has noted that we have a choice, since we can continue to participate as a partner in North American defence or we can stand down on principle. Either way, our government should exercise the courage of its convictions and take its responsibility as the ultimate guarantor of security for Canadians. He concludes there is no honour in procrastination.

Lester Pearson once noted that "politics is a skilled use of blunt objects," and Burney was a blunt, talented, and skilful agent on behalf of Canada not only in foreign affairs but in public administration at home. He could and did get things done. His book is a celebration of public service and a must-read for students of government. This is an outstanding contribution to the story of Canadian public affairs from 1960 on. It provides opinions on all the issues we faced then and now in our relationship with the rest of the world by one of our best and brightest. A lively and authentic Canadian autobiography!

Preface

Public service is little understood outside Ottawa and not always appreciated even in the nation's capital. I have often been asked how it was possible for someone from the public sector to move successfully to the private sphere. The question implies a certain ignorance about the nature of each. The objective in government is fundamentally to preserve and promote the national interest on behalf of citizens. In the private sector, or at least in managing a public or widely held company, the goal is to enhance shareholder value. The ends are different, but in many respects, the means are similar. Skills of analysis, communication, management, and motivation are vital in either enterprise. The dual experience – public and private – is rare, even though the qualities for success tend to be the same. Knowing what is needed or expected is a common prerequisite. Getting it done or meeting expectations requires a plan, and the skill and the motivation to execute it, in either sector.

Crisis management was, for me at least, more acute in the public sector (especially during my assignment in the Prime Minister's Office) than in the private. That is not to suggest it was absent in the latter. Rather, the scope for a crisis is more contained, hence more containable, in the private sector. In government, especially with issues or events involving the prime minister, the potential for the unexpected is limitless and therefore much more difficult to contain. Issues are much less predictable, can emerge with no warning whatsoever, and can last as long as the current mood dictates.

The primary difference between the two experiences is that the private sector is more private and, in some ways, less collegial. The foreign service is a career path, and while internal competition abounds, there is some sense of family, fuelled by assignments outside Canada, where individuals are drawn together during and after office hours. In the private sector there is, by comparison, less need and less inclination to "come together" after work. And at work there is also much less need for consultation, informally or formally. So the links tend to be more functional than personal.

Another difference is that in the public sector, particularly during my last ten years, I was more often on the defence than the offence – daily at the Prime Minister's Office and later mainly because of free trade. I often acted on the theory that the best defence was a good offence. In the private sector, I had the relative luxury of contemplating and executing an offence, notably in terms of a growth strategy at both BCI and CAE, but the market environment for each business also required periods of strenuous defence.

The bureaucracy in government is indeed more bureaucratic, involving much more analysis, more paper, more meetings, more attempts at consensus in shaping decisions, and less focus on "bottomline" considerations. Private sector decision-making is analytical but can also be more instinctual, less consensus-driven, and inspired by profitability considerations. Hierarchies operate in both, and their style or significance depends ultimately on the personalities involved rather than the structure. I have known vice-presidents in companies who would take calls only from their peers, much like assistant deputy ministers with similar habits.

There is, of course, no bottom line in government, and that is a major difference affecting behaviour and performance. Government departments do have budgets, and personnel are measured, to some extent, by their performance against budget. But the profit motive (and incentive) does not exist, and as the auditor general regularly points out, accountability in the public sector can be elusive. Public servants do manage programs and people, and the size of each can dwarf comparables in the private sector. Because it is virtually impossible to dismiss public servants for poor performance and because of politically correct attitudes and public service union militancy, the management and motivation challenges can actually be greater or more taxing in government.

This is a highly personal, hence subjective, account of my public service career, intended in part to disprove some myths about the value of public service. If there is an underlying theme, it is that serving the national interest – whether it was organizing Canada's first G7 Summit, concluding the free trade negotiations, or representing Canada in Washington – was the driving force for much of my public service career. Ronald Reagan once quipped that, while it was true that hard work never killed anyone, he figured, why take the chance? I had the privilege of taking many chances in my public service in a career more varied than most. This memoir attempts to capture the essence of each assignment.

It is dedicated to my wife, Joan, my life partner, who stood with me throughout, raised our family of four boys – Derek junior, Ian, Alex, and Jeff – and made her own unique contribution to every step of my career.

Getting It Done

ONE

Early Days: Lasting Influences

When you are born in a place called Fort William, Ontario, some challenges come with the location. For one thing, the mandarins at Queen's Park decided later on to merge the place with its "sister" city, Port Arthur, under a new name, Thunder Bay, ostensibly for reasons of synergy. When I served in Washington, Americans were puzzled by either name, and when they were informed that my home was about two hundred miles north of Duluth, their puzzlement deepened. "There is nothing two hundred miles north of Duluth" was a typical reaction.

In fact, while Thunder Bay is on the north shore of Lake Superior and roughly eight hundred kilometres east or west of the closest Canadian city, it is only eighty kilometres from the Minnesota border.* This fact of geography prompted some to opine that it had undoubtedly caused me – and presumably others born in Thunder Bay – to be closer in spirit, if not attitude, to the Americans.† Comments like that would certainly surprise many of my fellow citizens in the northwest pocket of Ontario. We were raised to be wary of anything emanating from Toronto, an attitude, I learned later, we shared with most Canadians, but we rarely spent time thinking about Americans. Duluth was a good place to shop when our dollar had value. Minneapolis five hundred kilometres south, had a stronger pull because it was much bigger in every respect. But growing up was closely confined to family and the community in Fort William. Even our twin city, Port Arthur, was relatively unknown terrain.

* The reason is straightforward enough. Prior to the American Revolution, the major North West Company's fur-trade post in this part of North America was in Grand Portage. When the boundaries were drawn after the Revolutionary War, Grand Portage fell on the newly American side, and the North West Company moved its operations to what became Fort William.

† See, in particular, Lawrence Martin's book *Pledge of Allegiance: The Americanization of Canada in the Mulroney Years* (Toronto: McClelland and Stewart, 1993).

My father died when I was eleven, and my mother, Annie, became, unexpectedly, the proprietor of our family business, a taxi and limousine operation combined with a service station and, very briefly, a Studebaker franchise. A bookkeeper by training, she ran the business initially with my much older half-brother, Jack. When he moved to California in 1953, my mother became the sole proprietor. The taxi business meant long days, holidays included. Christmas Eve and Christmas Day, New Year's Eve and New Year's Day were times when all in the family worked. We celebrated later.

I began as a gas-pump jockey and taxi dispatcher when I was thirteen, graduated to taxi and limo driver when I turned eighteen, and supported my mother throughout my years at high school and university. Even when I had a separate summer job each year – starting as a bellhop (low pay, good tips) and moving to the Great Lakes Paper Mill (very good pay at $3 per hour in 1956) and, for my university years, as a sampler and assistant inspector for the Grain Commission (government job; reasonable pay for not too much work) – I always found time to revert part-time to the family business. As my mother would say, "It gets in your bones."

Despite her full-time business activity (ten to twelve hours daily on average), my mother was the most powerful influence on my early life. The daughter of Roderick and Isabelle MacKay, she had immigrated to Canada from Scotland in 1918 at twelve and spoke fluent Gaelic, especially when she did not want me to know what was being said. She claimed that my name was a derivative of her father's. He had served in the Royal Navy and had also worked as a millwright in South Africa. My mother was born in Durban but moved to Scotland, near Stornoway on the island of Lewis, when she was three. My grandfather – Roddy, as he was known – emigrated to Canada in 1916 and was employed at Paterson Elevator in Fort William. He sent for his family a few years later. When I asked my mother why he had chosen Fort William, she said simply "Because he got a job there."

By all reports, my mother was an excellent student, but her father apparently saw little value in girls obtaining an advanced education. So after grade ten, Annie became a bookkeeper and went to work. She resented not having had the opportunity for more education and emphasized the importance of education to me time and again. She was also emphatic about work habits – "If you are going to do anything, do it well" – and generally had high expectations. A report card indicating 98 per cent in math, for example, inevitably elicited the question "And where did you lose the 2 marks?" I learned, by osmosis, the Scottish (or Hebridian) flair for speaking and acting directly, and for using sarcasm as a means of levelling dialogue.

My father's first wife had died in 1920, leaving him to raise his first two sons, Jack and Bob, who were close in age to my mother. My paternal grandfather, John Burney, had been killed in a mine disaster in Westville, Nova Scotia, at the turn of the century. This misfortune had prompted my father, George, the eldest of six children, to terminate his mining career and move his mother and siblings to Fort William. I never did learn why. After a stint at the elevators, he launched into the taxi business. He also had a political flair and served as an alderman in Fort William during the late 1940s until his death in 1951. He and a few civic colleagues were instrumental in getting the Fort William Gardens built that year.

My sister, Georaine, nine years older, had gone to teacher's college and become a kindergarten teacher, but she died tragically of leukemia at the age of thirty-six. My mother was determined that I would attend university. She thought that I should become a lawyer, and so did I for a while, but mostly she wanted me to "do well at whatever you do."

"Annie B" had a real thing for English grammar. She would correct anyone, anywhere, who failed to recognize that "the verb 'to be' never, never takes an object," including many puzzled taxi drivers in her employ. You could feel her wince when grammatical errors emerged, and you never wanted to be the focus of an "Annie Burney glare" if you had done something wrong. Her younger sister, Catherine, was even more formidable. Standing six feet tall, she had a penetrating glare that came from a higher level. In a man's world, Catherine was the assistant manager of the major hotel in Fort William. The manager was always a male, but everyone knew who was really in charge.

Growing up in Fort William, I played virtually all team sports – hockey, football, basketball, and baseball – but my favourite was hockey. When I graduated from peewee to bantam hockey at age twelve, I actually signed a card with the Montreal Canadiens and entered their then-extensive farm system. For this, I received a satin jacket and a pair of skates! A big deal in those days, but that is how things were done. The twin cities of Fort William and Port Arthur supported four Junior A teams at the time, each sponsored by one of the original six in the National Hockey League. Junior A was then the premiere "under twenty" league. Obviously, at age twelve, I had visions of NHL stardom very much in mind, but when, at age seventeen, I was given a tryout with the

Fort William junior Canadiens, my mother said, "No way," and she had a legitimate point. It was almost impossible to combine hockey at that level with grades twelve and thirteen. In any event, football had already damaged my left shoulder (several dislocations), so I stayed "in the minors" in hockey and concentrated more on attaining higher grades at school. I was also elected school president in my final high school year and was active, as well, in drama. So I was not short on diversions. Nonetheless, my interest in hockey prevails to this day.

Next on the list of major influences was a first-class high school history teacher, Dr Elizabeth Arthur, who was also the driving force behind Fort William Collegiate's annual theatrical productions. She was a terrific teacher who made history, especially modern history, come alive in the classroom, and I was easily hooked. My theatrical debut was in a production of Agatha Christie's *Ten Little Indians*, followed by *Pygmalion* and, in my final year, the lead role in James Barrie's *The Admirable Crichton*. (Twenty years later, our son Derek had the same role at Seoul Foreign School.) Miss Arthur also had a penchant for "doing things well," and she stimulated more of the same from many of her students.

At Queen's University* I was fortunate to receive similar inspiration and guidance from Dr. John Meisel, a political scientist in name but Canada's leading psephologist in practice. His classes – sociology and political science – were refreshing contrasts to the torpor induced by most university lectures. His inclination was to provoke new thinking, and as my MA thesis adviser and the one who suggested a foreign service career, he provided that, and then some, for me.

Apart from my studies at Queen's, I was active in drama (the Queen's Drama Guild, where I "starred" as Willy Loman in *Death of a Salesman* and won a $50 bursary for the effort) in student politics, first as president of my class, Arts '62 and then on the Alma Mater Society, and in campus politics and model parliaments as a young PC. This orientation may have been hereditary as my father had been a staunch Conservative. My mother, I suspected, voted Liberal primarily because Fort William's member of Parliament, the Reverend Dan MacIvor, was Scottish and Liberal and had conducted her wedding service!

---

* I chose Queen's in part because several high school friends were already there or planned to go, including my closest friend from those years, Jim Morris, with whom I shared accommodation for the first three years. It was also the university recommended by several of our High School teachers. The twin cities (Fort William and Port Arthur) had more than one hundred students at Queen's at that time ranking below only Toronto and Ottawa in total numbers.

As part of our MA studies, the students in John Meisel's class were assigned to cover each candidate running in Kingston during the 1963 election. Some of us became much more involved than others. For David Allin and me, our assignment to the PC campaign of J. Earle MacEwen took on much more than observation. MacEwen was the reeve of Kingston Township but had little in the way of organizational support in the city. Allin and I filled the vacuum, prepared his speeches, planned and implemented most of his newspaper and television advertisements, and organized many of his events, including one at Queen's. MacEwen had trouble with the word "economics" in a speech that had been prepared, and so the term was quickly amended to "business," which he fully understood. We became very involved in his campaign and, as a result, knew precisely what was spent. As a rule of thumb, we simply matched the Liberal incumbent, Edgar Bensen, ad for ad, TV spot for TV spot. When the election was over, we also declared the exact amount publicly, as we expected others to do. Much to our surprise, that was not the way for all in Kingston. In fact, the Liberals claimed expenses of about one-quarter the amount that we had reported for the PC campaign. Since 90 per cent of election expenses were for advertising, we knew that there was something fishy about the Liberal declaration. When the newly re-elected Edgar Bensen came to speak to our class (he had been a professor at Queen's), I could not resist asking why he had found it necessary to understate the amount spent by the Liberals. I remember his glare more than his response at that time, and when we met again years later at a reception in Tokyo, I saw a glint of that same glare! (MacEwen lost, but only by about 5,000 votes.)

The discipline and sense of achievement that came from completing my MA thesis during my first year at External Affairs was probably the most valuable experience of my university years. Not only did it give me more direct, personal association with one of Canada's leading scholars, but it proved to be an experience that stimulated a results-oriented discipline or "getting it done" approach to life more generally.

When I was growing up in Fort William, "foreign affairs" involved a date in Port Arthur! Eventually, I married a Port Arthur girl, although we actually met in Kingston. One summer day in 1961, when I was driving taxi, I received a call to pick up a passenger in Port Arthur who had requested me personally. The passenger turned out to be a fellow Queen's student, Joan Peden, whose Model A Ford had been immobilized because some lout had put sand in the gas tank, leaving her stranded. She also had no money for the taxi fare, which is what prompted the "personal" request. The taxi trip to her home in Port Arthur was illegal as well. Cabs from Fort William were proscribed from picking passengers up in Port Arthur for trips within that city. When I pointed this out, she simply smiled. It was a smile I would get to know all too well.

Shortly after, Joan called requesting another favour. She asked if I would accompany her to a Children's Aid square dance at Kakabeka Falls, primarily so she could decline a date to the same event from her boss at the Children's Aid, about whom she had some well-deserved reservations. I accepted, or volunteered, and that decision transformed into the most defining moment in my life. We were engaged five months later and married five months after that.

Joan supported me fully and financially during my subsequent graduate year at Queen's, and she has been the single biggest influence on everything that happened to me since. Raising four boys happily and successfully in various venues around the globe while I pursued my career is an achievement for which she deserves full credit, but her steadfast support, counsel, and patience in dealing with me is a commitment without parallel.

Growing up in Fort William, I was very much a product of the 1950s post-war enthusiasm and optimism in Canada, a simpler age when drugs were what you got at the pharmacy, when television offered one or two channels at most, and when the prospect of better times generally for the new generation seemed eminently attainable. John Diefenbaker gave a western face and a voice, albeit unilingual, to a new spirit of nationalism; the Montreal Canadiens prevailed in hockey; Montreal and Edmonton jousted for pre-eminence in Canadian football.

The world seemed smaller, more distant perhaps, but distinctly less threatening. The Korean "conflict" and events in Eastern Europe were symptoms of the looming Cold War, but both were far away. Multilateral institutions like the United Nations, the World Bank, and NATO were still relatively new and welcome instruments for a better world not yet jaded by cynicism or failure. Sputnik in 1957 had jolted American confidence and self-esteem, but by and large, times were good. It was a particularly good time to grow up in Canada, a time when university graduates from places as remote as Fort William entered government service with ideals and values intact, believing that we lived in a just society and that we could make a difference, or at least have the opportunity to make a difference, depending on what we chose to do.

TWO

Entering External, 1963–1965

I joined External Affairs in the summer of 1963 and actually completed my thesis and received my MA degree one year later. My thesis had been derailed by the 1963 election. The topic was "Canadian Political Parties and the Nuclear Arms Issue," and that unexpectedly became the issue in the 1963 election. Consequently, I had to let the election dust settle before I could produce a proper assessment. As the thesis involved interviews and questionnaires with members of Parliament, it also became my introduction to Ottawa politics. Little did I know then where all that would lead.

The decision to enter the Canadian foreign Service was anything but predetermined. After a sneak peak at the law courses thought during my undergraduate days at Queen's and the prospect of three more years of university, I abandoned the notion of a law career. I sat the foreign service exams and qualified – twice – but did not accept at first because I chose instead to do graduate studies. I took a master's degree because, for a time, I thought teaching might be the career of choice. And in those days you could teach at university with only an MA. Joan and I arrived in Ottawa in the summer of 1963 with one very young son, Derek junior, and one due in the fall (Ian). Starting a new life in a new city and with a fast-growing family – all on the princely income of $5,400 per annum and with very little support, if any, from my new employer in terms of relocation – was in sharp contrast to what I would much later discover is common practice in the private sector.

What a foreign service career offers is variety in spades – variety in terms of work, environment, and people. Assignments vary between two years on average at headquarters and two to four years at any one of Canada's more than one hundred missions around the world. Because of the rotational nature of the career, in and out of Ottawa, there is a continuous turnover of colleagues, superiors, and subordinates. It is hierarchical, as is any bureaucracy, and promotions are based primarily, if somewhat subjectively, on merit. However, for a department where communication skills are paramount, the quality of the performance report is occasionally more compelling than the performance itself! I suspect that the heavy emphasis on analytical and communication skills is what has enabled many foreign service officers to attain senior levels in other departments. (At one point in the 1970s more than a dozen deputy ministers had been drawn from the foreign service.) It is a career which, in general, has also attracted some, especially from Quebec, who might otherwise not have considered federal government service.

The foreign service has been criticized as elitist, even monastic or aloof from the domestic branch, and there may be some truth to this view. It is certainly seen by the barons of Treasury Board as pampered or privileged, in part because the foreign assignments convey additional perks or benefits in terms of allowances for cost of living, housing, and representation. While variety offers advantage to the career, the relevance of many duties is a source of continuing frustration. Foreign policy issues rarely hold centre stage in cabinet or Parliament; trade issues or negotiations do. Consular cases, incidents involving Canadians travelling abroad, command the attention of members of Parliament and the media, but as recent events confirm, stories of success or achievement run well behind those where the service provided is deemed to be less than expected.

When I joined the department, External Affairs still thrived on reporting. Dispatches of greater and lesser moment poured in daily from all parts of the globe to be analyzed, summarized, and, for the most part, filed by the responsible desk or division. Reports from major embassies got broader and more significant distribution in Ottawa and to other embassies. Instructions flowed from headquarters; replies and reports came from the embassies. If anything, the advent of modern telecommunications, computers, and the Internet have diluted both the quality and the brevity. With instant media available globally, the significance of diplomatic "reporting" has also declined, adding further to concerns about the relevance of the department's core function.

On arriving in Ottawa in the summer of 1963, and despite an advanced degree in political science, I knew very little about the workings of government; less still about the then "illustrious" Department of External Affairs. My first assignment proved enlightening, but when I was directed to obtain a "file" from "the Registry,"* I had no idea what either term meant. I was given an office initially in the Information Division "outfield" but was warned not to treat it as being "out of sight, out of mind," as had my immediate predecessor, who had spent most of his time golfing – or worse. My first task was not propitious. I was responsible for External's book donations to worthy institutions around the world. My first shipment of books to a university in Sweden sank literally en route, and I discovered that Her Majesty's government did not insure shipments – or anything else, for that matter.

My second effort was more eventful. I was ordered indirectly by a prominent canadian senator, John Connolly, to arrange a book presentation to the University of Notre Dame in Indiana. I challenged the directive on the grounds that, surely, Notre Dame had sufficient resources to buy books from Canada and did not need a "gift." I was overruled, alas, by the deputy undersecretary, Ed Ritchie, who explained, diplomatically, that the gift was timed to coincide with the award of an honorary degree to our prime minister, Lester Pearson. My first lesson in politics: when policy and politics collide, politics prevails.

Early days at External were anything but inspirational. There were many moments when I seriously wondered whether I had made a sensible choice of career. In time, I discovered that "moaning and groaning" was an External mantra, the not surprising consequence of many reportedly bright people in search of something more to do with less. But the department did very little to develop or inspire its new recruits. Assignments were ad hoc and the selection of postings was random, at best. All were expected, presumably, to learn "on the job," but the lessons were often as varied as the mentors. The hard reality is that many of the tasks are mundane, if not routine. Many of the posts are dull. Some are indeed arduous, even hazardous, but the opportunities for real influence and achievement were the exception, not the rule.

It is often said that the glory days at External were the post-World War II years, which saw the founding of the United Nations and various multilateral economic institutions and the launch of NATO as democracy's defence against the rise and spread of communism. There may be some truth to the legend. After all, at the end of World War II, Canada had the fourth largest army, a world-class navy, and a highly effective air force – in other words, significant components of raw power. It could also be argued that we chose to do fairly little with this power. As any reader of

---

* Departmental correspondence was organized in files that were kept in a registry within each division or branch of the department.

Churchill's World War II memoirs (or follower of Hollywood movies) can discover, Canada's substantial role in the war was muted somewhat by our subordination to British command. Our political role was stunted even further by the quixotic, if not ambivalent, attitude of Mackenzie King, our prime minister. In playing the customary balancing act with Quebec, King chose to express few views on the strategy of war and was similarly detached from political deliberations about the post-war world. (King's primary interest during the war seems to have been to secure ruins from wartorn London for his estate at Kingsmere.*) Whatever the reason, Canada, despite playing a more significant war role than, say, France, emerged in the late 1940s as a far less significant player in global affairs than our war effort might have afforded. We chose not to capitalize on our proximity with the United States and the enormous linkages that had been created by our common war effort. We nonetheless presumed a somewhat lofty sense of our role as a pivot or bridge between the United States and Europe.

This is not to disparage Canada's distinctive role in helping shape multilateral institutions or in initiating the concept of peacekeeping. But the "golden age" of Canadian diplomacy was something of a secret outside Canada, more by choice or abstinence than design. At any rate, by the 1960s, much of the "golden days" lustre had worn away, even in Canada. Once Pierre Trudeau succeeded Pearson as prime minister in 1968, External Affairs' role became less central. Trudeau had his own views on global affairs. In Ivan Head, he also had his own foreign policy adviser, and as Trudeau himself stated, he could always read whatever he wanted to know about foreign affairs in the *New York Times*. This did not, however, restrict him from some singularly quixotic foreign gambits of his own, for example, on Cuba.

While most countries, notably the United States, define their international role in terms of their national interests (and moral imperatives), Canada is concerned more about the role we should be seen to play. This penchant gave scope to the somewhat dilettantish forays of Pierre Trudeau, which had little relevance to Canadian interests. Much of what we actually did in foreign affairs was in reaction to events or global crises, rather than as a projection of distinct national interests. For instance, our lengthy role in Indochina was prompted essentially by the fact that we were a disinterested party, that is, had no direct interest in the region,

---

* For more on this subject, read Charles Ritchie's memoir of his time in London during the war years.

and yet it involved almost one-third of our diplomatic resources at the time. Our provision of nuclear power as aid to India backfired when the Indians used our technology to make a bomb. This outcome belatedly prompted Canada to adopt a very serious role on all issues relating to nuclear proliferation.

Our colonial heritage – British and French – inspired roles in the Commonwealth and the Francophonie which, while convenient in expanding our profile, bore little relevance to tangible national interests. I recall trying to explain to a Japanese foreign ministry official the rationale behind Canada's bilateral aid policy in Africa, namely, that it was concentrated and more or less balanced between anglophone and francophone African states – former colonies of Britain and France. He found this premise incomprehensible. "But what do they have that you need?" he asked. "Actually nothing," I replied. Our assistance was essentially humanitarian in nature, even though some was tied to Canadian products. My foreign ministry interlocutor suggested that multilateral channels were more appropriate for humanitarian or altruistic purposes. I explained that we did that too, and for those purposes. He remained confused about Canadian policy and priorities, concluding pointedly that Japan's bilateral assistance programs were targeted primarily at countries that had resources (such as uranium) that Japan needed for its own reasons. He may have assumed, of course, that, because Canada was rich in resources, we had no such need. I suspect he had even greater difficulty comprehending why a common colonial heritage should be a determining factor. This is not to suggest that either approach is preferable but rather that, on the issue of bilateral assistance, Japan followed a practice linked directly to its national interest.

Our perennial pursuit of a role in the Middle East – where the national interest is even more difficult to discern – is in a category of supreme overreach. Yet it consumes a good deal of departmental time and ministerial effort and has become a frequent source of criticism. The department and its minister are frequently accused of being "too balanced" on the issue, normally a position Canada cherishes in foreign affairs.

The Trudeau government's 1970 review of Canadian foreign policy purported to define our foreign policy objectives as extensions of domestic policy or national interest, a salutary benchmark. But there were two flaws. By avoiding reference to relations with the United States, the review ignored the paramount element of our foreign policy and the one most closely linked to domestic policies and national interests. Eventually, the "Third Option" – the notion of "counterweights" to offset Canada's "dependence" on the United States — attempted to fill the most obvious gap but proved to be impractical in its implementation. What this Third Option concept really reflected, however, was the ambivalent, somewhat apprehensive attitude of many in government about relations with our giant southern neighbour: a preference to dilute rather than enhance the value of our proximity. Nor did the review take into account the prime minister's penchant to set his own course on international initiatives, often unrelated to the basic principles and prescriptions of his foreign policy review.

The opening to China was a commendable initiative in itself by the Trudeau government, and the prime minister's intellectual commitment to the developing world ensured a prominent position for Canada in several attempts at North-South dialogue. But the results on the latter rarely matched the rhetoric. Trudeau's last attempt at global statesmanship – his "peace initiative" – may also have been well motivated, but it was as quixotic globally as it was fruitless. According to his principal secretary at the time, Jim Coutts, it was an "invention" intended more for domestic appeal than for genuine disarmament.*

Canada is unusual in its effort to define foreign policy by means of periodic reviews or, most recently, by nebulous dialogues or cross-Canada consultations. We search relentlessly for a distinct or "independent" role in international affairs, but in the process, we tend to neglect issues and relationships that are central to Canada's well-being.

Influence in foreign affairs requires more than good intentions. It demands commitment and consensus-building. Having forsworn nuclear weapons of our own and reduced our commitment to NATO in the early 1970s, Canada had little tangible influence on any serious arms control debate. Worse still, by tacitly accepting the security blanket of the United States during the Cold War, while at the same time appearing to adopt a stance of moral equivalence vis-à-vis the two superpowers, we marginalized ourselves even further from serious policy debate in Washington and within the alliance. Despite much activity and periodic headlines at home, our actual engagement in foreign policy became increasingly peripheral. The intellectual rigour, such as it was, produced more posture than substance, and tangible results serving Canadian interests were difficult to discern.

The absence of a serious focus on relations with the United States became all too obvious to me soon after I joined the department when I was assigned, in early 1964, to the USA Division. The responsibilities of

* See his article in *Policy Options* 24, no. 10 (November 2003).

the division included boundary issues, fisheries, bridges, migratory birds, parks, and International Joint Commission–related issues (the last being shared with External's Legal Division). Most of my work involved fisheries disputes on the West Coast. I did play a memorable role, however, in the creation of Campobello Park to commemorate Franklin Roosevelt's summer home in New Brunswick, helping move legislation through the necessary parliamentary hurdles. It was anything but controversial. Oh yes, and "drafty taxis." Perhaps because of my family background, I was tasked by my director, Paul Bridle, to do something about the "drafty taxis" servicing Ottawa's airport. Learning quickly about the power of delegation, I referred the matter to a colleague in External's Transport Division.

The economic dimension of our relationship with the United States was handled elsewhere in the department ("Economic Affairs") and by other departments, notably Finance and Industry, Trade and Commerce. Ditto for defence. The USA Division was definitely not within the power corridor at External. Any pretence at "managing the relationship" was remote. I recall once chiding our consul general in Philadelphia for spending too much time speaking to branches of the John Birch Society in Pennsylvania. He complained that this was the only message he had received from Ottawa during three years of "effort for Canada" in and around Philadelphia, and he told me, in essence, to mind my own business. He was, after all, a trade commissioner – in those days separate from External! (And now separate again – plus ça change.)

After about one year in the USA Division, I was posted with my family to Tokyo, Japan. Before departing, however, I was advised that I would have to "detour" for three to six months to Wellington, New Zealand, which, an obliging assignment officer explained, was "on the way." It proved a bit more complicated than that. I was told that the officer who had been intended to go to Wellington was being detained in Ottawa because the United Nations General Assembly session, normally scheduled in the fall, had been deferred until the beginning of 1965. He was deemed indispensable for that session.

What I was not told in advance was that the officer I was replacing in Wellington, a woman, Vivian Allen, had been "obliged" to leave prematurely because she had decided to marry a "native," a New Zealand ear, nose, and throat specialist. In those days, marriage per se by foreign service officers serving abroad was a matter for approval by the head of mission, and marriage to a citizen of the country in which the officer was serving was, in some cases, not permitted. For whatever reason, this marriage was not approved by Ken Burbridge, our high commissioner, the title used instead of ambassador by the senior diplomatic representatives in Commonwealth countries also having the Queen as head of state. The woman in question had been very popular with our office in Wellington and in New Zealand generally. The decision to terminate her assignment was not. Knowing nothing about any of this did not make me any more popular on arrival. To make matters worse, I was a "third secretary," the lowest rung on the diplomatic ladder, and was replacing a "first secretary." This meant I was not particularly welcomed by the high commissioner either, even though my assignment was temporary.

The office in Wellington was small in size and in operation. There were seven Canadians and a roughly similar number of New Zealand "locals." Relations between our two countries were pleasant, even quiescent. Wellington was not a hotbed of activity; as a result, internal human dramas normally held centre stage. Two events stand out. A visit by a trade mission from Vancouver created the kind of incident all Canadian foreign missions hope to avoid. One representative of the mission declared to the press on arrival that he regarded New Zealanders generally as "too lazy to pick up money lying on the street." This comment did little to advance Canadian trade interests but certainly put our erstwhile trade mission on the front page in Wellington.

Given the time zones and New Zealand's position at the most advanced position – fourteen hours ahead of Ottawa – we were also the site for the very first official raising of the new Canadian flag in February 1965. While this event provoked mixed emotions for our staff, some of whom revered the Red Ensign, as did many Canadian retirees living in New Zealand, it was memorable nonetheless. The flag is the ultimate symbol of nationhood or independence, and the Maple Leaf made an especially poignant statement in a country that used, and continues today to use, an ensign incorporating the Union Jack.

Our brief stay in New Zealand played a much broader dividend in the years to come. Canadians and New Zealanders do in fact have a lot in common. Our views on international issues are very similar, and our foreign services share information and intelligence openly and consistently. New Zealanders have attitudes about Australians which are not unlike those of Canadians regarding Americans. Socially and professionally, the links on foreign assignments are extensive and were among the most enjoyable for Joan and me in the years to come. Nevertheless, we were both relieved when our temporary stint in Wellington ended and, in April 1965, we embarked on our real destination – Tokyo.

THREE

Japan, 1965–1972

In the spring of 1965, Tokyo and Japan generally were beginning to emerge from both the devastation of World War II and the economic benefits derived from the Korean War. The 1964 Olympics had catapulted Tokyo into the international spotlight and regenerated a strong sense of national pride. Japan was already flexing its considerable economic power and was well on the way toward becoming Canada's second largest trading partner. Our commodities ("rocks and logs") helped fuel much of Japan's manufacturing prowess, and our wheat found a hearty appetite in the country's burgeoning middle class. There was real substance to our bilateral relationship and relevance in terms of embassy activities. The pace was very different from Wellington.

Initially, I was also third secretary in Tokyo, and that meant I was on the lowest rung of a much longer ladder. (Tokyo was, and is, one of the top ten Canadian embassies in terms of size.) My duties tended to reflect that very junior position. I was assigned primarily press and cultural relations, fisheries (again), and a portion of domestic political reporting. It was known generally as the "everything else" job, meaning everything that others preferred not to do. I was assured, however, that after one year, when I became a second secretary and a more junior officer arrived, I would vacate "everything else" and assume exclusive responsibility for Korea (which was then covered by our embassy in Tokyo), as well as an enriched package on domestic political reporting. That was a sufficient carrot to entice me into a stalwart effort on the hodgepodge, first-year chores.

Our first challenge, however, was to find housing in Tokyo. The plan had been for us to inherit the house rented for our embassy colleagues Fred and Eva Bild. But when they hosted a welcome reception for us in their home, the living room ceiling collapsed literally as the party began.

That obliged us to look elsewhere. After several weeks in a hotel, Joan and our two boys rented a small Japanese-style cottage in Kariuzawa, ninety kilometres north of Tokyo, for the summer. I lived in an embassy-owned house and commuted to Kariuzawa on weekends. By September we had found our own place in Ichigaya, a section in Shinjuku, which is often described as Tokyo's Greenwich Village. It was a western-Japanese "combo" house and became our home for the next four years.

If you come from northwestern Ontario, you may not have sampled the pleasures of pâté de foie gras (which I once described as "meatloaf," to the chagrin of my hostess), but you do know something about square dancing. It not only was the basis for my first real date with my future wife but also featured prominently during our first year in Tokyo. Our ambassador, Dick Bower, had a passion for square dancing. While stationed in London after World War II, he had been involved in the production of a special CBC recording of western Canadian square dance music prepared for Princess Elizabeth and Princess Margaret. As he told the story, the recording had been used in a demonstration for the young princesses at Buckingham Palace during the late 1940s. Ambassador Bower had his own copy in Tokyo and decided, on impulse, that it should also be introduced to the Japanese imperial family.

In the summer of 1965, Bower noticed a newspaper photo of the emperor's young brother, Prince Mikasa, observing square dancers during a visit to the United States. This photo provided the needed impulse, and the next thing we knew, those with square dance experience at the embassy were involved in the planning and training of what became a social high point for many unsuspecting diplomats in Tokyo and, of course, Prince Mikasa and his family.

Our military attaché, Ginger McColl, his wife, and the Burneys became the dance instructors and a dozen or more ambassadors and their wives were invited for weekly lessons prior to the main event. Separate lessons were arranged for the prince, his princess, their daughter (also a princess), and her fiancée. The residence was transformed into a gay nineties saloon or Klondike environment (I am not sure why), with the Japanese butler and staff wearing candy-cane vests and bow ties and sporting handlebar moustaches. Oh yes, and we even managed to rent an authentic player piano!

After weeks of training, and only two days before the event, we were advised that the prince urgently wanted to call on the ambassador. We feared the worst – a last-minute cancellation. After all, this was Tokyo, not the United States, and some in the Imperial Household Agency (the bureaucrats who assist the imperial family) must have wondered about the propriety of the affair. But the prince had a more elementary concern. Guests had been advised that the dress was "square dance fare," jeans and western shirts. His Imperial Highness simply wanted to know where he would be able to change into his black tie for dinner! "Not at all, Your Highness," explained our Ambassador. "We will all eat in our jeans." The prince broke into a full smile as he anticipated a first for him – dinner in jeans! It was a first for most of the ambassadorial guests as well, most of whom I doubt had jeans in their wardrobes beforehand.

The event itself was a smashing success – so much so that several ambassadors who had not qualified for the invitation list pressed for a second chance. And so we did it again, complete with lessons in advance. If nothing else, it made me slightly more comfortable posing in Tokyo as Canada's "cultural" attaché. It was also a telling example of cross-cultural engagement, a prerequisite of effective diplomacy.

There were still some vestiges of wartime at the embassy. The building manager in 1965 was Karl Westermark, a Finnish merchant mariner who had been languishing in jail in Yokohama until Finland switched sides during World War II. He was released and then assigned by the Swiss to guard the Canadian embassy and tasked primarily to put out fires from bombing raids during the last year of war. When the Canadian legation arrived in Tokyo in 1946 to resume diplomatic duties, they were greeted at the embassy by Westermark.

The embassy's local political assistant and interpreter, Genji Okubo, with whom I worked very closely during my early years in Tokyo, had been an associate of Herbert Norman, who had served in Tokyo before the war. While openly left-wing in his political views, Okubo had a remarkable network of contacts extending from academic to political and police circles in Tokyo. He provided shrewd insights and a host of valuable introductions. He also led a group of academics in and around Tokyo who shared his strong affection for Norman.[*]

Learning Japanese: "Stamina over Intelligence"

My decision in 1967 to study Japanese full-time for two years was driven more by emotion than analysis. The effort itself was more an exercise of stamina than intelligence. There were many contributing factors. I was twenty-seven years old with a young family living comfortably, if not

---

[*] Norman committed suicide in in 1957 Cairo, where he was serving as Canada's ambassador, following allegations during the McCarthy era in the United States about his political inclinations.

happily, in Japan. As an External generalist, I was frustrated by my lack of expertise in anything particular and welcomed the prospect of "specialization." (The "generalist" versus "specialist" debate within External is as old as the department itself.) Japan was beginning to emerge as a major economic power and External had very few Japanologists. In fact, the department's intensive language-training program for Japan had been suspended during an austerity drive in the early 1960s and was being resuscitated in 1967 only because a parliamentary committee had complained about the lack of language proficiency at the embassy.

What I did not know was that the entire 1966 class of foreign service recruits had been asked to volunteer for Japanese language training. All had declined. An attentive personnel officer noticed from my annual appraisal form that I was studying Japanese part-time on my own. Hence a letter came by diplomatic bag, asking seriously but politely whether I might "volunteer" for a two-year program, with one caveat. As this training would mean that I would have spent four years in Japan, the department wanted me to return to Ottawa on completion of the course! Otherwise, I might "go native." It was very concerned about young officers spending too much time away, especially on what was effectively for me a first foreign assignment. I challenged the logic of this proposal, requesting a minimum of "two years more," and eventually the department relented.

I had been invited to choose between the British embassy system: one-on-one tutorials, basically at home, and the US embassy's language school in Yokohama. I chose the latter, but ended up with a hybrid. The State Department, strapped financially, was looking for a paying customer. However, neither State nor I anticipated an edict from Congressman John Rooney of New York declaring, "No State Department facility should be used to teach non-Americans." As chairman of the House Appropriations Committee, he had the clout to make his edict stick. This created embarrassment all around, up to and including the then US ambassador to Japan, U. Alexis Johnson. A compromise was worked out. The US embassy also had teachers in Tokyo used primarily by students who had graduated from Yokohama for what were called "maintenance" courses, since language learning never ends. Various US embassy teachers taught me at home, two or three teachers per day, for six hours in total. I sat the exams in Yokohama, along with the American students, and the school director sent my performance results privately in writing to our Embassy.

It worked, and I had the benefit of top-notch teachers throughout, men and women. The highlight of the program was that, after each three-month semester, each student was given the equivalent of $100 to take a low-cost, one-week excursion anywhere in Japan, accompanied by a teacher. I visited many out-of-the-way parts of the country in this way, including some that had rarely seen a real live *gaijin* (foreigner)!

Progress was painfully slow, particularly learning to read. To read Japanese, you need to master a combination of Japanese hieroglyphics, two sets of 50 each – Katakana and Hiragana – and Chinese characters (Kanji), 1,880 of which are necessary to be able to read a daily newspaper. (This is the level achieved by high school graduates in Japan.) There is no quick way to master 2,000 symbols other than pure rote: 10 per day, 50 per week, 200 in four weeks, followed by a week of review to try to recover some that you inevitably lose along the way. That is what really absorbed the time. In addition to six hours of mainly oral lessons each day, the reading required two to three hours of repetitive writing each night. You move slowly, ever so slowly, from children's nursery rhymes to primary school texts, middle-school texts, and eventually – nirvana – a real newspaper. To this day, I can remember the first news story I was able to read: "Indonesian President Sukarno arrived in Tokyo today to sign a treaty on Navigation and Commerce." It was as if blindfolds had been removed. But the depth perception was limited. The embassy course vocabulary concentrated heavily on politics and economics with some military or security terminology blended in. Venture into kabuki theatre or No drama, and I was hopelessly lost.

There were also incidents on the home front. My two older sons, Derek and Ian, who were six and five years old at the time, were mastering street Japanese much faster than I. (They attended a Japanese public school.) For one thing, my teachers refused to delve into "colloquialisms." Such were "not appropriate" for diplomats. They erred on the side of excessive politeness, and on occasion – in a bar, for instance – I would often be rebuked for "talking like a woman," in other words, for being excessively polite. My children had difficulty accepting the hierarchical nature of the Japanese language: different terminology for older versus younger brothers, between children and adults, and so forth. Often they used vocabulary I had difficulty comprehending. On one occasion, Derek reported that Ian had called him a *debeso*, the dictionary translation of which I discovered was "protruding belly button." When I asked my female teacher the next morning what it really meant, she blushed and suggested I ask Mr Ota, one of my male teachers. Mr Ota also declined to explain but told me sternly to avoid using the term at all costs.

The study of Japanese did give me a deeper insight into the culture and the habits of the people and many aspects of Japanese life. But after only ten months of study, I was suddenly and unexpectedly called on to perform. In those days, Canadian and Japanese cabinet ministers met from time to time in an effort to boost the relationship. In 1968 it was Tokyo's turn, and our ambassador, Herb Moran, decided it would be an excellent opportunity to feature his prize language officer. I was asked to interpret the after-dinner remarks of the secretary of state for External Affairs, Mitchell Sharp. Not having much choice, let alone capability, I agreed, subject to two conditions: that I be given some idea in advance of what the minister intended to say and that he not tell any jokes. Sharp gallantly accepted the first condition but balked at the second. Surely, he contended, if he explained the joke in advance, I would be able to translate. Wrong! Humour does not travel well, especially to Japan. Besides, as it turned out, Mr. Sharp's joke was not funny even in English!

Fortunately, I had been taught many tricks of the interpreting trade, especially how to improvise when presented with a formidable translation challenge. When Sharp concluded his joke in English, I said carefully in Japanese: "Those of you who understand English will know that the minister has just told a joke. All of you know that jokes are very difficult to translate. You also know that I am an inexperienced student, still learning the intricacies of the Japanese language. I would therefore be very grateful if you would laugh right now." They did and Sharp was duly impressed. "I told you it could be done," he said.

The embassy butler was more perceptive. "Burney-san," he said, "you were very nervous," "Yes, but how could you tell," I asked. "I could see your heart beating," he observed. Somehow I got through this translation adventure and many more after with the same ambassador.

Years later, when I accompanyied Don Jamieson to Tokyo, I again learned the difficulty of conveying humour across cultures. "I understand, sir," said Jamieson's counterpart in careful English, "that you are known in Canada as the bionic mouth." Jamieson was not amused by the label, and that night I saw our then ambassador's heart almost stop beating.

While I was studying Japanese, Herb Moran told me, in effect, that I was crazy. "You'd be better off learning French." In retrospect, he was probably right. But at the time, it posed both a challenge and an adventure. I wanted both. The sense of achievement was helpful personally, and the element of specialization strengthened my uncertain commitment to life in foreign affairs. It also gave my family and me a unique seven-year experience in Tokyo at a time when Japan flourished.

Although I did not return later as ambassador, as I had hoped, I did develop a long-standing appreciation for the country and its importance to Canada and the world.

Ambassador Moran was one of the most senior officers in the department. After serving on Field Marshal Montgomery's staff during World War II, he had joined External well above the entry level. I used to tease him, gently, that he had "only" served as an ambassador, first in Turkey, then in Pakistan, and, after being the first head of what is now CIDA, in Japan. He was tough, even irascible, but shrewd, well connected (notably to Prime Minister Pearson), and highly effective in getting his way.* His attitudes about people were more or less instantaneous and seldom subject to change. Officers in External were rated annually (and privately in those days) on a scale of 1 to 10, with the vast majority converging around 8 (e.g. 8+, 8-, and so forth). Moran was known and feared for having given marks of 4 or 3 to some who, in a highly competitive career, had difficulty recovering from "one black mark."

He could be quirky. When the Japanese were not able to schedule his credentials presentation ceremony in August 1966, the time he had arrived, he decided to go first to Korea, where he was also accredited. As the officer then responsible for Korea, I was in charge of the arrangements for his visit and, as well, for a return trip via Nagasaki, in Japan's southern-most island of Kyushu. The climate was hot and humid and so, increasingly, was the atmosphere around our new ambassador. He sent me back to Tokyo directly from Nagasaki as being "of no further use whatsoever," while he and his wife returned more sedately by ship and train pending the credentials ceremony with Emperor Hirohito in Tokyo.

My initial reporting efforts did not elicit a more positive response from Ambassador Moran. When I prepared a draft for his approval on the latest machinations of Japan's Democratic Socialist Party (a minor force of even more minor significance), he strode into my office, glared at me over his glasses, and without uttering a word, crumpled the draft and threw it on the floor. He then chomped on his cigar and marched out before I could ask what had provoked his reaction, which, while clear, was not particularly instructive. Over time, I fared better with my dispatches, but Herb Moran rarely left anyone in doubt about his opinions.

---

* Both Moran and Lester Pearson liked baseball, and so when Pearson visited Tokyo shortly after stepping down as prime minister in the fall of 1968, the ambassador invited two local peewee baseball teams (which included children from local embassy personnel who lived in a small embassy compound) to play in an empty lot directly in front of the embassy. The "ball field" as it was then called eventually became the site of the new Canadian embassy in Tokyo.

In time, our working relationship improved substantially, especially when my language proficiency became an asset to the ambassador but also because I managed to work through his occasional outbursts. He could be highly effective, especially with economic issues, on which he had spent considerable time in his early days at External. Moran was also politically astute. On one occasion, when I was going to the airport to provide emergency visas to the parents of a young Canadian boy scout who had been injured in a car accident in Tokyo, Ambassador Moran assigned an extra duty. John Diefenbaker was travelling through Tokyo en route to Taiwan at about the same time. Although Canadian embassies had been directed *not* to provide "the usual courtesies" to our former prime minister, Moran chose, not for the first time, to ignore the Ottawa order. "Introduce yourself and see if he needs anything" was my instruction.

When I arrived at the airport, I found Diefenbaker standing for a photo in front of a sign to a VIP lounge. His name was featured incorrectly and in two words – "Mr. Diefen Banker" – and after my introduction, he embarked on a series of amusing stories about how his name had been mangled over the years. At one point, he quizzed me: "Now, young man, I know you are not here to greet me. So why are you at the airport?" When I explained my real mission, Diefenbaker pulled some stationery from his briefcase and proceeded to write a personal note to the incoming parents. "But," I asked, "you do not even know if they are Conservatives?" "Oh," quipped the Chief, "many Canadians who are not Conservatives have voted for me."

Some time later, when Senator Paul Martin visited Tokyo, he complained to our ambassador about the fact that the Trudeau government had cancelled the "usual courtesies" for Diefenbaker. According to Moran, "they [Diefenbaker and Martin] are like two peas in the same pod." I was flabbergasted, but it was proof in spades that politics does make strange bedfellows.

Japan and the Japanese

Japan is not an easy country for foreigners. I sometimes thought it was not easy for the Japanese either. It is highly homogenous, relatively egalitarian, but very tightly wound. Japan rarely gets the respect internationally that its economic power alone would command. This is partly a carry-over from World War II. It is also attributable to the weak foreign-language skills and short duration in office of Japanese leaders and, more generally, the reticence of Japanese to speak and act as individuals.

Becoming the number two global economic power was no mean feat for a country that had been literally flattened during World War II. Industrial production vanished in the wake of Japan's defeat. Unfortunately, its politics, operating under an American-drafted constitution but with power effectively in the hands of bureaucrats and political chieftains, failed to match its economic growth. The stability of virtually one-party rule drifted gradually into stagnation, and when, in the 1990s, Japan's speculative financial bubble burst, the "system" – the tight network of banks, industrialists, and government officials – had no effective response. Japan remains prosperous today, but its future is less than certain. The homogeneity that is its most distinctive feature can also be its Achilles heel, inspiring a degree of insularity and resistance to change. Pressure for change exists, but how and whether it will be channelled is an open question.

It is often said that, if you want to write a book about Japan, do so after a six-week visit, otherwise, it gets very complicated. It is, in fact, easy to generalize about Japan, much more difficult to explain. "Conservative," "predictable," "efficient" are adjectives that arise easily from much of what one sees. Easy to respect; hard to admire. The Japanese have borrowed extensively and highly successfully from other cultures, but excepting xenophobic outbursts such as those that propelled them into World War II, they have been known more for caution than innovation or leadership in global affairs. Political leaders change frequently, albeit with some notable exceptions, but rarely leave much of a legacy. Politicians preside, but bureaucrats rule.

The singular economic achievement cannot be understated, but Japan never seems able or willing to seek a global political role commensurate with its economic power. Its foreign policy and its security are linked firmly to the United States. A vocal and sometimes violent minority opposes both spasmodically. But apart from the American alliance, Japan is very much alone in the world and has little stature of consequence in any international association other than the G8. Its neighbours, notably China and Korea, bitterly resent their periods of often brutal subjugation by Japan, a resentment that spills over into other parts of Asia as well, despite generous dollops of economic assistance and flourishing private sector investment from Japan. These immediate neighbours are wary because of history, and their continuing sensitivity undoubtedly contributes to Japan's low global profile.

In many ways, Japan resembles one of its own creations: the bonsai, a carefully cultivated and nourished but tightly controlled, miniature tree, natural to a point but with its growth stunted to an unnatural degree in the name of form. I will resist a sociological diversion but make one other point. Japan has trouble gaining respect, and those who specialize in the country are acutely aware of the challenge. The relative appeal of China over Japan was a continuing source of annoyance for those of us in External who specialized in Japan. Countless visitors would "pass through" Tokyo en route to China. (We referred to this practice as *pissoir* diplomacy.) Few wanted to spend much time in Japan, but the allure of China was pervasive.

In Ottawa the Chinese embassy never had difficulty attracting any number of Canadian cabinet ministers to social events. But for functions at the Japanese Embassy, extra effort was often required. And yet the disparity in significance of our relations with Japan versus China, at least in those days, was striking. Japan was our third largest trading partner – a major economic power in its own right – but you would never know it from the time, attention, and priority given to Japan by Canadian ministers. With some exceptions, the Japanese themselves did not do much to right the balance.

Japan hands at External had a dual challenge. Raising attention in Canada to the importance of Japan was one; raising attention in Japan to the importance of Canada was another. The latter was bedevilled by the overwhelming attraction, almost obsession, in Japan for all things American. In the Japanese Foreign Ministry, Canada and the United States both fell under the two "North American" divisions (Mexico did not). But the ratio of attention never even came close to the 90/10 ratio to which Canadians are accustomed. In the 1960s and early 1970s there was still a proconsul tinge to relations between Japan and the United States, a focus that dwarfed virtually all other relationships, except perhaps those of Japan with China and Taiwan. The continuing American occupation of Okinawa added to this equation, giving the United States a prominent position on what was in fact a domestic issue. As one might expect, the imbalance gave rise to tensions – personal and professional – in the management of this paramount relationship. All others, including Canada, held a distinctly secondary status.

Diplomatic Reporting: "Keeping Ottawa Informed"

Following two years of intensive Japanese language training, I rejoined the embassy as first secretary (political), with responsibility for international political reporting (foreign policy issues) and oversight of domestic political affairs and the duties of the embassy's new third secretary. As well, I became the ambassador's unofficial interpreter, particularly for his visits outside Tokyo.

The war in Vietnam was a major topic for exchanges with the Japanese Foreign Ministry and for sessions with counterparts from "friendly" embassies. As Canada moved in 1970 to establish relations with the People's Republic of China, this also became a topic for regular exchange with the Japanese and made it easier for us to glean information in return. It gave us relevance on a topic of considerable interest to Japan. It was obvious that the Japanese would have preferred to be briefing us on their opening to China, rather than observing what we were doing, but Japan had a much deeper relationship with the Taiwan regime (Taiwan had been a Japanese colony until the end of World War II). And it was unlikely in any event to move on China ahead of the United States. But the dominant topic in Tokyo in the early 1970s concerned renewal of the US–Japan Security Treaty and the reversion of Okinawa from US occupation to Japanese rule. The Security Treaty prompted massive student-labour demonstrations in the streets of Tokyo; however, these were, for the most part, more ritualistic than threatening.

Domestic politics in Japan during the 1960s and 1970s and right up to the present time concentrated almost exclusively on battles within the ruling Liberal Democratic Party. The LDP, in one form or another, has ruled Japan for all but one year since the end of World War II. It is essentially a coalition of conservative factions centred around powerful chiefs or kingmakers, some of whom are labelled reform-minded, others right-wing, but all of whom share a fundamental reason for being – and remaining – in power and taking advantage, whenever possible, of the spoils of power, especially lucrative public service infrastructure projects that generate cash to sustain the factions. The multi-member constituency system for Japan's Lower (and more powerful) House, allowing citizens to vote for one candidate only in three-to-five member constituencies, helps both the largest party and the smaller but highly organized parties such as Komeito, which represents an evangelical-style Buddhist sect. The opposition, more generally, is highly fragmented. The largest of these groups – in the 1970s the Japan Socialist party – had a platform of domestic and foreign policies that virtually guaranteed its perennial opposition status.

The LDP dominance of government provided consistency and stability of sorts and worked efficiently enough in good economic times. The faction leaders often preferred to rule from behind the scenes and nominate proxies to serve in cabinet. In the absence of a singularly powerful faction leader, they often opt for a low-common-denominator consensus (least-offensive) candidate to serve as prime minster. Cabinet portfolios changed hands almost annually, leaving little scope for policy initiative by ministers and maximum control of the status quo by officials. There have been notable exceptions – for example, Yasuhiro Nakasone, who also had the advantage of speaking English – but by and large, Japanese politicians have had little impact on global issues and are, for the most part, undistinguished in Japan itself. When the economy was booming, as it was from the early 1960s until the early 1990s, there was little concern about the mediocre government performance. But when the economy faltered, the limitations of Japan's political structure and its politicians became much more obvious. The reforms needed for country's financial institutions proved all too elusive for those wielding power and the superficially smooth management by Japan Inc. sputtered all too noticeably, even for its jaded electorate. Instead of genuine policy reform, however, events produced a series of seemingly charismatic leaders who proved to be fresh as personalities but lacking in resolve or direction or in the internal support needed to generate results.

My time in Japan was one of unusual political stability. Eisaku Sato, a faction leader in his own right, was prime minister for almost the whole period. His major skill was in maintaining a careful balance between his and other major factions while presiding over a rapidly growing economy. In retrospect, his tenure is seen as more positive than it was at the time. He was succeeded in 1973 by the much more flamboyant Kakuei Tanaka, whose nickname was "the Bulldozer." Tanaka was more forceful and less subtle than any of his predecessors. Eventually, however, his tactics overwhelmed his leadership skills. He resigned over a series of corruption charges and spent the rest of his life trying to avoid sentence.

The objective of discussions with the Japanese Foreign Ministry, as well as with journalists, academics, and colleagues in other embassies, was primarily to "keep Ottawa informed," a task that could be as subjective as it was selective. The real purpose was to keep ourselves informed so that we could provide compelling briefings to visiting dignitaries and participate intelligently in discussions with others who had similar duties in Tokyo.

The value of political reporting is difficult to quantify in any foreign service. Assessments of domestic political developments in a major country such as Japan are important in terms of either the stability of the government or the consequences, in policy terms, of a change in government or within government. Exchanges on global issues with representatives of foreign governments are essentially intended to acquaint or influence one another with the status of policy on a given issue or on developments where one has more direct information than the other. These in turn are intended to help guide the evolution of policy and decision-making at the home office. The same is true of notes taken during meetings between ministers and/or heads of government. Embassies are able to track what is being reported by their counterparts in other capitals, and the policy process is either enriched or diluted by the breadth of these exchanges. It is intelligence-gathering in a fundamental sense, requiring analytical and communication skills as well as an ability to network with counterparts from a wide variety of cultures.

Not surprisingly, reports from the major embassies – the G8 countries, for instance – carry more weight in Ottawa than information exchanges at smaller missions, which involve fewer people, should be more selective, and are used primarily as briefing material for visitors. In all cases, relevance and brevity are important, but not always observed, guidelines. If officers are sensitive to the relevance of what they are observing to Canadian interests, their reports are more likely to attract attention. If they are crisp and to the point, they are more likely to be read, especially by senior officials and ministers. Before the computer age, External prided itself on the quality of its reporting. Many drafts were customary, and bottles of whiteout ink were handy staples. The higher the rank, the sharper the editorial pen, and External had some excellent editors.

Treasury Board concepts of "program management" and "quantifiable objectives" were difficult to reconcile with the core of diplomacy, particularly political reporting. That is one reason why External usually fared poorly in budget allocations. The inability to quantify the value of much of its departmental effort was a continual drag on resources generally and a source of frustration for those who, all too frequently, saw their efforts being misunderstood and unrewarded. Besides, those who were strong at articulating policy positions and rose to the most senior levels of the department were not as strong at managing the affairs of the department, especially in negotiating budgets with Treasury Board. (The brightest may not always be the best!) Trade commissioners had the advantage of a constituency for consistent support – the export community. Political officers from External had no equivalent.

Trudeau in Japan

I first met Pierre Trudeau in the summer of 1970 when he visited Japan at the end of a six-week prime ministerial tour of South Asia and the South Pacific. It was not an auspicious beginning, and the Trudeau entourage, on arrival, seemed more like a football team returning from a weekend loss: tired and irritable.

The embassy had tried repeatedly to obtain some information about the prime minister's preferences – what he wanted to do or not do during the Japan portion of his visit. A major component was the Osaka World Fair. Trudeau was one of more than one hundred heads of state and government visiting Japan to see the Exhibition. The Japanese, being meticulous about protocol and swamped with visitors, wanted information about individual preferences months in advance and down to the last detail. (A colleague mused that in Japan, when it comes to "programs," even the coffee breaks are a matter of negotiation!)

In any event, we were unable to provide much in the way of preferences. We knew that Trudeau had visited Japan privately on a few occasions and apparently had stayed and studied briefly at the main judo school in Tokyo. We were aware, in short, that he knew a good deal about Japan and would undoubtedly have some particular preferences, but despite repeated requests, we had been unable to obtain answers from Ottawa. Very late in the planning we were advised that Trudeau wanted to visit a steel mill in Kawasaki, an industrial, working-class suburb of Tokyo. The mill imported coal from Alberta, and we were asked to arrange a "photo op" of the prime minister shovelling coal onto a conveyor belt. We were also told that, in terms of cultural activities, judo and kabuki were his favourites. The Japanese hosts wanted to know what his favourite popular song was, so that could be featured at the state dinner in his honour. "Try to Remember" was the answer. All in all, it was a visit that was hard to forget.

After an "official day" in Tokyo, the Canadian delegation set out for Osaka by train. All the senior officials accompanied the prime minister in one car. I was in a separate coach, seated with various Japanese protocol and logistics officials. After about an hour, I noticed one of the senior officials from the Prime Minister's Office, Gordon Gibson, entering our car. "Which one of you is Burney?" he asked pointedly. His tone was not warm. "The prime minister wants to see you NOW," he added. I was ushered forward and seated beside the prime minister. Our ambassador and the senior government officials from Ottawa were all looking concerned, but at the same time, were keeping well away.

"I understand you are responsible for this program," said the prime minister.

"Yes," I acknowledged, "but it really reflects what we were told to arrange by your office." No way was I going to assume responsibility.

"Well, Mr Burney, you have me going to a steel plant in Kawasaki. If I want to go to a steel plant, I can always go to Hamilton."

"Yes, Prime Minister," I replied, "but we were told you wanted to highlight the Kawasaki mill's use of Alberta coal."

"And you also have me going to see a demonstration of judo. I spent six weeks at that facility many years ago. I would much prefer to see kendo." (This was a different martial art, involving wooden swords).

"By the way, I also prefer bunraku [puppet theatre] to Kabuki." I was on a roll, downhill, and all I could say was "Well, Prime Minister. I will do what I can to make some of the changes you want, but I guess I should have written to you directly to get advance information on your preferences!" He smiled wanly.

On arrival in Osaka, I spent the entire evening with Japanese protocol and security officials reshaping the balance of the prime minister's program. The Japanese were not amused by the sudden change of plans, but they responded with their customary efficiency. At 7:00 a.m. I pushed a handwritten, revised version under Ivan Head's door saying, "Unless I hear to the contrary by 8:00 a.m., this is the new program." (Neither Ambassador Moran nor the undersecretary, Ed Ritchie, the senior department official, wanted to take the responsibility. That is why I went to Head). Hearing nothing, I advised the Japanese to proceed accordingly.

My challenges were not over. Later that morning, I was asked to brief Trudeau on what he would see and do at the Osaka Fair. At the Canadian pavilion, I used a large map of the exposition site and a pointer to explain the route being suggested. At one point I said that, depending on the time remaining, he would have two alternative routes to complete the tour. (Remember that I had been up all night.) "Oh, Mr Burney you are such a bureaucrat. Always with a contingency ..." I lifted the pointer and started to aim it. He glared back and, I think, dared me to throw it. I didn't but it certainly was tempting. When dignitaries completed a major visit, it was customary for the embassy grunts to have a "wheels up" party. The one we had during the summer of 1970 was one of the best in my memory.

There was a more serious and sensitive side to Trudeau which I saw first in 1976 when he made another official visit to Japan. Although he did know a great deal about the country, he wanted advice on dealing with the then Japanese prime minister, Masayoshi Ohira. By this time, I was director of the division responsible for Japan, and Ivan Head had included me in a pre-visit briefing for the prime minister. My advice was that he be extremely patient in his one-on-one session and try to get the Japanese prime minister to move away from his formal script – the briefing note prepared by officials. Too often, I explained, foreign visitors are so anxious to make all their points that they mistake the translation of their views as a response from their interlocutor. Sometimes they do not even let the translator finish and jump in with more. As a result, the exchanges in Tokyo are usually very one-sided and the Japanese impart little more than set-piece notes prepared by officials.

One of the best techniques I had learned in Japan was the power of silence in one-on-one sessions. Canadians get very uncomfortable when there is silence; Japanese do not. I urged Trudeau not to try to fill every vacuum but, above all, to wait and try to elicit comments from his host. He did exactly that during this and subsequent meetings in Tokyo and made an obviously positive impact on his Japanese counterparts.

In a moving ceremony at the embassy during his 1976 visit, the prime minister apologized formally for Canada's treatment of Japanese Canadians during World War II.* His eloquence on that occasion made us all stand a bit taller as Canadians. (In Fort William I had played baseball with the sons of many Japanese who had been transported from British Columbia to Canada's interior. At that time, I knew nothing of events that had prompted the transfer.)

Several years later, at the Montebello Summit, I had more protocol "discussions" with Trudeau but also again saw his sensitive side. Just before the Japanese delegation arrived, I mentioned to him that our interpreter was a woman and that it was important to her that Trudeau allow her to translate for him and not be over-ridden by the male interpreter for the Japanese prime minister. "Does she speak French?" he asked. "Yes, she does," I answered. And so, Trudeau greeted Prime Minister Suzuki in French and spoke to him entirely in French during the arrival ceremony. Suzuki's interpreter was visibly perturbed. Score one for Canada.

---

* I do not recall any similar apology from Japan for the treatment of POWs captured in Hong Kong.

FOUR

Headquarters, 1972–1978

After more than seven years in total in Japan, we were obliged to head home in the summer of 1972. By this time two more sons had joined the family – Alex (1968) and Jeffrey (1969). Both were born in Japan and spoke Japanese before they mastered English.

I joined the Officer Assignment unit in External's Personnel Division with responsibility, first, for the assignment of officers at my own level in the department and subsequently for officers at all levels below ambassador. There was no real science to the assignment process at External. Coincidence, luck, and the whim of fate were often contributing factors. A colleague who joined the department with me left his galoshes in the office of our assignment officer one morning after our French lesson. When he returned at noon to pick them up, he was asked, "Where do you want to be posted?" He replied, "Africa," and within weeks, was on his way to Tanzania – only nine months after joining the department! His was not an isolated incident.

About a year after joining External, I had been offered a position at the consulate general in New York as my first posting because, I was told, as one of the youngest officers in the class of '63, I "could afford to waste four years in New York." I explained that, with two young children and a salary of $5,400 per annum, I could not afford to live in New York. For turning down that posting, I was left to cool my heels six months longer in Ottawa but, eventually, received the posting to Tokyo, albeit via Wellington, New Zealand.

There were very few rules governing assignment selection. The newer you were and the less Personnel knew about you, the more limited was your say on assignments. Bachelors were natural candidates for assignment to the truce commissions in Indochina (in Vietnam, Cambodia, and Laos) but, for security reasons, were generally barred from serving in

Soviet-bloc countries, the theory being that they might succumb to the temptations of Moscow Mata Haris and be compromised. The fact that married officers might not only be as easily tempted but were also potentially more likely to be embarrassed and therefore co-opted by such dalliances did not seem to register. In time, and with the benefit of greater exposure, assignments became more negotiable, and actual qualifications took on greater relevance. But in the beginning, it was very much the luck of the draw.

Throughout my career, the only assignment I negotiated successfully for myself was my posting as ambassador to Korea. (More on this later.) During my thirty-year foreign service career, I had only one job – ambassador in Washington – that lasted more than three years. Variety was and is the spice of life for all who serve – different assignments with different people and in different parts of the world. No two careers are alike. Nothing is preordained. Being in the right place at the right time (or the wrong place at the wrong time) can be a major factor in determining career paths. But what you do with the choice is ultimately left to you.

It would be tempting to say that talent in the department rose, like cream, to the top or at least, like water, found its natural level, but promotions were inevitably somewhat subjective. It could not be otherwise for a service scattered over more than one hundred locations around the world, with all the attendant vagaries in terms of responsibilities, supervision, and assessment. Nonetheless, the rating system at External was rigorous, albeit inflated, and the competition for promotions was fierce. Demanding assignments were often the ultimate test and determinant of promotability. The principle that busy people attract more work was very much in practice.

Judgment was inevitably a significant, if not decisive, factor for both assignments and promotions. Personnel Division held the judgment responsibility for assignments, but these were also a matter for negotiation with the individual and the receiving supervisor. Both aspects required differing degrees of salesmanship. Promotions fell to committees appointed annually by Personnel for each officer rank and reflecting as much balance as was practical between headquarters and the field and across the range of departmental functions.

My stint in Personnel (1972–75) was beneficial in many ways. I was introduced to the breadth of talent in the department, warts and all, as well as to some fundamentals of management: convincing officers to accept difficult assignments; explaining to officers why they were not being promoted; persuading senior managers to accept less-than-all-star candidates for positions. All of this taught me valuable lessons about people and about effective management – more so, in many ways, than would have a comparable position in an "operational" division. I learned a lot in a hurry about human nature – or at least the qualities of human nature represented by the officer contingent at External Affairs.

One special challenge involved a visit to Saigon in 1973 to "negotiate" with the members of the Canadian truce supervisory team to accept an extension of their period of duty in Vietnam. Under heavy US pressure, Canada had reluctantly agreed to serve initially for sixty days on a reconstructed four-nation supervisory team in Vietnam, but as this deadline drew near, we were strongly encouraged by the Americans to extend our assignment. To achieve this objective, I was sent to Saigon with offers of "rest and recreation" weekends in Hong Kong – which many accepted – in exchange for extended duty. The net result of the commission's effort, however, was no more salutary than that of its lengthy predecessor: Saigon fell to the North Vietnamese in April 1975; Canada's contingent had been withdrawn only weeks before.

In 1973, External recruited a record eighty-five new officers, almost 50 per cent more than the normal annual intake. Knowing in advance that not all would eventually make the grade, I drafted a Vietnam veteran, Manfred von Nostitz, to "babysit" the new arrivals. Manfred had served in Can Tho as the political adviser to our military contingent on the initial supervisory commission. He arrived in Ottawa with Montagnard bracelets on his wrist and hung an AK-47 machine gun on his wall. It proved somewhat intimidating to some of our new recruits but had the right effect overall. The class had more than a few characters, and not all were really cut out for foreign service.

The new probationary officers were rotated through various divisions for on-the-job training and if their performance was satisfactory during the first year, they were confirmed. Not all passed. One individual presented a real challenge. He had performed in outstanding fashion during his initial assignment, which had included a period of duty on a delegation to India. On his second assignment, he had failed miserably. We assigned him next to a director in whom we had a lot of confidence for the judgment required. We received a pungent verdict in only three weeks, which declared "This guy is as phoney as a $3 bill." On checking the recruit's credentials, we determined that he had in fact entered with fraudulent claims regarding his educational background. He was promptly dismissed. Years later, however, he re-emerged in public after successfully negotiating a settlement for a Canadian mining company with Idi Amin in Uganda. Our former recruit had used his diplomatic passport (obtained for his stint in India) to present himself in Kampala as a "special emissary" of Prime Minister Trudeau. He got the settlement, along with a hefty commission and, presumably on the basis of more of the same, established a splendid lifestyle for himself in London, complete with a white Rolls Royce. Who knows how far he might have gone if we had confirmed him in External?

During my stint in Personnel, I also spent time attempting to meet the bilingual language requirements of the department. After only a six-week study period at Laval in the summer of 1974, I passed the test, essentially by translating experiences from Japan into pedestrian French for an easily enthralled instructor. This got me through the test but disqualified me for any further training, even though I was a long way from being proficient in French, something I regret to this day.

The rule of thumb in the Canadian bureaucracy (and it may not be limited to Canada) is that 20 per cent perform better than most and carry a disproportionate share of the load, 60 per cent perform in a generally satisfactory manner, and the remaining 20 per cent are underperformers. This standard was probably accurate for External Affairs, even though performance ratings suggested that 80 per cent fell into the top category. "Walks on water" and "jumps over buildings in a single bound" were common appellations that we in Personnel gave heavily inflated ratings. These assessments usually revealed more about the calibre of the rating officer than about the individual being assessed.

A frequent challenge in Personnel was to try to sift fact from fiction in the appraisals and ensure as much objectivity as possible in identifying and rewarding top performers with assignments involving higher responsibilities and with timely promotions, though not necessarily both at the same time. Unlike the bureaucracy at large, External had the flexibility to assign officers to positions that did not necessarily match their rank or job classification. It gave assignment officers more flexibility in moving people to and from difficult environments or positions on short notice, and it served to counter some of the delays stemming from the strict, often litigious, promotion process.

The assignment and promotions system was anything but perfect, and assignments to Personnel Division were not regarded as luxurious or even career-enhancing. At the time, I very much missed the action in the department's mainstream, but looking back, I would acknowledge that valuable lessons in personnel management were learned, ones that helped significantly as my managerial responsibilities increased both in the public and eventually in the private sector. I also think that the 20/60/20 rule holds true for the private sector as well. The main difference is that in the private sector you can release unsatisfactory performers. In the public service, you can only assign them to less crucial functions.

After three years in Personnel, I was re-assigned to the mainstream and promoted to the position of "director" of the Pacific Affairs Division, one of three in External's Asian Affairs Bureau. (There were four geographic bureaux – Western Hemisphere, Europe, and Africa–Middle East being the other three, along with several functional bureaus – Economic Affairs, Public Affairs, Personnel, etc.) Geographic units had broad managerial responsibility for bilateral relations within their respective region and were the primary point of contact both for our embassies in the region and for representatives of embassies in Ottawa from countries in the region. Pacific Affairs covered a large portion of Asia: Japan and Korea in the northeast; and Malaysia, Indonesia, the Philippines, and Singapore in the southeast, along with Australia, New Zealand, and several smaller island states in the South Pacific. Most of the action in my time centred around Japan, Korea, and Australia. Since I had actually served in two countries within our region, I had the advantage of some local experience.

Our principal task was to shape policy issues involving our region, monitor developments having significance for Canada, and respond with advice on unforeseen events. One such surprise was Indonesia's sudden invasion of East Timor in the spring of 1976. Along with most of our allies, Canada expressed "regret" over this action at the time but did little more. But years later, as evidence of Indonesian belligerence mounted, Canada adopted a firmer position, and East Timor has since become independent. Most of my time, however, was spent trying to breathe new life into relations with Japan, prodded persistently by our colourful ambassador in Tokyo, Bruce Rankin, who thrived on his assignment and expected all others to share his enthusiasm.

The Minister's Office: Life with Mr J.

After less than a year in my new role as director of Pacific Affairs, I was dispatched as the External "hostage," along with a CIDA "hostage," Vic Lotto, on a trade mission to Southeast Asia in September 1976 led by Don Jamieson, then the minister of Industry, Trade and Commerce. Little did I know how pivotal this assignment would be for my future career.

Accompanied by forty Canadian businessmen and several trade officials, Jamieson carried out a two-week blitz of Indonesia, Singapore, Thailand, Malaysia, and the Philippines, ostensibly to promote Canadian trade interests in the region. The External and CIDA "hostages" were along on an "as needed" basis. I was there primarily to accompany the minister on political meetings with heads of government or state and to brief him appropriately for such meetings. Otherwise, the CIDA representative and I were expected to leave the "business" of the mission to our trade colleagues.

For whatever reason, "Mr J." and I hit it off. He had a deep interest in the history and politics of the region and, as the relatively new director of the division at External responsible for four of the five countries being visited, I was delighted to respond whenever asked.

Mr J. was a man of prodigious girth and habit. He enjoyed good food and fine cognac. A masterful storyteller, he was also a consummate orator, delighting in speaking eloquently anywhere, any time, and usually without the benefit of a text ("stemwinders," as he called his speeches), much to the chagrin of officials in tow. It was said that when he delivered the news on TV in Newfoundland, he often did so without a script!*

In Kuala Lumpur one evening during the trip, he delivered a speech almost Churchillian in tone and substance. He described Malaysia as the "new flower of parliamentary democracy in Southeast Asia" and in terms that literally brought tears to the eyes of many in the audience. For our acting high commissioner at the time, Mr J.'s speech was too much. It rendered him speechless. When the minister left the podium, he slapped the acting high commissioner on the back and asked what he thought. Hearing only an incomprehensible croak in response, Jamieson then bellowed "External" (what he called me) and posed the same question. "Well," I said carefully but firmly, "tomorrow we will be in Manila, and I suggest you steer clear of the 'Parliamentary democracy' theme."

"Oh, you mean I should stick to trade."

"Yes, Minister," I replied (long before the eponymous TV series).

And he did, more or less, but the meeting with the president and Madame Marcos at the Macapagal palace the next day was extraordinary

---

* Don Jamieson held a variety of portfolios – Transport, Industry, Trade and Commerce, and, ultimately, External Affairs. He had been attracted to Ottawa by Lester Pearson but served primarily under Trudeau. Jamieson left federal politics in 1979 to become leader of Newfoundland's Liberal Party. He served as high commissioner to the United Kingdom but died shortly after and before completing his memoirs. He had promised that his chapter on External would be entitled "No Bottom Line." It would have been a delightful read.

in other ways. Oil had been discovered on or near one of the outer Philippine islands the day before the arrival of Team Canada. Evidently, the Marcoses were busily in contact with Hong Kong bankers to try to secure title or leases to the area in question before markets opened. Hence, our Philippine hosts alternated, almost kabuki style – first the president and then his wife – on a platform in front of the Canadian delegation. One presided over the meeting while the other huddled in a corner with a senior adviser. Mr J. maintained his poise throughout the erratic encounter and remained firmly on message – trade, trade, and only trade in Manila!

The mission as a whole was, to say the least, a rollicking affair from start to finish. What it did for Canada's trade relations in the region, I cannot really say. After all, this was not External's terrain. But the personal dividend came very soon thereafter. One month later, in fact, Mr J. was named secretary of state for External Affairs, but before taking up his new responsibilities, he was determined to conclude one last trade function, a visit to the Soviet Union as the guest of his Soviet counterpart. Aboard a private train en route to Leningrad (St Petersburg), the two ministers virtually disappeared from all contact, much to the consternation of the then undersecretary, Basil Robinson, who feared he had "lost" his minister in the Soviet Union, of all places, and at the height of the Cold War.

Before embarking on this trip, Mr J. had shunned explicitly any notion of having, as was the tradition, an External official in his office, primarily to move the paper but also to provide a consistent communications link to headquarters. Most of his predecessors had had such an arrangement, and the position had taken on an aura of significance, as well as danger, for each occupant. Mr J. had been indoctrinated at Industry, Trade and Commerce to be wary of the "cocktail-squeezing, cookie-pushing" functionaries at External, and he acted accordingly, spurning all offers of direct departmental assistance.

After the Soviet escapade, however, the undersecretary was adamant. (He may have been helped by Trudeau.) In any event, Robinson met Mr J., presented the department's "stud book," the biographies of all officers, complete with photos, and pleaded that the minister "take anyone you want, but please take one" for his office. Mr J. did not waste time. He quickly got to the B's in the book, saw my photo, and declared, "That's External. I'll take him." And that is how I became his senior departmental assistant in 1976. The "media spokesman" role was added essentially because neither Mr J. nor his political staff could determine what their newest "Assistant" would do. I said at the time that being named Mr J.'s "spokesman" was like being drafted to write letters to the editor for Eugene Forsey. Mr J. was one of the government's very best spokesmen, and he usually did it without a script.

Like virtually all ministers since the election of the Parti Québécois in 1976, Jamieson was preoccupied with the topic of national unity. As a Newfoundlander born before the province joined Confederation, and therefore an adopted Canadian, he was more passionately committed than many of his colleagues who were born Canadian. In cabinet he was consensual, never confrontational, and took his cues primarily from the prime minister or from the deputy prime minister and fellow Atlantic Canadian, Allan MacEachen. Foreign policy issues, in any event, were rarely predominant in sessions of cabinet or Parliament during the late 1970s. Mr J. had a strong moral compass, manifested clearly in his staunch commitment to nuclear non-proliferation and in his efforts to impose economic sanctions on South Africa in December 1977, despite complaints from the business community whose views he normally shared.

Apart from running External's Press Office, my principal task was to brief the minister daily before Question Period on topics of the day, move the departmental paper to and from his office, and accompany him during official visits and meetings. It was, for the most part, as delightful as it was varied. Mr J. did not take to lengthy briefings. I was lucky to capture his attention for a minute or two before Question Period – usually right after a cabinet or cabinet committee meeting and, more often than not, as he stood at a urinal with his attention on other matters. But he knew enough to respond diplomatically when necessary and prudently at all times. One technique he used selectively but effectively in Question Period was to say that he had indeed been briefed on "that very issue" on his way into the House, but rather than take the time to provide a full reply, he promised that the honorable member would have "a written reply on his desk before 4:00 p.m. that day." On sitting down, he would give a quick look up to the gallery where I sat and an even quicker wink. We both knew where matters were headed.

Part of the spokesman role was to convey a Canadian view of events or encounters involving the minister, and on occasion, that would involve some embellishment or "spin." For instance, when Mr J. "summoned" the Soviet Union's ambassador, Aleksandr Yakovlev, to his office to "complain" about the treatment of refuseniks in the Soviet Union and to present to him a list of potential émigrés, Mr J. handled the exchange with diplomatic charm. But the press headline the next day proclaimed,

"Jamieson Tackles Russian Bear," and the newspaper account described the exchange in more assertive terms. Yakovlev was surprised by the media report and, at a subsequent reception, challenged me on the spot. "Are you the one who spoke to the press?" he asked pointedly.

"Yes, but I don't write their reports," I answered.

"Well," he muttered, "I do not want you to give them the impression that I go around eating babies!" When Mr J. was called upon to expel several Soviet diplomats on charges of espionage, he was solemn and to the point. There was no need for embellishment on that occasion.

Mr J.'s two favourite cities to visit were New York and London. Not surprisingly, he attached a high priority to relations with the United States and Britain, undoubtedly reflecting his Newfoundland heritage. Similarly, he put a premium on good relations with his US and UK counterparts, Cyrus Vance and David Owen respectively. They met frequently at summits and in the context of their shared "Group of Five" responsibilities for Namibia. He had more of a problem with Henry Kissinger. As Jamieson tried gamely to explain a fisheries dispute "off the tip of Georges Bank" to the secretary of state during a NATO meeting, Kissinger was uncharacteristically speechless and obviously unaware of the meaning of the phrase, let alone the nature of our dispute.*

One of my zanier but most memorable moments with Don Jamieson occurred at the London G7 Summit in May 1977. This was President Jimmy Carter's first trip overseas as president and, as Mr J. and I learned first hand, was the cause of some apprehension for the newly elected man from Georgia. As is their habit, the Americans had declined to use the fleet of three official cars offered by the host government for the principals attending the summit from each country (the head of government or state, the foreign minister, and the finance minister). Instead, President Carter was to be conveyed in a gigantic, fully armoured, super-stretch and specially made Lincoln. There was only one hitch. As the leaders and their ministers were meeting at Lancaster House in the morning, the American limo (known by then as "the aircraft carrier") ventured into the inner courtyard, but much to the consternation of the more than two hundred American, mainly security, officials in attendance, it could not get back out. As the delegations emerged from the morning meeting and set off for lunch in their three car convoys to No.

---

* In his own memoirs, Kissinger makes a point of indicating that relations with Canada involved largely technical issues best left to the technicians, and he uses fisheries as the example. He did not think that his time was well spent on such issues, much to the frustration of Mr Jamieson, other ministers, and Canadian ambassadors to Washington, who rarely succeeded in gaining an audience.

10 Downing Street, a somewhat frantic American delegation searched in vain for the president's limo.

The ever-alert National Security adviser, Zbigniew Brzezinski, (a McGill graduate!) spotted the Canadian vehicles, Maple Leaf flags being a dead giveaway, and quickly ushered his president to the second car in the Canadian contingent. As I was about to join Mr J. in the back seat, I felt a hand on my shoulder and heard a soft southern voice. "Y'all don't mind giving me a lift do yuh?" said the thirty-ninth president of the United States. Mr J. quickly grabbed my arm and, with "help" from a Secret Service agent, propelled me into the jump seat, where I was joined immediately by the same agent. Another Secret Service agent jumped into the front seat, slapped our driver on the knee, and shouted, "Take off, buddy!" The driver looked in the mirror and blanched. He also drove his foot to the floor. "Slow down for Chrissake," shouted the frantic agent. "Don't you know you're driving the president of the Yewnighted States?"

Our driver got the message. We slowed down and proceeded more presidentially toward No. 10. Meanwhile, Mr J. and the president were getting on like a house on fire. At one point, Mr Carter expressed concern that, with the exception of Trudeau, he was the only leader attending the G7 summit who had no previous finance or treasury experience. "Don't worry about that," advised Mr J. "The sign in front of your seat says U.S.A. You can say any damn thing you want and, believe me, everyone will listen." Carter relaxed visibly on hearing this, encouraged no doubt by the fact that many in the crowd on the sidewalk as we drove noticed him in the Canadian limo and shouted out, "Jimmy, Jimmy." "Well," he observed, "as long as they're calling me Jimmy, things should be allright."

The chemistry between Mr J. and Jimmy Carter paid dividends during the 1977 G7 Summit in London. The president made a quick trip to Geneva during the Summit for a secret meeting with President Assad of Syria, to "push the Mideast peace process" (yes, even back then). He gave Mr J. a first-hand account over coffee the next morning. "Do you think the boys in Ottawa might be interested?" asked the secretary of state for External Affairs. "Well, Minister," I said, "your sources are pretty good!"

Two years later, when I was in Korea, Mr Carter came on a state visit. As is the custom, the resident ambassadors were lined up along a red carpet at the airport as part of the greeting party. We were intended to serve as fence posts, not participants, but I could not resist. When President Carter came by, I said, "You may not remember, Mr President, but we once shared a car ride in London." He beamed and lied, "Of course I do." We exchanged a few pleasantries, much to the consternation of the Korean (and American) officials, who realized the schedule was, as a result, already one or two minutes behind. When I met Brzezinski years later, he too remembered the "failed aircraft carrier" at Lancaster House in the spring of 1977.

My job in the minister's office involved two delicate challenges. One was balancing the wishes of the Minister and his political staff with the needs and advice of senior officials of the department, notably the under-secretary. The second involved on-the-record and background briefings on the minister's and the department's position with the Canadian media. The risk of exposure was high with each. Fortunately, Mr J's positive disposition towards most things proved to reduce the threat to me on both counts. With the first of these tasks, I was essentially an expediter, getting information to and from the minister, as well as decisions or approvals when such were required. The overall challenge taught me valuable lessons which served to enhance my effectiveness in future roles. Having daily experience with the pressures on ministers from Question Period, cabinet meetings, or what are often over crowded schedules, I learned the value of brevity and precision for briefings – orally and in writing. Attempting to brief media representatives of varying depth and quality, I also learned, sometimes the hard way, what works and what doesn't work. While Don Jamieson was definitely his own best spokesman and, as a man from the media, had a genuinely positive rapport with them, I learned from him and from them techniques that ultimately influenced what I later did more on my own as ambassador, as chief of staff, and as summit sherpa.

The line between politics and policy is less clear for an official working in a minister's office, although External Affairs is usually one of the least partisan portfolios. To be successful in such a role, a public servant must not only satisfy the minister's wishes but also get along with the minister's political staff and avoid upstaging the senior echelon of the department. Mr J's main political assistants were David MacNaughton, his executive assistant, who handled political matters relating primarily to Newfoundland and Atlantic Canada, and Allan Lever, his administrative assistant and schedule coordinator. Both were congenial and professional and accepted me openly as part of the team, though with a clear delineation of who did what.

The paper flow from the department was enormous. Lengthy memos on topics as diverse as the countries where Canada was represented were the order of the day. Mr J. was often frustrated by memoranda that avoided clear policy choices and seemed wishy-washy – "on the one hand ... and on the other." Brevity was never a strong suit at External. I was asked, more than once, by the minister to condense or summarize the lengthier memos. I was scolded, more than once, by the undersecretary when he learned that I had deigned to summarize a memo that he had signed. (Most were signed or initialed by the undersecretary or his designate.)

Mr J. had a technique of his own to streamline the flow. Many memos would be returned to me marked "Desk File." After a few days on the job, I asked what he intended me to do with papers so marked. "Hang on to them, Derek, my son, and every few weeks we will go over them again." Which we did, and lo and behold, more often than not, events overtook the analysis. Rarely, only rarely, did memos he marked "Desk File" ever require action. Mr J. told me he had learned the technique from Brooke Claxton, who had served in various portfolios over an extensive career in Parliament. My job was to try to get answers or signatures whenever, wherever I could. He often said, "When they lower me into my grave, I know that you will be there, tapping on the coffin saying, 'Just one more to sign, Minister.'"

The paper flow did not stop when Mr J. travelled, but the dialogue with headquarters occasionally came unglued. The danger in the job came from the fact that the departmental assistant often spent more time with the minister than the undersecretary, the department's most senior official. The chemistry between the departmental assistant and the minister is one thing, but for the job to work, there also has to be a "zone of confidence" between the assistant and the undersecretary. My relationship with Allan Gotlieb was not the same as I had had with Basil Robinson. I had suggested to Allan when he was appointed that he might want to have his "own man" on the 10th Floor (the minister's floor), but he demurred. It worked for a while, but eventually, things came to a head. Messrs Jamieson and Gotlieb were polar opposites in personality, and I like to think that was part of my problem. Instead of being a buffer, I sometimes became an obstacle. When the undersecretary did not appreciate the message from his minister, his inclination was to shoot the messenger.

When travelling from Paris to Turkey and then to Cyprus, I was being chased for a reply from the minister to a lengthy report and recommendation from Marcel Cadieux on a fisheries issue. Cadieux was one of the department's brightest luminaries, having had stints as undersecretary and as ambassador to the United States and to the European Community. At this point in time he was negotiating the highly sensitive East Coast Fisheries Treaty with American envoy Lloyd Cutler. As legal adviser, he had also been Gotlieb's mentor. I knew all that and realized too that timing was important. The problem was that I could not get Mr J. to take the time to read and react to a very detailed report (one I did not dare condense). At long last, over breakfast in Istanbul, I managed to get a reply, one that reflected the annoyance of a minister being "hounded." I scribbled the reply – too hastily, I am sure – in the back of a taxi en route to the airport, handed it to our ambassador as we moved to our plane, and departed for Cyprus.

By the time I reached my hotel room in Nicosia, the telephone lines were purple. The undersecretary did not appreciate the response received and his message was explicit. Mr Cadieux would resign if he received this reply from the minister, and I had shown a profound lack of judgment in dispatching it. Allan Gotlieb's bursts of outrage were not uncommon. On that occasion, the minister intervened, urged the undersecretary to calm down, and said he would take another look at the memo. If only he had marked it "Desk File."!

I had other moments of tension with the undersecretary and was therefore pleasantly surprised when, years later, Allan Gotlieb spoke quite positively about my role with Mr J. and more generally with External Affairs: "Derek suited him [Jamieson] to a 'T,' gruff, blunt, no bull, where do you stand, let's get it done approach." And, with respect to the Montebello Summit: "He got the ball and ran. He learned how to make the system work." Gotlieb added, "He did what was necessary to get the job done."[*]

In any event, by the spring of 1978, I was itching to go abroad again and told both the minister and the undersecretary that I would welcome a posting. I was nominated first as high commissioner to Malaysia, a suitable full-circle ending to my Jamieson moment. Fortunately for me, the Malaysians took their time granting agreement. Meanwhile, the ambassador's position in Korea came open. I volunteered for more familiar territory, and in the summer of 1978 we embarked for Seoul.

---

[*] Quoted by Hugh Winsor in the *Globe and Mail*, in October 1987.

FIVE

Korea, 1978–1980

The biggest challenge I faced on arriving in the Republic of Korea was the adjustment down from the centre of action in External to the management of a dynamic but somewhat peripheral embassy.* The bread and butter of Canada's relationship with the country in 1978 was trade, which had expanded vigorously, as had Korea, since my last visit in 1966. I had little experience or knowledge of trade issues at the time but decided to give this dimension maximum attention. I was blessed with a first-class group of trade commissioners, led by an articulate and hard-charging senior officer, Axel Conradi. We made a good team, reinforcing one another in our effort to put Canada squarely on the map in Korea.

Our biggest advantage was that Canadian businessmen saw the potential of the Korean market but knew very little about the country. Consequently, they relied heavily on the embassy for advice and knowledge. We were relevant and could help, and that made our task meaningful as well as satisfying. I suspect that Korea was unusual in this respect. In any event, we were able, for instance, to help Nortel win its first major contract in Korea, lobbying strongly with key policy-makers – given that the customer was the government. We also promoted Canadian coal, Canadian canola, Canadian beef, and Canadian nuclear reactors, bolstered by regular visits by representatives of the respective Canadian firms and occasionally by provincial premiers and ministers. During my two-year stint, no federal minister visited Korea. None of us at the embassy, however, complained about the oversight.

---

* Despite more than five thousand years of history as one people, the Koreans had been divided geographically and arbitrarily following World War II and, more bitterly, after the Korean War, which lasted from 1950 to 1953. The southern portion of the peninsula is officially the Republic of Korea; the north is the Democratic People's Republic of Korea. Except where otherwise indicated, references in this chapter to "Korea" or "Korean" apply to the Republic of Korea.

Although small in size – about forty people, Canadians and Koreans, in total – the Canadian embassy in Seoul was very active, probably one of the top five foreign missions in Seoul in terms of influence and relevance. While trade promotion was the major function, the embassy had four other program activities: general relations or political affairs – domestic and global; military liaison, as Canada continued to serve on the nascent UN Command in Korea, participating in the regular but fractious dialogue in Panmunjon (where the truce had been signed in 1953); immigration, processing a steady flow of Korean applicants, and Customs, essentially monitoring the burgeoning Korean exports to Canada.*

The domestic Korean political scene was anything but tranquil. The Korean War had had a devastating impact on the country, and the 38th parallel, dividing North from South, was as forbidding in 1978 as it had been when a truce had been declared in 1953. The truce was brittle and inconclusive, and the two Koreas were locked in a frigid, unrelenting stalemate.

My first visit to Korea had been in the spring of 1966. Because Canada had not yet opened an embassy in Seoul, relations were handled from Tokyo, and as the second secretary (political), I had responsibility for Korea as part of my duties. In 1966 it was just beginning to embark on its economic miracle – ten years of 10 per cent GDP growth annually – transforming from one of the poorest countries in the world to one of the twenty-five richest. On my first visit, Seoul had a population of 3 million, and the city still showed the ravages of the Korean War, during which the capital had changed hands three different times. There were no automobiles except those for diplomats and the US armed forces. But there were thousands of Jeeps, converted after the war with cabs made essentially from jerry cans – black ones for the government, green ones operating as taxis. In 1966 it was not unusual to see labourers in downtown Seoul carrying immense cargo in A-frames on their backs, the traditional mode of moving material in Korea.

The Koreans were rugged, in-your-face direct, a startling contrast to the Japanese, their former and much-despised colonial masters. Relations between the two had been frozen since the end of World War II, but a "normalization" process had begun in 1966. While, to this day, relations

---

* On one occasion, when our customs officer visited a Korean manufacturer, he was asked which set of books he wanted to see: "The ones we have for the Americans, the ones for Japan, or those for our own government?" The truth could be an elusive commodity in Korea.

between the two run from frigid to brittle, the economic links have become substantial; the security links are obvious.

Unquestionably, the period of Japanese colonialism had been rough on Korea. The Koreans had been forbidden to use their own language and forced to adopt Japanese names. Thousands, especially those with any skill, had been deported to Japan. Many had served in Japan's armed forces. The president, Park Chung-hee, had been a Lieutenant in Japan's army. Some of the nastiest POW guards were, in fact, Koreans anxious to please their colonial masters. On my first visit, a Norwegian missionary had explained to me that in 1945 there were no Koreans who knew how to operate a train. That had not been allowed. Others noted that Korea had been occupied and subjugated at various times in its history by all the major powers: the Chinese, the Mongols, the Japanese, the Russians, and the Americans. Those who remained were, above all else, survivors, people who lived by their wits or by whatever means possible.

Koreans, by and large, are tough, proud, and resourceful. Their long history of civilization, colonization, war, and internal division has contributed to each facet of their national character. I used to explain to visiting Canadians that there were twelve different denominations of the Presbyterian Church in Korea, and since Christians made up only 20 per cent of the population, it gave some indication of the fractious nature of this otherwise very homogeneous society.

Park Chung-hee had seized power in a military coup in 1965. His authoritarian rule suppressed much of the political opposition but channelled the underlying spirit of resourcefulness and industry of Koreans into a dramatic period of economic development. Democratic reform played second fiddle to economic growth and the perennial concern for security. But, even under tight internal controls, including curfews and heavy press censorship, there were sparks of opposition, led primarily by students. They had a proud tradition dating back to the end of the Korean War, when student demonsrations had helped unseat the government of Syng Man-rhee, resulting eventually in the coup led by Park Chung-hee.

When I returned as ambassador in 1978, the city of Seoul and the country had been transformed by the economic miracle, but the politics were virtually unchanged. Park was still very firmly in control. Seoul now had 12 million people and was flourishing. Taxis were now much more plentiful and featured Korean-made Hyundais and Daewoos. There were no more A-frames. In little more than a decade, Korea had moved through two hundred years of development from a feudal colony to an emerging economic power, and despite the paralysis of a cold armistice along the 38th parallel.

I suspect that the secret of Korea's economic success is simply its people – industrious, cohesive, proud, reasonably well educated, and fiercely competitive. While authoritarian, the government under Park gave a free rein to US-educated technocrats, who introduced economic development prescriptions in a style similar to that of Lee Kuan-Yew of Singapore, a prescription many others in South and Northeast Asia sought to emulate. It led, of course, to cronyism and corruption and stunted Korea's democratic development for some time, but the threat of another invasion provided a cohesion of sorts until the economic progress itself galvanized political change as well.

Anti-communism was a powerful and legitimate cause in Korea and was ostensibly the excuse for South Korea's authoritarian style of government. North Korea had FROG* missiles targeted at Seoul, had constructed at least three tunnels under the DMZ, and sporadically launched secret attacks against the South. In 1968 a squad of North Korean commandos had launched an unsuccessful raid on the Blue House, the residence of the South Korean president. Park's first wife had been assassinated at a political rally, an event blamed on radical North Korean influences. Park himself had presumably been the target. All of this was used by government officials to reject Western concerns about "human rights." They claimed, in effect, that their circumstance was unique and that their priority was survival.

For a diplomat, Korea had a lot to offer. Canada's trade was mushrooming. The peninsula was one of the last global flashpoints in terms of potential war. More than one million military personnel were stationed on each side of the DMZ. Forty thousand Americans were in Korea "to preserve the peace," still ostensibly under the mantle of a United Nations Command. We had our own CINCPAC (commander in chief Canadian forces Pacific), a major who, along with a sergeant, made up the entire Canadian contingent. Representatives of the UN command, along with South Korean military officers, met roughly once a month with North Korean officials at a table in the middle of a room at Panmunjom. (The Chinese no longer participated.) And I mean roughly. They attacked and counter-attacked verbally in a manner that was as coarse as it was sterile.

---

* The FROG (free rocket over ground) family of Russian-developed, unguided, spin-stabilized artillery rockets had a range of 70 km and a 550 kg warhead. They were first introduced in 1965 and eventually replaced in the USSR by the SS-21 tactical ballistic missiles with greater range (120 km) as well as greater accuracy.

There were occasional skirmishes of a military nature within the DMZ and no progress whatsoever towards peace. Millions of Koreans had died during the war. Millions of families were divided at the end of the conflict and had had no contact of any kind since. The atmosphere was as harsh as a Korean winter, and the prospect of a unified Korea was remote in the extreme.

What had changed most notably between the mid-1960s and the late 1970s was the economy of the two Koreas. In the 1960s North Korea had been a model of Soviet-style development, second only to East Germany, transforming the mineral wealth of the north into production, civil and military. The South, which had been the breadbasket, was more or less a basket case economically, undermined by corruption, neglect, and a series of bad governments. By the end of the 1970s, the situation was reversed. The North had stagnated under the almost theocratic leadership of Kim Il-sung, while the South had flourished under Park Chung-hee and his Western-educated economic planners.

Even under the strict rule of Park Chúng-hee, politics in South Korea remained rambunctious and, other than the all-powerful president, revolved essentially around three men each named Kim. Kim Jong-pil had been a supporting colonel in Park Chung-hee's coup in 1965. He had been in and out of Park administrations since, serving intermittently as prime minister, defence minister, and head of the Democratic Republican Party – Park's party. In 1978 he was out of government but still quite active and with ambitions to become president.

Kim Young-sam was the leader of the Official Opposition when he wasn't under house arrest. He eventually became president, serving one term in the early 1990s. When Prime Minister Brian Mulroney visited Seoul in 1986, he asked me to meet privately with Kim Young-sam, who was then under house arrest. Much to the annoyance of our Korean hosts, I did, thereby asserting Canada's continuing commitment to democratic reform in Korea.

Kim Dae-jung was under permanent house arrest when I arrived back in Korea. He had been defeated twice by Park in bids for the presidency and had suffered physically for his opposition tendencies, having been jailed, tortured, kidnapped from Japan, and threatened more than once with assassination. He was the personification of Korean survival. A Roman Catholic, Kim Dae-jung also had an international following. His treatment was monitored carefully by many non-Koreans. As ambassador, I visited him several times during his house arrest and, knowing that our conversations were being monitored, asked pointedly each time how he was being treated.

Kim Dae-jung was not a communist, though that is how he was often labelled. He was the least anti-communist of the major, mostly conservative politicians in the South and was from Cholla province, in the southwest corner of the peninsula, one of the poorest regions, which conspicuously had received little economic munificence from the Park regime. Park was from the northeast. Kim's support was concentrated in his home province but extended to unions – such as they were – and students, who frequently took to the streets to assert their opposition to Park's administration.

Our oldest boys, Derek and Ian, were teenagers by this time and, witnessing the mounting student demonstrations in the streets, were inclined to join. I received calls both from their school and from the Foreign Ministry suggesting that their activity was "not appreciated." I tried to explain to the boys why their conduct as the sons of a diplomat was questionable, but I am not sure it registered.

A more troubling incident on the home front was a bomb threat telephoned to the Residence. My wife received the call. We reported it immediately to the Korean authorities, and within minutes, we were deluged by special investigators, dogs, and army units. Nothing was found and the call was not repeated, but for several weeks after, we had a special guard surrounding the Residence, marching around at all hours and periodically shining a huge spotlight on the interior, including the bed in the master bedroom, in the middle of the night. It kept us on our best behaviour. The caller was never traced, but because the call was in English, strong suspicion focused on classmates of our older boys.

In "normal" times, my duties as ambassador were divided equally between trade promotion and political reporting. In times of crisis, my activity concentrated on sifting intelligence from various sources, interpreting and reporting events to keep Ottawa and interested other Canadian embassies (e.g., Tokyo, Washington, NATO) fully informed. There was no regular rhythm but a series of unexpected events that spasmodically catapulted Korea into the world spotlight. An invigorating ambassadorial debut all around – more so, I suspect, than Malaysia would have been.

Apart from regular contact with Korean officials to glean information and report Canadian positions, I maintained a systematic dialogue, professionally and socially, with the American ambassador, William

Gleysteen Jr, and with several top US military officers in Korea. With 40,000 troops in Korea and a substantial economic development program, the United States had the largest and most significant diplomatic presence in Seoul. Gleysteen was clearly *primus inter pares* among ambassadors, but proved to be an open and articulate interlocutor, particularly in the sensitive times following Park's assassination and, later, in the aftermath of the Kwangju uprising. The Australian ambassador, Geoff Miller, and Ken Cunningham of New Zealand were very much kindred spirits of mine in the intelligence gathering and sharing aspect of diplomacy, even though we were competitors when it came to agricultural exports.

While serving as ambassador in Korea, I was expected to also act as a policeman of sorts over certain activities of our Canadian staff, particularly potential black-market currency activities. This was a problem for the department not confined to Korea, but there had been embarrassing incidents involving embassy personnel elsewhere using the black market to exchange currency and reap personal advantage. The proposed solution was neither appealing nor effective. Ambassadors in countries where currency black markets were active were instructed to have each employee and his or her spouse fill out a form each month recording the particulars of all currency transactions and verifying that they had been conducted in official channels. This requirement prompted a mini-mutiny among staff members in Seoul. Some objected on the grounds that their spouse's spending activities were no business of mine or the government's. (Some spouses were independently employed in Seoul.) Those who agreed to play by the rules were offended in principle. Still others pointed out, no doubt accurately, that miscreants would sign any form without compunction. (In fact, one embassy employee had applied for a fake degree in theology from a "paper university" in order to claim a 10 per cent discount on airfares!) Many objected to being monitored with a system that presumed guilt.

I appealed to the department for assistance in responding to what seemed to me to be legitimate concerns about the new procedure. I was told, in effect, to comply "or else" and to ensure that signed forms were available in the event of an inspection from headquarters. Eventually, I persuaded the more principled of my embassy colleagues to complete the forms monthly and give them to me in a sealed envelope, to be opened only in the event of an inspection. It was an honour system of sorts, and it worked, despite the initial aggravation.

Social life in Seoul had memorable moments. On one occasion, a black-tie dinner hosted for Korea's foreign minister, Park Tong-jin, I had invited a professor from Seoul National University whom I had not met but who was well regarded and considered by some to be less than enamoured of the Park government. We made a point of establishing contact with both "official" and "unofficial" opposition representatives.* Professor Lee Sang-ock arrived at the Residence a bit late and without his black tie. No big deal really, but I was determined, nonetheless, to make him feel less conspicuous. So I quickly changed my jacket, shirt, and tie to match his and continued hosting the dinner. No one seemed to notice anything untoward, and the dinner proceeded without incident. Almost twenty years later, however, I received a call from Ottawa telling me that the Korean foreign minister had been at dinner the previous evening and had related this incident and the "unusual courtesy" displayed to him by Canada's ambassador at the time. It turned out that Lee Sang-ock, my informal guest at dinner, had become Korea's foreign minister.

In October 1979, during a raucous debate over a different dinner about when and how to respond to the latest round of massive student demonstrations in the streets of Seoul, President Park was shot and killed by his KCIA director, Kim Jae-kyu. For a few short months, South Korea experienced the spirit, if not the substance, of a genuine democracy. Press censorship was lifted. The prime minister, Choi Kyu-ha, became acting president, and Kim Dae-jung was briefly released from house arrest. To commemorate the latter event, the publisher of a major Seoul newspaper, Dong-a Ilbo, hosted a "coming out" birthday party for Kim Dae-jung to which I was invited along with the American, British, and Japanese ambassadors and several Korean dignitaries. Kim Dae-jung's name could not be used in the press while he was under house arrest. He had been referred to as "a dissident from the South" or by some such label. Everyone knew even then who it was, but now his name was legitimate, hence the "coming out" party.

Park had been feared more than admired as president, although it had been difficult to glean any candid assessment from Koreans while he held office. His assassination evoked little sadness but immediate concern about who would fill the power vacuum. There was genuine fear about what North Korea might do to exploit the situation. Suggestions that the North or the CIA had been involved or that there was a sinister conspiracy behind the assassination surfaced briefly but inconclusively.

---

* The "official" opposition was somewhat tame and therefore somewhat tainted. Members of the "unofficial" opposition, like Kim Dae-jung, were usually under house arrest, labelled as dissidents, or in academic and labour union circles.

North Korea was then, as now, hermetically sealed, heavily armed, and highly unpredictable. Administered in the most totalitarian system anywhere in the world, it provided the rationale as well as the rationalization for authoritarian or "firm" rule in the South. The threat from the North also ensured that the military would have a determinant say in whatever happened politically in Seoul.

In the immediate wake of Park's assassination, my Korean interlocutors – businessmen, politicians, government officials, academics, and religious leaders – were remarkably candid in assessing what had happened and what was needed. Most believed that Korea needed stability first and then democratic change, not the reverse. Its earlier experience with Western-style democracy after World War II had been marred by corruption and ineffectual government. This was a major reason why the military remained very suspicious of politicians generally and of some in particular, such as Kim Dae-jung. Army leaders were similarly wary of businessmen who had ostentatiously flaunted their wealth. That is why Park, and the generals who followed, cracked down from time to time on lavish entertainment and golf games.

Some Koreans concluded (after the fact!) that Park had reached the limit of his education and military background and no longer had the capacity to handle the challenges of modern Korea. The longer he had been in power, the more he had been surrounded by sycophants who had shielded him from reality and intimidated others in the inner circle who showed any spine. All with whom I spoke stressed that an accommodation between the military and any new president was essential. Accommodation was not a Korean strong suit, and as the situation became more fluid, Korea's younger generals became more restless. The brief interlude of openness and candour was too good to last. In December, General Chun Doo-whan and his cohorts elbowed their army superiors aside, and in April 1980 they seized full power from the acting president in a military coup.

Chun was a paratroop general, a veteran of Korea's famous Tiger Battalion, which had fought in Vietnam and most recently had been in charge of the elite presidential guard at the Blue House. Unlike Park, he had no political experience in juggling the various Korean factions, less still in administration. He was determined, nonetheless, to re-establish order and relied on Park's brain trust to maintain economic growth. The power elite in South Korea welcomed the return of an iron fist. Stability was more attractive than democracy. The students reacted quite differently. In May 1980 they demonstrated furiously in Kwangju, capital of

Kim Dae-jung's home province, and were put down savagely by the Korean army. It is estimated that more than two hundred students were killed. Adding insult to injury, Chun had ordered soldiers from the northern provinces to do the dirty work – and they did. Remarkably, the students in Seoul did not mobilize. They may well have been shocked into submission by reports of what had transpired in Kwangju.

The Kwangju uprising, or "massacre," as it came to be called, created shock waves in Korea that resonate even today. The victims became martyrs, galvanizing demands for retribution and reform and ultimately fuelling electoral victory for Kim Dae-jung as well as a death sentence for the president who had directed the assault, Chun Doo-whan. The Americans were also blamed by many for "allowing" the Korean army to be used in this incident, but it is unlikely that they would have been able to prevent the Korean generals from acting as they did, even if they had wanted to. Clashes involving students and riot police were not unusual in Korea. What was unusual about Kwangju was the number of casualties and the brutal actions of Korean soldiers against their own people.

After the uprising in Kwangju in May 1980, Kim Dae-jung was rearrested and summarily sentenced to death as "the ring leader." For my farewell call later that year on President Chun Doo-whan, I was instructed by External to ask that this death sentence be commuted. It was not normal to raise any issue of substance during a farewell call, and mine turned out to be anything but normal. I arrived at the Blue House and met the president in a small anteroom. He was accompanied by the foreign minister, Park Tong-jin, who spoke English, a few Blue House advisers, military aides, and the president's interpreter. After a few pleasantries, I said that I did have an issue to raise, namely that my government respectfully requested that he consider commuting the death sentence of Kim Dae-jung.

On hearing the translation, the president bristled and the friendly demeanour of our meeting vanished. He grabbed the arms of his chair and started to yell at me in Korean. His interpreter gave a lively imitation in English. "What would Trudeau say if my ambassador asked him to commute the sentence of a Canadian thug?" If words were daggers, I had been jabbed. I had to think quickly, very quickly. "It would never happen, Mr President, because we do not have the death sentence in Canada. Mr Trudeau doesn't have that kind of power anyway. Very few leaders do. Not even," I added, "the president of the United States. You are one of a very few in the world who have such power."

At that point, as the translator was relaying my message to President

Chun, the foreign minister jumped in, in English. He was furious. "The president of the US does have the power," he declared. "No, he doesn't." "Yes, he does." "No." "Yes." The room was heating up. The president had had enough. He slapped the souvenir ashtray (my farewell gift) on the table. His aides lifted it and me up – me by the elbows – and marched me unceremoniously out of the Blue House.

A few months later, the newly elected president of the United States, Ronald Reagan, made a similar request, and it was reluctantly accepted. Kim Dae-jung was "deported" to study at Harvard in the early 1980s as a Nieman fellow. In 1997 he was elected president of the Republic of Korea. By that time, Chun Doo-whan was in jail under a death sentence relating back to the events in Kwangju. His death sentence was eventually commuted by Kim Dae-jung. You could never say that life was dull in Korea.

Many years later, and shortly after Kim Dae-jung had been elected president, I returned to Korea as the CEO of Bell Canada International. We made a major, and ultimately very profitable, investment in a Korean wireless company, and our Korean partner was convinced at that time that my support for Kim almost twenty years earlier helped win government support for the transaction. On this occasion, the circumstances for my meeting with the newly elected president were certainly different from those during his incarceration!

The Maple Leaf flag raised officially for the first time anywhere in the world, February 1965, Wellington, New Zealand,

Square dance lessons in Japan, September 1965: Derek H. Burney at centre; US Ambassador Edwin Reischauer in foreground (right); his wife, Haru, to the right of Burney; Barbara Bower, wife of Canada's ambassador, at left

Derek junior at his Japanese school, April 1966

With Don Jamieson at a Washington press conference, February 1977

Presenting credentials to President Park Chung-hee in Seoul, September 1978

Credentials
presentation day
at the Canadian
Residence, Seoul,
Korea, September
1978: Derek and
Joan Burney

First day on the job at the PMO, February 1987: Brian Mulroney and Derek H. Burney

At the Venice G7 Summit, June 1987: Derek H. Burney with President Reagan

Derek,
That where a guy from Thunder Bay should be!
with gratitude
Brian Mulroney

Accompanying the prime minister in a call on President Reagan in the Oval Office, 1987. The US note-taker is Ty Cobb, assistant national security adviser.

*for Derek, in the 'gallery'!
"FREE (Trade) at last".
with thanks Brian Mulroney*

Prime Minister Brian Mulroney looking at Simon Reisman and Derek Burney in the Members Gallery, October 1987

Presenting the final agreement to Prime Minister Brian Mulroney in Ottawa, December 1987: *left to right*, Gordon Ritchie, Derek H. Burney, the prime minister, and Simon Reisman

Brian Mulroney signing the Free Trade Agreement in Ottawa, 2 January 1988

Full support on the home front, Ottawa, December 1988:
left to right, Ian, Derek, Alex, and Jeff Burney

SIX

Ottawa, 1980–1987

The Montebello G7 Summit

Following my initial two-year stint in Seoul, I was advised that my appointment had been extended for a third year. That was not what happened. During a summer break in Hawaii in 1980 and after settling our oldest son, Derek, in the University of British Columbia (the closest one to Korea), I received an urgent message to call headquarters. When I did so, the officer in charge of Personnel, Daniel Molgat, read me a telegram he said I "would have received had you been at your post." I was being summoned home – by Allan Gotlieb, no less – to serve as the administrator of the 1981 G7 Summit in Canada. Technically, I would report to the clerk of the Privy Council, Michael Pitfield, but functionally the link was to Gotlieb, who was then the Canadian sherpa, or senior official, involved in the substantive summit preparations. My responsibilities involved logistics – security, media relations, and all transportation, hospitality, and hotel arrangements.

My first question was "Why me?" On receiving the predictable response, "You have been selected by the undersecretary," I asked," What exactly do you expect me to do?" I was told to return post-haste to Ottawa to begin to assemble a team and to get a better grasp of what was involved. As this was the first G7 Summit that Canada would host, the relevant information was skimpy. We had hosted a Commonwealth heads of government meeting, but that, as I was told, was in a different league. Indeed.

It was suggested that I visit Venice and consult the Italians, who had organized the 1980 summit. Only later did I discover that Gotlieb's first choice for administrator had actually attended the Venice summit to learn first-hand. His appointment had been vetoed by Michael Pitfield because Gotlieb had failed to consult Pitfield about his selection. Such are the ways of bureaucracy and the whim of fate in shaping careers.

Our son Ian was not impressed. He declared solemnly in Hawaii, "There must be a hundred guys in Ottawa who could do that job. Why did they have to pick you?" With visions of his high school graduation in Korea, girlfriends, and lifestyle in Seoul vanishing, to be replaced by grade twelve and thirteen in Ottawa, he was inconsolable and refused to speak to me for several weeks. Despite this highly annoying experience with the vagaries of foreign service assignments Ian is, ironically, the only one of our sons who eventually chose a foreign service career.

I headed to Ottawa to get started. Joan took the family back to Seoul and started to pack. I returned for six weeks to pay farewell calls – notably my call on President Chun Doo-whan – and brought the family home in November. For the summit, I started from scratch. I was told emphatically that Prime Minister Trudeau wanted to return to the simpler milieu that had initiated the whole summit process, a library at Rambouillet. The summits had become much grander events in each subsequent year, with each leader trying presumably to outdo the preceding host in terms of grandeur.

The Chateau Montebello seemed to fit the bill. A 1930s log structure, situated halfway between Ottawa and Montreal, it was remote but reasonably luxurious and could handle about fifteen guests each for the eight participants. (Although called the G7, the European Commission's representative made it eight.) But Montebello by itself was not enough. Because we were unable to get satisfactory assurances for co-operation on security from the separatist Quebec government, we had a second or backup site established in Ottawa. Consequently, half the summit was planned for Montebello; half for Ottawa. Double the logistics; double the headaches; double the challenges.

I recruited several key organizing team members: John Robinson from External as my deputy in all respects but with major responsibility for media relations; Harry Stewart from the PCO for all administration and finance issues; Assistant Commissioner Bill McKibbon from the RCMP for security; and Ron Lemieux for protocol and logistics. Security was a major concern, which was why we sought explicit security assurances from Quebec. The year 1981 saw attempted assassinations on President Reagan and the pope. So we were on high alert, contemplating all sorts of plots and contingencies. A special RCMP squad was trained by Britain's famous SAS for hostage retrieval (our Armed Forces having declined the honour). Thousands of soldiers were drafted, along with police, to provide perimeter protection around Montebello and along the Ottawa River.

Special armoured cars (Chevrolets!) were acquired for each head of government. And Canada's modest military helicopter fleet was upgraded to transport delegations to and from Montebello. The Americans spurned all Canadian transportation, bringing Marine One to transport the president, along with their own armoured presidential limousine. (Shades of London and Lancaster House.) I took a small revenge. When the Americans asked to use the golf carts at Montebello so that the president could drive to the adjacent Manoir Papineau for a private breakfast with the president of France, I said, "No, you brought your own helicopter and your own limo. Get your own golf cart." I subsequently relented, but I think they got the point.

The media aspect was anything but straightforward. Apart from the logistic challenge of housing, feeding, and lubricating some two thousand media representatives from the participating countries, Canada was also the host broadcaster for all public portions of the summit, providing the basic television feed to all other networks. Unfortunately, the CBC's technicians' union went on strike in June of 1981, just weeks before the summit, and threw a major monkey wrench into our plans. We turned to CTV, only to discover that they did not have enough equipment to handle the task. CTV was then a network of independents, as opposed to a true network.

I called Michael Pitfield and explained that our only recourse was to have the prime minister order CBC management to take up the task. He agreed and so did the prime minister. Fortunately, the CBC vice presidents proved to be up to the challenge, but not without incident. As a summit session began at Montebello, one of them, operating a camera, mistakenly bumped into Prime Minister Thatcher as she searched for her place. She swatted him firmly with her handbag, all the while being recorded by another senior CBC cameraman.

Even protocol had its moments. There are certain established international customs, one of which is that heads of state outrank heads of government. Therefore the presidents of France and the United States have higher status than prime ministers when it comes to transportation (the first shall be last to arrive, etc.) and other matters of protocol during events. I had assigned the US and French delegations to the ground-floor river-view wings at Montebello, and the senior (by time in office) prime ministers were given the second-floor river-view wings, while the more recent leaders and the host were assigned initially to the wings facing the highway.

Trudeau, however, did not accept conventional protocol, especially any notion that presidents outranked prime ministers. He insisted very late in the day that he and his friend Helmut Schmidt receive the pride of place at Montebello, and he did not really care where the others were lodged. That would have been fine if only we had known before each delegation's advance party had visited the site and, in the case of the Japanese, taken photos of each of their rooms and the furniture they were to use. Nonetheless, I was obliged to comply with the host's and my prime minister's wishes.

Most delegations accepted the abrupt change of allocation with minimal fuss. However, the Japanese ambassador persisted in asking why the change had been made at the last minute. To accommodate Trudeau's wishes, I had rearranged the delegations in an abstruse but somewhat alphabetical order – to give some logic for the change – but the Japanese still wanted to know why. I said that a change had been made because one delegation had complained about the original allocation. On checking one by one with his ambassadorial colleagues in Ottawa, the Japanese ambassador discovered that none had requested a change. After the summit, he confronted me with his findings. "Ah, Mr Ambassador," I explained, "you missed one delegation – the Canadian delegation." He was stunned into silence.

Canada's first G7 summit proved to be a testing ground for organizational and managerial skills and, most of all, direct involvement in crisis management. Events of this kind, I learned in time, are destined to succeed primarily because of the enormous political capital invested. The ingredients for success are the interpersonal relationships between and among the G7 leaders, which can pay dividends between annual summits. As the most junior (in power) player at the G7, Canada is particularly privileged just to be there. The substance of the discussions and the communiqué issued at the end of the summit are the real focus or determinant of success. Logistics, even security, are secondary, but as in much of international affairs, form is as important as substance. Canada has a well-earned reputation as a master of the form or, more simply, for being a good host. With the success of Montebello, I was happy and greatly relieved to contribute to that proud tradition.

The American priority at Montebello, if not at all summits, was to ensure that the United States' view gained top billing with the attending media. To preserve the informal atmosphere of Montebello, we had established the press centre and all the media in Ottawa, which is where the summit concluded. Delegations were expected to brief their media on events at Montebello by returning to the Ottawa media centre for that purpose. The Americans short-circuited this plan and the "understanding" among all summit participants by commandeering a church in Montebello, which became their on-the-spot briefing centre and gave them a clear jump on all others. The following year, the French hosts abandoned the notion of informal seclusion and hosted the summit in the palace at Versailles!

After the Montebello Summit, I was appointed assistant undersecretary (director general) for the Economic Affairs Bureau at External. This was a prize assignment and my real introduction to trade policy. The bureau had three divisions: Commercial Policy, headed by John Weekes, with Louise Fréchette as one of his deputies; General Economic Relations (summitry, OECD relations, and, more generally, international financial institutions involving, primarily, liaison with the Department of Finance), headed by John Paynter; and Economic Development (north-south issues, aid, and relations with CIDA), headed by Aubrey Morantz. These divisions each had top-ranking officials or "high flyers" at the helm. They had the knowledge and the experience. My job was to steer. My main task was to serve as "sous-sherpa" to our associate undersecretary, de Montigny Marchand, who was Trudeau's personal representative or sherpa at the Versailles (1982) and Williamsburg (1983) G7 summits.

I had become a summit "groupie" of sorts, having attended London in 1977 and Bonn in 1978 with Don Jamieson and having served as the administrator of the summit that Canada hosted in 1981. Involvement as the sous-sherpa and later the sherpa for a total of nine must have set a record, but it imbued me with a strong sense of the importance of these annual gatherings for Canada as well as of their potential utility in global affairs. Quite apart from the "show biz" imagery and the lack of concrete action, these summits do provide a unique forum for major world leaders to get to know one another, to share concerns and differences, and occasionally to nudge a clearer consensus on major economic issues and provide a direct collective response to hot political topics of the day. During the early 1980s, these inevitably related to developments in the Middle East.

Our bureau was also responsible for providing regular guidance and instructions to our OECD mission in Paris, the GATT mission in Geneva,

and other embassies directly involved in multilateral trade and economic affairs. The 1982 GATT Ministerial in Geneva, which Canada chaired,
was, unfortunately, unsuccessful in launching the next trade round, but
I learned that even failure involves a lot of detailed work. The Uruguay
Round was ultimately launched at Punta del Este in 1986. This experience was also sobering for me personally regarding the efficacy of global
trade negotiations. The tempo was glacial.

The 1983 UNCTAD VI Conference proved similarly revealing on the
difference between ideological rhetoric and tangible progress on the
problems faced by developing countries. UNCTAD (the United Nations
Conference on Trade and Development) was, of course, related directly
to the North-South dialogue, a concept championed by Prime Minister
Trudeau at the G7 summit chaired by Canada in 1981, but the emphasis
was disproportionately long on dialogue and short on commitment,
reflecting fundamental ideological differences on the most appropriate
economic model for developing countries. The overlaying test of wills
between the United States and the Soviet Union also diverted attention
and action on this topic and fuelled the ideological split.

The Trade Policy Review

Our bureau also became involved with a "trade policy review" which the
government had initially assigned to the Department of Industry, Trade
and Commerce (ITC), in conjunction with External and Finance.
However, early in 1982, the clerk of the Privy Council, Michael Pitfield,
decided to reorganize ITC, and Regional Economic Expansion (DREE),
essentially by merging the Trade Commissioner Service and some policy
branches from ITC into External and leaving the sector branches to join
with DREE in a new Department of Regional Industrial Expansion (DRIE).
It also provided External with two ministers: the secretary of state for
External Affairs (Mark McGuigan at this point, but soon replaced by the
veteran Allan MacEachen) and a new minister for International Trade
(Ed Lumley).

What followed was a revolving door of new senior or deputy minister
appointments, much bitterness among trade commissioners everywhere,
and a good deal of internal confusion. The concept was clear, but the
integration process had not really been thought through. I learned later
in life that reorganizations rarely achieve what is intended and usually
generate confusion for about two years. This was certainly true of the

1982 reorganization of External and ITC. An example: as a result of simply moving groups alongside one another without really integrating them, the "new External" had seven separate divisions dealing with the United States, reporting to three assistant deputy ministers and to two deputy ministers, as well as two ministers, a prescription for policy paralysis, if not confusion.*

But with one exception: the trade policy initiative now rested squarely with External Affairs, much to the annoyance of Finance. We decided to make the most of it. Michael Hart† held the principal pen. Tough-minded, even acerbic at times, Hart had a formidable knowledge of trade policy at all levels and a clear-eyed view of practical, as opposed to ideal, solutions. He was indispensable in moving matters forward within our department and in the seemingly endless interdepartmental consultations that ensued. He quickly earned my full confidence. My job was to try eventually to move the result through the juggernaut of process to which all new policy was subjected under the highly centralized Pitfield system: endless reviews by committees of senior officials before anything got to cabinet.

It meant that something like "trade policy" was reviewed by senior representatives from departments such as Indian and Northern Affairs or Defence which had neither an interest nor any knowledge of the topic. Nonetheless, they had views. It was Parkinson's law at its bureaucratic worst. There were days when my main task was to try to restrain my younger colleagues from using Canadian hockey tactics at these meetings and to motivate them to keep at it, despite the frustratingly slow pace of progress through the system and the ill-informed nature of much of the discussion. Among other things, we discovered during this policy review that no courses were being taught at Canadian universities on Canadian commercial policy. Consequently, as part of the initiative, we produced a textbook of sorts on the history and practice of Canadian commercial policy.

During the consultative process conducted in parallel with the private sector, we were told repeatedly that it was essential "to get things right with the US," a theme our trade minister, Ed Lumley, encouraged and welcomed. He also inspired our small group to keep at it, in spite of all the

* It took even longer for the system to accept that the Lester B. Pearson Building now housed trade officials. The sign in front of the building was not updated until 1992, just before the department underwent a name change from External Affairs and International Trade to Foreign Affairs and International Trade. Of course, the single department has now been dismantled and replaced by separate departments of foreign affairs and international trade.

† Hart's book *A Trading Nation* (University of British Columbia Press, 2002) is an excellent primer for students or practitioners of Canadian trade policy.

bureaucratic backsliding. When he moved to Industry the following year, he maintained his constructive and supportive attitude on the review.

The Trade Policy Review offered a comprehensive description of Canada's approach to trade negotiations and of the options for further liberalization. It presented various options but stopped short of any recommendation. When our new trade minister, Gerald Regan, brought it to cabinet in the summer of 1983, he nonetheless gave particular emphasis to one option – the prospect of pursuing additional sectoral agreements (like the Auto Pact) with the United States. As bureaucrats, we were both surprised and encouraged by this emphasis and by the positive reaction to a review that would prove ultimately to have a much larger purpose. The minister's support proved instrumental in establishing a small task force charged with exploring further the prospects of sectoral arrangements. Tony Halliday, an experienced trade official recently returned from an assignment in Washington, took on responsibility for this task. While, in the end, this task force did not succeed in negotiating any such arrangements, its work proved critical in preparing the ground for a much more expansive initiative to address Canada-US relations. More about that later.

The US Branch

By this time (September 1983), I had moved up the ladder to become assistant deputy minister (ADM) for the United States, handed the task of blending the seven disparate US divisions into a coherent force – a "refinement" of the 1982 reorganization. I had not expected the assignment. In fact, I had expected to become the ADM for economic policy, a more natural extension of the job I had. Bob Latimer (from ITC) had been expected to be the US head. In the event, we reversed roles.*

The initial realignment of the two departments in January 1982 had, as mentioned earlier, not integrated the various units dealing with the United States. Instead, they were left standing as they had been in various buildings and with very different reporting structures. Grouping all into a single branch posed a challenge, but the more clearly defined responsibilities and more coherent structure reinforced the basic objective. The new US Branch was to manage all dimensions of the bilateral

---

* I am not sure why this happened. One theory is that de Montigny Marchand, one of our associate undersecretaries, wanted an "External" head of relations with the United States. He also knew me better than he knew Bob Latimer.

relationship. It was assigned the lead role on trade – both trade policy and trade promotion – and the coordinating responsibility on trans-boundary issues such as environment (acid rain), energy (the NEP), and transportation. The latter often involved difficult consultations with line departments in Ottawa as well as with American officials. What were loosely labelled "political" relations were at the core of the branch's responsibilities and covered everything from highly sensitive issues such as cruise missile testing to high-level visits to and from the United States. The branch had managerial oversight of the embassy in Washington and more than a dozen consulates general and consulates in the United States, duties that spanned budget preparation, personnel assignments, and officer appraisals. All public affairs activities in the United States (cultural events, media relations, Canadian studies, etc.) were also coordinated within the branch.

The new US Branch reported to the troika of deputy ministers – the undersecretary, Marcel Massé, the deputy (political), de Montigny Marchand, and the deputy for trade, Sylvia Ostry – and also to the two ministers. I was on call, literally, to each at any given time.* Despite the heavy superstructure, the new realignment provided a much more cohesive basis for managing our relations with the United States and a new team spirit for all. Other geographic branches, such as for Europe, Asia, Africa, and Latin America, were organized in a similar manner at the same time, but none had the breadth or depth of bilateral issues and interests of those now concentrated in the US Branch.

Structure is one thing, but people are what make a difference and are what really make any organization work. I inherited strong, experienced individuals from "old" ITC and External respectively and added some key officers to reinforce our new responsibilities. For instance, a special unit headed by Michael Hart and Bill Dymond and reporting directly to me was put in place to spearhead consultations and developments arising from the Trade Policy Review. Percy Eastham and Doug Waddell brought wisdom, experience, and solid tactical judgment to a lengthy list of trade disputes and to an ongoing dialogue on each with our embassy and the Americans. Bob Gaynor, Ed Bobinski, and, later, Garrett Lambert were seasoned veterans from the Trade Commissioner Service who guided trade promotion plans, events, and export assistance programs with our consular offices in the United States.

---

* This divided responsibility vis-à-vis ministers became a bone of contention between the two ministers, each of whom wondered whom I really worked for. I suspect this irritant fed the desire to resplit the department in 2004.

Our political and transboundary responsibilities were led by a complementary blend of External "high flyers." Manfred von Nostitz and John Noble were strong-willed, tenacious, and articulate. They had exactly the temperament and negotiating skills I wanted and more than held their own both in intra-departmental discussions and with their American counterparts. They also handled most of the managerial oversight duties with the embassy and our other offices in the United States. Stan Gooch and, eventually, Brian Buckley provided a more genial approach in coordinating the transboundary issues (energy, environment, etc.) for which other Canadian departments had the major policy role. I had a very strong team overall, and the clear focus of our new branch's duties energized our effort across the board. I always enjoyed working with people who were clear-headed and determined, and I tend to give maximum scope to those who demonstrate that they can deliver.

I have often thought that the ADM positions, at least at that time, were the most attractive and, in many ways, the most significant operational slots in the newly reorganized department. Later, as associate under secretary or deputy minister, I obviously had higher rank and broader responsibilities, but the duties were less hands-on and lacked the collegiality or camaraderie of a tightly knit and clearly focused branch. For one thing, ADMs had their offices "with their troops." Deputy ministers were on a floor by themselves.

My job as ADM was to manage and direct the full range of bilateral issues or irritants – from the major to the mundane – in this all-encompassing relationship. I had to assert as well as defend positions within the department and in interdepartmental consultations with counterparts at Environment, Energy, Transport, and Agriculture. A regular dialogue with senior US diplomats based in Ottawa, including the ambassador, was an essential part of the job. I was in almost daily contact with our ambassador and others in our Washington embassy, receiving their views on American concerns and representations as well as fervent opinions the embassy held on Canadian policy. Our ambassador, Allan Gotlieb, was not shy with advice. On all fronts, the dialogue could be spirited since virtually every Canadian has a view on relations with the United States, and many pride themselves to an unwarranted degree on how well they understand or know the United States. Direct oral briefings with our two ministers were very much part of the duty, both with the soon-to-be outgoing Liberals and with the incoming Conservatives. This was definitely not a "desk job" and the US Branch was a far cry from the USA Division in which I had laboured almost twenty years previously.

In the fall of 1983, relations with the United States were strained. The

National Energy Program (NEP) had antagonized the Americans as much as it had Albertans. What the Americans found particularly egregious were the confiscatory aspects regarding their assets. The NEP had not been subjected to the Pitfield process of consultation but had sprung from two or three senior officials, presumably with political prompting. External had not been involved in developing the policy and yet was the recipient of much wrath from the United States. The Foreign Investment Review Agency (FIRA), established by the government in 1975 to "review" all foreign investments and ensure that they were "of net benefit to Canada," smouldered as another irritant, despite Ed Lumley's best efforts to "defang" its operation. Acid rain was a prominent irritant on Canada's side. Trudeau's ambivalence on NATO and his hints about moral equivalence between the United States and the USSR were anathema to the Reagan White House. His 1983 peace initiative aroused similar concerns.

My attempts to question the practicality of this initiative within External were singularly unappreciated. I contended essentially that the prospects for success were much lower than the potential for annoyance in Washington. The latter may, of course, have been a secondary part of the motivation. Trudeau's initiative was supported and promoted by colleagues in External Affairs, very much in the spirit of projecting a "distinctive Canadian voice" in world affairs with undertones of "Third-Option" yearnings for counterweights to our "dependence" on the United States. (Similar attitudes prompted the "soft power" initiatives and emphasis of Lloyd Axworthy when he served as Canada's foreign minister in the late 1990s.)

Like most US ambassadors, the ambassador to Canada, Paul Robinson, was a political appointment rather than a trained diplomat. He had no hesitation in offering advice bluntly and publicly to Canadians on matters that went well beyond the scope of our bilateral relationship and traditional understandings of his diplomatic role. His counterpart in Washington was my former boss, Allan Gotlieb, no shrinking violet any day of the week. Whenever I accompanied the new Conservative ministers to Washington, there tended to be a common feature at the end of the visit. Gotlieb unfailingly advised the visiting minister that it had been the "best visit" he had experienced during his time in Washington. After several of these similar appraisals, I finally asked the ambassador how every visit became "the best." "Because," Gotlieb deadpanned, "they just get better every time!"

The ADM assignment proved to be stimulating, and for ten years, the challenge of managing this complex and primordial relationship for Canada was central to almost everything I did. While, for the most part, the objective was to maintain and facilitate smooth diplomatic relations through regular lines of communication between the two governments, the Trade Policy Review was building momentum for what became a rare but major policy initiative on trade, which would set the dominant tone for the relationship over the better part of the next decade.

Trudeau and Reagan

It is unlikely that there were two more incompatible personalities on the world stage than Pierre Trudeau and Ronald Reagan. Topics of common interest were difficult to define, and there was little meeting of minds on policy issues, domestic or global. They each had a flair for showmanship and each aroused strong support, even adulation, on their respective home fronts, as well as equally passionate opposition.

On one occasion when they met in Washington, Trudeau had been advised to open with a joke in order to "ease into" the discussion. Reagan was known to enjoy telling and listening to jokes, but Trudeau's bombed. It was decidedly "off-colour," prompting grimaces and no laughter on either side of the table. From that point on, the meeting went downhill. Reagan's advisers were visibly displeased. It was evident from leaks to the US media that they did not see Trudeau as someone they could work with – more like their "left-leaning liberal" opponents in the United States. Trudeau did not seem to mind. After all, keeping a safe distance, especially from a Republican-led US administration, had political appeal in Canada (and not just during his time).

Nonetheless, when President Reagan visited Ottawa in 1981, he was greeted on Parliament Hill by hundreds of demonstrators demanding action on acid rain. Trudeau stepped up and urged the demonstrators, in effect, to give the president a more civil reception. With each bilateral meeting, however, the differences became more profound and the chemistry at the top was cool at best. Their lack of compatibility put more weight on relations between Reagan's secretary of state, George Shultz, and Canada's secretary of state for External Affairs, Allan MacEachen. Their personalities were much more compatible, but they could not bridge the major differences on policy.

Because relations were fractious at the very top, MacEachen tried to use his previous personal association with Shultz to contain the damage. They had been classmates at the University of Chicago, and both were, after all, economists with academic credentials. MacEachen was determined, above all, to explain the rationale behind the National Energy

Program in a manner which, he thought, would prove to be persuasive with his former fellow student.

The NEP had been initiated with little interdepartmental consultation, despite all the PCO committees that were in place precisely to ensure coherence and extensive deliberation for all government policy. Not only were the Americans, who had major investments in Canadian energy resources, in the dark, along with the province of Alberta, which had the most to lose, but so were those of us whose task it was to explain government policy to the Americans. It is difficult to defend what you do not know, and in the initial weeks and months, we scrambled to develop a plausible response to complaints from Washington. There is always a fine balance between the need for secrecy on major initiatives and the need for consultation, but the NEP broke all the rules on process. The substance of the policy initiative did not fare much better.

MacEachen sought valiantly to fill the void. In what became the first in a series of regular quarterly meetings between the two, he selected the lieutenant governor's residence in Halifax as the site for his meeting with Secretary Shultz. With the assembled delegations flanking a boardroom table, the secretary of state for External Affairs gave a detailed discourse on the evolution of the NEP, tracing the historical distinctions, particularly the role played by government, in the development of Canada, as opposed to the United States. It was a scholarly effort, tightly presented and with only one flaw. At the end, Mr MacEachen said in a light manner, "Well, George, I have used every arrow in my quiver." "Yes, Allan," Shultz blurted, "and you didn't hit me with one." On that note, the Canadian side of the table slumped visibly, and the rest of the discussion made little headway.

At best, these meetings served the purpose of focusing attention on or drawing the poison from priority issues on the bilateral agenda, an exercise which, in turn, obliged the bureaucracies in Ottawa and Washington to rethink or, at least, restate long-standing points of difference. They acted to relieve pressure on some, even if efforts at resolution proved more difficult. Much depended on the commitment of the principals and the chemistry between them. Shultz was genuinely committed and referred to the routine get-togethers as "good gardening." On the Canadian side, both MacEachen and his Conservative successor, Joe Clark, were similarly committed, but both were, in conventional Canadian style, wary of getting "too close" in the process. The quarterly meetings helped soften the tone of the bilateral relationship, but the pending general election in Canada would provide new impetus on the policy side as well.

SEVEN

New Government: New Direction

With the election in September 1984, many at External Affairs expected that relations with the United States would be given priority, but my first meeting with our newly elected government was anything but cordial. The day after the Progressive Conservative government of Brian Mulroney was sworn in, I was summoned, along with our undersecretary, Marcel Massé, and Bob Fowler from the Privy Council Office to the Prime Minister's Office to discuss his plans for an early visit to Washington. It was immediately clear to us that the prime minister's aides were furious. News of Mr Mulroney's plan to visit Washington had leaked the night before, and they were convinced that the leak had come from Canadian civil servants, many of whom they suspected of being loyally Liberal. Attempts to suggest that the leak had come from the Americans, who had already been advised, were spurned. The atmosphere was brittle.

At one point in the meeting, I was asked bluntly how I expected to help with such a visit. I carefully explained that, ordinarily I would oversee preparation of a briefing book for the prime minister setting out the specifics on bilateral and global issues. "What makes you think you can prepare a briefing book for us?" asked the PMO official in charge.

I paused. "Well," I said. "We will set out the United States position for you on each of the issues and you can fill in the paragraph on what our position is going to be." That broke the ice a bit and was the beginning of my relationship with Prime Minister Mulroney. I accompanied him on his first summit meeting with President Reagan later that month and was closely involved in all subsequent sessions.

The tone and priority of our relations with the United States was about to change dramatically. Although Mulroney believed that good relations with the United States were in Canada's best interest, this did not mean that he had an ideological affinity with the US administration.

In fact, despite the Conservative appellation of his party, Mulroney, along with many others in his government and Canadians generally, was more closely aligned in political terms with Democrats than with Republicans, especially on social policy issues – fiscally conservative, perhaps, but socially progressive.

Brian Mulroney acknowledged publicly that he had been attracted to politics initially by the example of a young, Irish American Democrat, Jack Kennedy, whose "new generation" appeal resonated throughout North America. As prime minister, Mulroney cultivated relationships with Democrats, including Senator Ted Kennedy, and Republicans, recognizing implicitly the balance of power that existed between a Republican administration and a Democrat-controlled Congress and the need for access to both.

On assuming office, Mulroney was acutely aware that the bilateral relationship was in need of high-level attention and new direction. He was determined to undo some policies that not only had antagonized the American administration but, more fundamentally, he also saw as undermining Canada's economic well-being. The National Energy Policy and FIRA were at the top of this list. The PCs had campaigned openly against both in the 1984 election. So there was no surprise when steps were taken to change them shortly after the election. The NEP had been as offensive to many western Canadians for restricting development as it had been to Americans for confiscating value on a retroactive basis. FIRA had been more of a procedural annoyance than a restrictive mechanism. It had done little of any consequence for the Canadian economy but had become a symbol of excessive interventionism. But the most dramatic change of all would involve a major initiative on trade.

Free Trade Underpinnings

My own involvement with free trade had begun with the government's Trade Policy Review in 1981–82 and my own immersion in trade policy following the Montebello G7 Summit. As a student of Canadian history, I was generally aware of the political debates over reciprocity and free trade that had been at the forefront in Canada's early days as a nation. But I had no idea the Trade Policy Review would open the avenue for a full-scale negotiation and a riveting national debate culminating in the 1988 election.

The prospect of free trade between Canada and the United States predated Confederation. As prime minister of the Province of Canada, John

A. Macdonald had tried to negotiate a reciprocity agreement on trade with the United States following the demise of the 1854 Reciprocity Treaty. His initiative was rebuffed, but when given a broader prime ministerial role for all of Canada in the aftermath of the American Civil War, he tried again. Again he was rebuffed. Only after gaining his second mandate in 1878, did Macdonald institute his National Policy, aimed at nurturing and developing a manufacturing and trade base within Canada. His imprint on trade had a long life and eventually spawned a branch-plant phenomenon for manufacturing, notably in Ontario.

Wilfrid Laurier tried, in 1911, to rekindle the flame for free trade. He and his finance minister, W.S. Fielding, successfully concluded a modest new reciprocity agreement, but lost in an election campaign noted for its hyperbole (shades of what was to come). Mackenzie King succeeded in placing Canada-US trade policy on a more principled basis with the conclusion of the Trade Agreements of 1935 and 1938. Carefully never described as either free trade or reciprocity, these two agreements reduced tariffs and committed the two countries to extend most-favoured-nation (MFN) status to each other. King also flirted briefly, and largely privately, with the concept of a bilateral free trade agreement immediately after World War II but decided, presumably, that the political price might exceed the economic gain for Canada. Instead, he stuck with the politically safer, and much slower, process of trade liberalization introduced with the successful conclusion of the multilateral General Agreement on Tariffs and Trade (GATT) in 1947. While GATT may have been slower and safer, some of the later negotiating rounds, particularly the Kennedy (1964–67) and Tokyo (1973–79) Rounds, provided a framework for continuing liberalization of Canada-US trade, and the Auto Pact of 1965 consecrated the concept in one of Canada's most powerful manufacturing sectors.

The Trade Policy Review covered the waterfront on Canada's existing trade commitments, the strengths and weakness of the Canadian economy, and the extent of bilateral and other trade links, and outlined possible options for the future. Probably more for political than for economic reasons, the trade minister of the day, Gerald Regan, as I have previously mentioned, emphasized the notion of additional sectoral arrangements (like the Auto Pact), though this had been a minor theme of the review. Any suggestion of broader free trade was muted by bureaucratic caution. Regan's political motive, I suspect, was to find a potentially positive point of dialogue with the Americans, at a time when there were few positives on the bilateral agenda.

The Auto Pact was a compelling example. It had moved Canadian auto production out from the inefficient, branch-plant shelter of producing only specific models for the Canadian market into an integrated North American market in which plants in Canada, primarily in Ontario, produced for both the Canadian and the United States markets. And it worked very much to Canada's advantage. We produced about one-third more automobiles for the Big Three – GM, Ford, and Chrysler – than Canadians bought. It became a tonic for improved productivity in Canada and a major engine of growth for Ontario's economy.

Attitudes in the country tended to be divided roughly on regional lines. The Atlantic region and western Canada generally favoured the concept of free trade, but possibly more for negative than for positive reasons. Atlantic Canada, in particular, resented the growing dominance of a protected, high-cost Ontario manufacturing base. The West was philosophically and politically more disposed to favour closer ties with the United States but also resented the protected manufacturing dominance of central Canada. Ontario and Quebec were much more guarded, if not outright negative. Ontario did not want to risk its place of economic privilege within Canada and was fundamentally more leery of getting "too close" to the United States. The "cultural nationalists" were primarily from Ontario and were congenitally fearful of American domination of their domain. Quebec was sensitive to its clothing, textile, and footwear industries and to its supply-managed agricultural operations (dairy and poultry) but less fearful about cultural domination.

A combination of forces in the early 1980s triggered changes to the landscape, notably in Quebec and, to a lesser extent, in Ontario. The success of the Auto Pact was evident to all, but relations, more generally, with the United States had become fractious on many fronts. The National Energy Policy had unnerved Americans about investment in Canada. Pierre Trudeau's foreign policy flirtations with Castro and Moscow did little to encourage positive attitudes in Washington, and American stonewalling on acid rain had perturbed many Canadians. Whereas, as I have said, the recurring message during contacts with the Canadian business community was "Whatever you do (on trade policy), you need first to 'get things right' with the Americans," I learned that the definition of "right" tended to differ from source to source.

Nevertheless, public opinion was shifting on the concept of free trade, notably in Quebec, where sentiments towards the United States were basically less sensitive (and less apprehensive) than in Ontario. The West was solidly supportive; Atlantic Canada, possibly for nostalgic reasons, remained favourable. These facts fit well with Mr Mulroney's power axis, which combined the West and Quebec.

In the early 1980s, Canada faced a twin dilemma on the trade front. Increasing protectionism in our major market, fuelled by individual or sectoral congressional pressures, aroused concern throughout the Canadian business community and in the minds of those in government dealing with the many of irritants vis-à-vis the United States. On the multilateral front, efforts to expedite a new round of global trade negotiations, including a ministerial session of the GATT chaired by Canada in 1982, were failing dismally. The European priority was internal integration and preservation of its Common Agriculture Policy. The GATT was proving to be powerless, like a "sheriff without a police force,"* in adjudicating or resisting a host of "managed trade" solutions. These sentiments underpinned a series of consultations with Canadian business representatives and became a catalyst for fresh thinking among some bureaucrats in Ottawa, including me.

Trade liberalization, whether bilateral or multilateral, was perceived as positive in policy terms and as an instrument, by no means exclusive, for promoting greater competitiveness and greater efficiency in Canadian industry. Canadian firms were obliged to adjust to changes in technology and to tax and fiscal policies in order to compete successfully, but for an economy as dependent on trade as Canada's, an assertively open approach to trade was critical. Less certain was the degree of political will to move against vested interests and the decidedly mixed emotions in Canada about any major initiative involving the United States. What was increasingly evident, however, was a mood favouring improved and more secure access to the vital US market, which consumed a steadily increasing share of Canadian exports. By the early 1980s, three-quarters of Canada's exports went to the United States.

The Shamrock Summit

One day in December 1984 I opened a letter in the mail at home. It was from the prime minister, putting me in charge of all policy preparations for President Reagan's visit to Quebec City in March – what came to be known as the "Shamrock Summit." The manner of the appointment was unusual. It sidetracked all normal procedures in government. The un-

---

* A description usually attributed to the EC's ambassador to GATT at the time, Roy Denham.

usual process itself betrayed the PMO's lack of familiarity with the ways and levels of Canada's bureaucracy. It also ruffled a few feathers of those above me in the bureaucratic hierarchy at External. Normally, the PCO would have acted on the prime minister's behalf and perhaps delegated the responsibility to External. Nonetheless, I was instructed to put together a task force using "all the resources needed for success" and to develop, with my American counterparts, a substantive agenda for action by the leaders at the meeting.

The newly re-elected Reagan administration was warm but somewhat wary of the newly elected Canadian government. Political leadership had changed, but policies and officials in Ottawa, had not. Canadian officials were well aware of the political change in Ottawa but many had been bruised from earlier encounters with their American counterparts and had no illusions about the prospects for tangible results. The Americans were completely unfamiliar with the parliamentary system wherein elected leaders changed but the officials representing them did not. The whole Canadian civil service, right up to deputy ministers and the clerk of the Privy Council, is made up of permanent, professional officials. The US system is very different on that score. When an administration changes, it means up to four thousand senior officials resign, to be replaced by new people appointed by the new president.

Nonetheless, both sides saw the Shamrock Summit as an opportunity to change the tone and chart a new direction for bilateral relations. It was evident that this was what both leaders wanted. In our planning for the summit, we focused on three dimensions of the bilateral relationship: trade and investment, which I led on behalf of External Affairs on the Canadian side, assisted primarily by Finance and DRIE; environment, specifically acid rain, led by Jim Bruce of Environment Canada, assisted by External; and Defence Production and Trade, led by Bob Brown* of DRIE, assisted by Finance, Defence, and External. Reflecting my G7 sous-sherpa experience, as well as convention, our interdepartmental task force decided that an all-encompassing communiqué would be the best umbrella for action.

Defence production and trade proved to be the least productive of our three "initiatives," essentially because the "hawks" from the Pentagon were more anxious to see a unilateral increase in defence spending by the dovish Canadians than any mutual benefit on production or trade. Acid

---

* The same Bob Brown who eventually became chief executive officer of Bombardier and in August 2004 succeeded me as chief executive officer of CAE.

rain posed a major obstacle because the positions on both sides were deeply entrenched. Neither side was ready to blink, as this would only be construed as weakness. The best we could muster was an agreement to consign the issue to "special emissaries" for further study. The dispute was elevated but made little progress.

That left trade and investment, which was by far the most important and the most promising element on the bilateral agenda. By signalling its readiness to dismantle the NEP and FIRA, the new government in Canada had already indicated that change was happening. In December 1984 the prime minister had declared to a business audience in New York that Canada was "open for business" and he meant it. As officials, we knew there was interest on both sides in moving the trade relationship forward. We also knew that there was opposition, particularly in Canada, to much more than an incremental approach. The concept of "free trade" caused much more of an allergic reaction in Canada than in the United States, and while President Reagan had spoken publicly about a North American accord – "from the Yucatan to the Yukon" – Mr Mulroney was on record as being opposed to free trade. However, other influential cabinet members, such as Michael Wilson in Finance, John Crosbie at Justice, and Jim Kelleher at Trade, were openly in favour.

Because of sensitivity about the term "free trade," we had to avoid using it explicitly. The Americans were no less sensitive. They preferred to speak about "free and fair trade," fairness always being in the eye of the beholder. The major test, therefore, for the Shamrock Summit was to devise a wording that launched something like the exploration of free trade without calling it that. Even that proved a hard sell within Ottawa. There were two major and many minor opponents. The minister of Industry, Sinclair Stevens was adamantly opposed; one of his deputies, Gordon Ritchie, was obliged to endorse his minister's position, but I suspect that he also resented the fact that External was dealing with a subject he thought belonged more appropriately to his department. We often referred to Industry as the "Department of Protection" and saw Commerce in Washington in the same vein.

Within External, there was also strong opposition to a bilateral trade initiative from the "GATTologists," the multilateral brigade, primarily from my former Economic Affairs Bureau, and from those who continued to see value in a more hands-off approach to the United States generally – in other words, those who still saw life in the "Third Option." The head of the multilateral, or GATT, team at External was Reid Morden, who had joined External with me in 1963. Despite the different emphasis we gave to trade policy, our relationship was one of mutual respect. When I subsequently moved to the PMO, Reid was the assistant secretary for foreign policy and security at the PCO. When I was in Washington, he was the undersecretary at External, following a stint as the head of the Canadian Security and Intelligence Service (CSIS). We had both served in Japan, although at different times. Close personal relationships often help to mitigate differences and, equally, can stimulate co-operation under fire. Morden was skeptical but not obstructive, about the free trade initiative.

Our Foreign Affairs minister, Joe Clark, was cool to the trade initiative and remained neutral at the outset. Some of the prime minister's political advisers were similarly dubious. We pushed ahead regardless. After all, we were simply proposing communiqué language calling for an "exploration." We were a long way from any actual negotiations. Ultimately, and following preliminary consultations with US officials, the draft communiqué stated that the president and the prime minister "pledged to give highest priority to finding mutually acceptable means to reduce and eliminate existing barriers to trade in order to secure and facilitate trade and investment flows." And that was precisely the intent.

But even the "success," relatively speaking, of the communiqué language on trade and investment was short-lived. On returning to Washington from Quebec City, President Reagan shuffled his cabinet, moving Bill Brock to Labor and installing Clayton Yeutter as the new US trade representative (USTR). We knew Bill Brock and his personal team well, and we knew that we could work reasonably well with them. We did not know Clayton Yeutter, and therefore we were really back to square one on trade.

Under the Liberals, we had tentatively pursued with Brock the prospect of broader sectoral trade arrangements in four sectors: steel, agricultural implements, urban transit equipment, and information technology. None of these had anything like the potential significant of the Auto Pact. More to the point, it became extremely difficult to find a balance or mutual advantage within a given sector; some might benefit Canada more; others would be better for the United States.* As these sectoral talks sputtered, more thought was gradually given to a broader package, a big agreement in which it would presumably be less difficult to find a balance of mutual advantage, namely, a free trade arrangement.

At this early stage, I was neither an advocate nor a critic. I was pre-

---

* Sectoral agreements were technically violations of the GATT, but the United States had succeeded in getting a waiver for the Auto Pact.

pared to advance the policy scope, the analysis of Canadian interests, and the consultative process to better determine what might be negotiated and to see whether there was a political appetite in either government for something bigger.* While free trade was a political issue at all times, it did not start as a partisan issue. Within the two major parties, there were strong proponents on either side of the debate. Traditionally, the Conservatives had not been free traders and the Mulroney cabinet itself was divided. The Liberals had traditionally been more in favour of free trade and in the early 1980s many, including Ed Lumley, Gerry Regan, and eventually Paul Martin and Roy MacLaren at the federal level and Robert Bourassa in Quebec were very much in favour. So, it was assumed, was John Turner.

Donald Macdonald's royal commission on economic prospects for Canada, initiated by Trudeau and concluded in September 1985, recommended a "leap of faith" in favour of free trade. All but one of the thirteen commissioners supported this recommendation. That became a significant catalyst in terms of political and public opinion. It provided substantial, intellectual underpinnings for the initiative.

Attitudes were one thing, progress was quite another. On various occasions, usually meetings to discuss softwood lumber, I had exchanged views generally with Mike Smith, the deputy USTR, about how to move the bilateral trade agenda onto a more positive footing. Neither of us really knew what our respective governments might be ready to support. Equally, neither of us wanted to be perceived as the *demandeur* in the dialogue. These exchanges led to a very informal sailboat picnic on Chesapeake Bay in Mike's boat *Wind* in July of 1985. I was accompanied by Michael Hart of External and Bob Martin from Finance (our colleague on the Trade Policy Review). Mike was joined by his wife and Bill Merkin, the deputy assistant USTR with primary responsibility for Canadian trade issues.

Smith and I both recognized that the "crunch" issues of any free trade negotiation would be trade remedy rules (for Canada) and investment restrictions (for the United States). I made it clear that an agreement that did not give Canada some relief from US trade remedy rules would not fly politically. I emphasized, too, our acute sensitivity about cultural issues. Smith was equally adamant that some change in Canadian foreign investment restrictions would be a *sine qua non* for the United States. He

---

* I became, in the words of one of my associates at the time, Bill Dymond, a "policy entrepreneur."

added that a phased approach on lowering tariffs would have to be symmetrical, even though Canadian tariffs were, on average, double those in the United States. We concluded that if these issues could be addressed, there would be prospect for a full free trade agreement. I reported the essence of this informal discussion to key Canadian ministers Kelleher and Wilson.

Within External, shortly after the PCs were elected in 1984, my US Branch had prepared a comprehensive memo to cabinet on the management of the US relationship. The paper contended essentially that we had much to gain by trying to harness the power and proximity of the United States to Canada's advantage. It was a not-too-subtle rebuttal of the "Third Option," which had characterized much of the previous government's approach to Washington. The consequences of that posture – of trying to find counterweights to offset US influence – had, in my view and that of some but by no means all of my colleagues, left Canada less relevant, less engaged, and with less generally from our most important bilateral relationship. It was remarkable that relations with the United States had been conducted without a comprehensive policy framework, other than a desire to establish counterweights against the relationship.

Relations generally between Canada and the United States could be categorized by long periods of benign neglect from Washington, accompanied by calculated ambivalence from Ottawa. From time to time, personalities or issues prompted outbursts of engagement or irritation. Party lines in Canada did not make much difference. Prime Minister John Diefenbaker's position against Bomarc missiles in the 1960s provoked fury from Washington not unlike that directed at Jean Chrétien for his opposition to the Iraq War in 2002. Canada's loyal, if somewhat innocuous, service as Washington's proxy on the Indochina Truce Commissions during the Vietnam War did not temper the annoyance of President Lyndon Johnson when Prime Minister Lester Pearson gently cautioned publicly against US efforts to bomb North Vietnam into peace. Diefenbaker's attempt to divert 15 per cent of Canada's trade to the Commonwealth proved as futile as Trudeau's Third Option, yet the motive was similar – to reduce Canada's "dependency" on the United States.

The risk of getting "too close" conditions virtually all Canadian attitudes toward the United States and at all levels. Our fetish for multilateralism as a goal in its own right, rather than as a means to a goal, echoes this sentiment, as does our periodic preoccupation with global issues where Canada has no readily definable interest at stake (e.g. the Middle East). Efforts to engage our proximity to the United States to our advantage are the exception, not the rule. This attitude may explain why, for the most part, Canada has resisted a coordinated or coherent overall approach to its major relationship, allowing ad hocery, inspired or otherwise, to carry the day-to-day conduct of relations. And when we do decide to engage, as the free trade negotiations demonstrated, it is not easy to arouse the needed attention from our American counterparts, who can be supremely oblivious to the risk for Canadian leaders in such initiatives.

Sensitivity about sovereignty looms over any discussion in Canada about relations with the United States. We try to define ourselves, too often, by the manner in which we differ from Americans, betraying, it seems, a lack of confidence in our own distinction. I fell into this mould myself from time to time. I recall chastising my sons for drinking American beer (produced in Canada of course, it being beer). They shrugged. "Hey, Pops, do you really think we will become Americans just because we drink their beer?" To this day, they laugh or cringe as I religiously point out to them actors on TV or films who are Canadian. I suspect (or hope) that the new generation of Canadians will be more confident, more positive about their distinctiveness as Canadians, and will not have to resort to an espousal of differences with Americans as a means of defining our distinction.

I spent two years as assistant deputy minister for US affairs and in the fall of 1985 was elevated to deputy minister status as one of two associate undersecretaries at External supporting the new undersecretary, Si Taylor. (The other associate was Deputy Minister of Trade, Bob Richardson.) In this capacity, I assumed overall responsibility for relations with the United States and with Asia, as well as the Economic, Communications, and Administrative Management functional bureaus of the department. Don Campbell, a seasoned veteran with important experience on economic and energy files with the United States, was brought back from his posting as ambassador to Korea to succeed me as ADM for the United States.*

Si Taylor was the quintessential Canadian diplomat: fluently bilingual, intelligent, articulate, and uncontroversial. He had no enemies and many admirers. I was among the latter, having worked closely with him on various G7 Summits, where he, as Canada's political director, unfailingly produced a summary report of the political discussions in as precise and compellingly clear form as his distinctive, almost calligraphic, writing style. His specialties were Europe, East-West (Soviet) relations,

---

* Don went on to become deputy minister for International Trade, ambassador to Japan, and deputy minister for Foreign Affairs. Upon his retirement from the public service, I recruited him to join me as an executive vice-president at CAE.

NATO, and security issues more generally. He was also highly experienced on the sensitive "triangular" file – Canada, France, and Quebec. Our respective backgrounds and expertise complemented one another.

Responsibility for US and Asian affairs sustained my close and regular contact with the new prime minister, as did my continuing role in the evolving free trade initiative. Shortly after his appointment as Canada's chief negotiator, Simon Reisman invited me to join his newly formed Trade Negotiations Office, the separate status of which I had staunchly recommended to Simon as the best means for shedding bureaucratic interference. I declined his offer, in part because I thought I might be of more use to him from outside. There were other reasons as well. I did place two of my best lieutenants, Michael Hart and Bill Dymond, in the TNO. who not only injected valuable insight and expertise to the negotiating team but were also a continuing source of opinion and private intelligence to me on the progress of negotiations.

Hart and Dymond were an unusual pair. Hart has already been introduced earlier. Dymond was the more philosophical of the two but equally determined, knowledgeable, and pragmatic. He also had a splendid dry wit. As a team, they were highly effective in providing the grist for consultations within the department, with other departments, and with the private sector. Ideal colleagues when the going got rough, as it often did.*

Joe Clark had been appointed to chair a special cabinet committee on the trade negotiations, and I supported him in that capacity on a regular basis. Clark was a good foreign minister but a difficult politician to define. Thoroughly decent, articulate, and painstakingly persistent in searching for consensus, he served loyally and effectively in a cabinet led by the man who had defeated him as leader of the Progressive Conservatives. Less clear were Clark's core convictions and, from time to time, his political judgment. On occasion, he had trouble distinguishing action from achievement, seeming to relish initiatives for their own sake without calculating the end results, let alone the objective motivating them. The Charlottetown Accord probably reflected the best and the worst of his attributes. He worked conscientiously and dutifully to fashion a compromise because he knew something was needed to fill the vacuum left by the collapse of the Meech Lake Accord. But his need to bring everyone on board degenerated into a rudderless process and a lumpy package which proved in the end to be unpalatable to the elec-

---

* Michael Hart currently holds the Simon Reisman Chair at Carleton University. Bill Dymond served subsequently with me in Washington and is currently senior executive fellow at Carleton's Centre for Trade Policy and Law. Together with Colin Robertson, they wrote the definitive book on the free trade negotiations, *Decision at Midnight: Inside the Canada-US Free Trade Negotiations* (UBC Press, 1994).

torate. As foreign minister, he represented Canada well and inspired pride and support from many associates at External Affairs, but one had the impression that his career was, in a real sense, unfulfilled.

In the summer of 1986, Mr Mulroney made an official visit to China and Japan, and I accompanied him as the senior external official and as the background spokesman to the press contingent. The prime minister was distracted daily during this trip by allegations evolving on the home front regarding the conduct of his minister of industry, Sinclair Stevens. But his meetings in China with Deng Xiao-peng and others were as colourful as they were memorable.

During their meeting, Deng Xiao-peng smoked incessantly and used a spittoon selectively but accurately. At one point, the prime minister asked what Deng's biggest challenge was as leader. He replied in one word, "Envy." He added that in China some were now getting washing machines or televisions; many were not and resented the fact that others were now "better off." When everyone had nothing, he added, things had been "easier to manage."

Mulroney went to some length to soften Chinese attitudes about the United States, pointing out the contrast between Canada's long, unde-fended border with the US and the heavily manned and armed border between China and the Soviet Union. Sensitive to the Chinese attitudes regarding "old friends," he brought Alvin Hamilton along on the dele-gation. As agriculture minister in the Diefenbaker government during the early 1960s, Hamilton had negotiated the very first western wheat contract with the People's Republic. The Chinese remembered well and were still significant customers.

Throughout the Asian trip, my main task was to brief the accompa-nying media contingent on the objectives for each event and on the results of major meetings. These were done "off the record," as was the custom for briefings by officials. On one occasion, I was described, un-named, as being in "a rumpled tuxedo whispering in the prime minister's ear" before his calls on Asian counterparts. This prompted a call from the home front suggesting that I get my suit pressed! The media experience, nonetheless, reflected some degree of confidence on the part of the prime pinister who, along with his PMO entourage, remained generally leary of the public service. Little did I know at the time where this experience would lead.

EIGHT

The Prime Minister's Office: The Most Foreign Assignment of All

In early February 1987 I made an inspection visit to our consulate general in Los Angeles, after which my wife and I had planned a one-week vacation in La Jolla. At about 8 a.m. on the first day, the telephone rang. It was the prime minister's switchboard saying that Mr Mulroney wanted to speak to me. "Where have I reached you?" he asked. I answered. "Who are you with?" As I replied saying, "My wife," she sat up in bed wondering what on earth.

"Have you noticed what happened over the weekend in Washington?" Mr Mulroney inquired. (Donald Regan had been replaced summarily by Howard Baker as the president's chief of staff.)

"It is probably good for the President," I replied, "but I am not sure whether it will be good for Baker."

"Well," continued the prime minister, "how would you like to become my chief of staff?" Just like that, right out the blue. While there were persistent stories about problems in the Prime Minister's Office, there had certainly been no speculation about me as a possible solution. I had no quick comeback. To fill the vacuum, he next asked, "What is your impression of how my office operates?"

"How candid do you want me to be?" I responded, trying desperately to think about what to say honestly but diplomatically. Finally, I suggested, "Well, your office seems to me to be a bit like a wagon wheel without a rim. We all know you are the hub, but there are several people representing your views to the bureaucracy and the messages do not always connect."

"How do you think I feel," he interjected, "going home at night and finding three memos from my staff on the same subject but each with different recommendations. I need someone to organize the place." Mulroney elaborated on the other changes he was contemplating: Bruce

Phillips to replace Bill Fox as director of communications and Marjory LeBreton to become deputy chief of staff. I was still having trouble taking it all in.

"But I am not a political strategist, Prime Minister. I am a public servant and have worked for governments of different political stripes."

"I don't need a strategist," he implored. "I am the strategist, but I need someone to organize my office. I want to focus my time on major issues like free trade and tax reform, not tainted tuna. You know those major issues and you can help."

"What does Paul Tellier think?" I asked. As clerk of the Privy Council and the senior public servant, as well as the prime minister's principal adviser from the Public Service, he was my boss and might not relish a senior colleague in a position so close to the prime minister.

"I don't know," he said, "but that is a good question." I asked a few more questions intended primarily to give me time to think. He agreed to think them over, and I did the same about his proposal. It was not clear-cut. When I explained that I was planning to return to Ottawa on Saturday (this was Monday), he said he would call again on the weekend with some answers. "But," he added, "if it doesn't work out, this conversation never took place."

Needless to say, his call ended any sense of vacation. I was very uncertain about the whole proposition but did not see how I could turn down a direct appeal from the prime minister. I had no idea whether I could do the job, let alone whether I wanted to do it. I did feel that I should try to help, but I did not want to walk away from twenty-five years in the foreign service. I did not see how the job of chief of staff could be isolated from the politics of governance, even though the prime minister had assured me I would not have to do anything with the party or act in a manner that would jeopardize my civil service status. At the time, neither of us knew how political, how partisan, and how central to the next election free trade would become. (During the subsequent campaign in 1988, Opposition Leader John Turner declared that, if elected, he would change my assignment from Washington to North Korea!)

Saturday came but no call. Then on Sunday evening, during a family dinner, the prime minister did call. He gave some answers and said he wanted to move quickly. I asked if he had alerted Clark, secretary of state for External Affairs. "Not yet" was his reply. I mentioned that I was going to Washington with Clark the following Wednesday. Before that, I attended a cabinet meeting, along with the secretary of state for External Affairs. The prime minister presided but did not speak to me at all. The next day, in Washington, I was called out of Mr Clark's meeting on the Hill with Texas senator Lloyd Bentsen. It was the prime minister again. "We are going to announce it tomorrow," he said. And that is exactly what happened, even though to that point I had not had a face-to-face meeting to discuss any of it with him.

There are many stories about why I had been selected. Stanley Hartt, a long-time Mulroney adviser and then deputy minister of Finance, among others, takes credit for the suggestion. Joe Clark said he was asked to provide a rating of my strengths and weaknesses versus those of a senior colleague at External. But I never did learn the real answer. Presumably, the prime minister had concluded that he needed someone running his office who knew how the bureaucracy functioned and who was familiar with major policy issues.

For him, it was an extraordinary gamble. While he knew me to some extent from my involvement with Canada-US relations, notably the Shamrock Summit, and from the Asian trip the previous summer, he did not really know much about my skills or my personality. For me, it was also a major risk. Even if I succeeded, my foreign service career would be forever affected by a stint in the PMO, whereas failure could have an even more disastrous effect.

Others have suggested that the gamble worked because I brought a degree of order to the PMO and a degree of harmony to relations with the public service, notably the PCO. Ultimately, my involvement in concluding the free trade negotiations added policy and political substance to the prime minister's record and proved instrumental to his re-election in 1988. His confidence in me certainly helped my role in the PMO and also made my subsequent assignment in Washington more relevant and, I believe, more productive.

My appointment came as a surprise to just about everyone else too and consequently raised few immediate criticisms. Paul Tellier, for his part, warmly welcomed me and expressed the hope that I would establish a sense of order in the Prime Minister's Office, something he deemed useful for the bureaucracy as a whole. As for me, I often said it was my "most foreign assignment": the most demanding, the most exhausting, and the most exhilarating of all.

Working in the PMO

The major task for the chief of staff is to focus the prime minister's time and his message on key issues and to ensure consistency between the message and the delivery of government action. As well, there is a major control function, resolving or containing disputes and crises as they inevitably but unpredictably arise in government. The proactive element, giving shape and direction to the prime minister's agenda, was challenging; the firefighting or crisis management was often frustrating but also stimulating. The combination was very demanding, mentally and physically, but the pressure of it all paled in comparison to that on the prime minister himself.

It is true that, in the Canadian system, a prime minister with a strong majority has substantial power and authority on appointments, on policy, and on decisions. But even with a huge majority, the prime minister needs to maintain a careful balance within cabinet and caucus, mindful of the regional and linguistic fundamentals of politics and governance in Canada. The leadership skills that Brian Mulroney demonstrated in maintaining balance, commitment, and direction was, in my experience, his most unheralded achievement.

The high point was his weekly meeting on Wednesday morning with caucus. As the polls ebbed and flowed, and particularly when they ebbed, the prime minister had to rally the spirit of his huge caucus and, above all else, keep it united behind him and government policy. There was no limit on candour during these sessions, and the Progressive Conservatives had a notorious history of devouring leaders in caucus. Time and experience in government can provide a glue of sorts for party unity, but the critical ingredient is the leader and his or her ability to instill confidence and optimism. Mulroney excelled as the leader of an unusually large and diverse caucus, and he did it skilfully in both languages, week in, week out, despite low polls.

My immediate challenge on entering the Prime Minister's Office was to take stock of the operation as best I could and develop a plan of action. That sounds bureaucratic but, after all, it was precisely what I was. On closer examination, the Prime Minister's Office struck me more as a collection of individuals rather than as a team. Loyalty and dedication to the prime minister was not the issue for any, but some of the senior officers had different, sometimes competing, views on how best to serve him. One of his complaints to me had been that he would often receive memos from his staff with different assessments or recommendations on the same topic. A greater degree of order and cohesion was needed, but I concluded that, first and foremost, some changes in personnel were essential. My problem was that the individuals concerned were in many ways much closer personally to the prime minister than I. He might not accept my recommendations for change. Many had been with him as friends and advisers for more than a decade and were veterans of both his leadership campaign and the 1984 election. They had brought him to 24 Sussex.

My conclusions were formed when I read a newspaper article one morning in which two of my senior Prime Minister's Office colleagues were quoted in a manner that clashed openly with the views of our minister of Finance, Michael Wilson – at that point, one of the most credible members of the cabinet. At an early morning PMO meeting, I asked pointedly, "How does this kind of freelance criticism serve the prime minister's agenda?" There was no answer. But staff in the Prime Minister's Office were accustomed to operating in a fire-wagon style, one that had served them well during the highly successful leadership and election campaigns but was not as suited to good governance.

A few years later, I read a book on the Reagan Administration by Hedrick Smith, *The Power Game*, in which he described the difference between stage craft (elections) and state craft (the art of governance). His conclusion was that the people who get you elected are not necessarily the best to help you govern. That was obviously true in Canada as well. Even without Smith's analysis, I had reached a similar conclusion and prepared my recommendations accordingly. I thought that they might be too hard for the prime minister to accept and so prefaced my private session with him by offering to return from where I came, if that were the case. I had prepared (bureaucratically) a small briefing book – "Purpose," "Analysis," and "Recommendations" – and started to summarize the contents. He stopped me moments after I began saying, "You do whatever you have to do to get that place organized."

"Yes," I said, "but when I ask some of these fellows to move along, they will go right to you. What then?"

"I will support you all the way," he replied. And he did. But when I delivered the message the next day one by one to each individual, that proved to be my most difficult day at the Prime Minister's Office.

Instead of recruiting a series of replacements, I relied on my new deputy, Marjory LeBreton, as my key link to the party and to oversee appointments. She was dependable and unfailingly optimistic. Both were qualities that endeared her to me. She listened, patiently and sensitively, to complaints and concerns from all quarters within the PC Party in a manner that I could never have emulated. Marjory had served the party loyally and, for the most part, thanklessly since the days of John Diefenbaker. Almost four decades of dedicated networking gave her an unusual range of contacts and views. As the saying goes, she "knew where all the bodies are buried" and was an indispensable political force for our office and for me personally.

The team I brought with me from External – Brian Hambleton and then Jim Wright, along with my trusted secretary, Marilyn Connolly – gave rhythm and focus to my office. Brian had been the principal drafter of the US Branch's memo on US relations for the new government. He and Jim were both talented foreign service officers with the skills and background needed to make things work. Brian died tragically on his subsequent posting in Japan. Jim has gone on to an excellent career in the foreign service as an assistant deputy minister for political affairs. I rearranged duties for others, brought in Ross Reid as my "issue firefighter," and forged much closer links with the deputy prime minister, Don Mazankowski, and his top-notch staff, notably Jamie Burns, Phil Evershed, and Margaret Martin. Ross Reid got along with just about everybody, not a claim I could make. He spent endless hours containing crises and forging consensus long after most others had given up. Loyal and tactful, he possessed excellent requisites for the challenges faced daily.

As chief of staff, I was often called upon to vet key appointments, such as senior, non-career diplomatic assignments and some Senate appointments. The task varied but invloved, especially with relatively unknown individuals, routine checks to avoid embarrassment to the government. On one occasion, as part of a standard drill, I recall asking a Senate candidate from Newfoundland whether there was anything in his past that might prompt a news headline if his nomination went forward. There was a pause on the other end of the line, followed by a barely audible "Aw, shit." I waited, somewhat perplexed. Finally, some elaboration: "I was caught in a raid on a whorehouse in Montreal many years ago. It was a setup by Joey Smallwood!" I did not really want to hear the details but asked simply, "Does your wife know?" When told that he had not been married at the time, I asked the prospective candidate to review the offer and the reaction the story might elicit with his wife if it became public and then advise me whether he wanted his nomination to proceed. He did and we did. A one-day, minor item about his youthful escapade appeared in the media, but by all reports, he went on to serve with the distinction in Canada's upper chamber.

Most of all, I endeavoured to become the single funnel of views and decisions to and from the prime minister and the regular controller and coordinator of his ever-changing agenda, conscious at all times of a principal rule of politics: the need to concentrate his time and his message on key items and not be diverted, as he had put it, by "tainted tuna." Some have suggested that I was a "control freak" and overdid the concentration of power in the PMO. There is some validity to both charges, but the latter goes with the territory. As to the control aspect, it was presumably the objective of my appointment. In any event, as Mr Mulroney was a "phoneaholic" with a network all his own, my control of his agenda and face-to-face meetings was never total.

Agenda and message control was vital. Inexperience was obvious, and expectations had been excessive, but the public had witnessed too many stumbles, petty scandals (inflated by the media), and diversions that knocked the government off stride. Much of the criticism about "the gang that can't shoot straight" focused, rightly or wrongly, on the PMO.* The prime minister's agenda was driven primarily by the issue or event of the day or week and by planning for events, speeches, and travel, including his international activity. These, in turn, were reviewed through regular consultations with the PCO and the Deputy PMO and were decided or adjusted in periodic one-on-one sessions with the prime minister.

There was a lot of suspicion in Tory ranks about what I, as a bureaucrat, was doing in the chief of staff position. Clearly, I could not be identified with any faction from the PC party, although some presumed that since I came from External, I was probably a "Clarkie." When I brought Ross Reid in (he had been John Crosbie's campaign manager), that simply added to the confusion. Many in caucus were suspicious of government and assistants of any kind, including particularly the staff in the Prime Minister's Office. As a result, they would give the prime minister notes and requests by hand in caucus rather than through any normal channel, including, specifically, his own office. On several occasions, we were obliged literally to strip search the prime minister as he left caucus so we could act on these missives, ensuring at all times that the replies went back from him only and by hand, either at caucus or during Question Period.

Among my bureaucratic colleagues, the reaction was decidedly mixed. Some were openly critical, saying I had "ruined my future career" simply by accepting a PMO position. Others saw it as potentially positive, on the theory that it might indeed bring some order to the Prime Minister's Office. None, as I recall, had any compelling advice to offer on "how to say no to your prime minister."

---

* During a brief Easter break on the island of Bequia in St Vincent in 1988, I learned a valuable political lesson from the prime minister, James ("Son") Mitchell. Diversions, he explained, are what experience in politics teaches leaders to deploy. To demonstrate, he added that his remedy for drug dealers – temporarily – was flogging! That apparently served to divert the attention of everyone in St Vincent away from everything else. There were certainly days in Ottawa when the lesson and the example had considerable appeal!

While most days in the PMO were highly unpredictable, there was a rhythm of sorts. PMO senior staff met twice weekly at 8:00 a.m. to sort through major issues and/or events. Central issues in my time were free trade and Canada-US relations more generally; Meech Lake; the budget, notably plans for what was initially called the business transfer tax (which became the GST); defence policy; Canada-France issues (fish and "ships" – both France and the UK were vying to supply Canada with nuclear submarines); incidental or pop-up issues, like South Moresby, which involved the prime minister; and two "wild card" social issues – capital punishment and abortion.

Major events reviewed included the 1988 G7 Summit in Toronto, hosted by Canada, which for that reason required regular briefings and updates from Canada's sherpa, Sylvia Ostry, as well as pre-summit visits to each G7 capital. Visits to Canada by foreign dignitaries – Presidents Reagan and Chirac, Prime Minister Thatcher, and president-to-be Nelson Mandela, to name a few – also required advance preparations and briefings. Crises erupted without notice and usually involved a minister, a ministry, or a caucus member. Containing or minimizing the damage for these is what Ross Reid and my own assistants performed most admirably.

Speeches by the prime minister required careful attention. L. Ian MacDonald and Paul Therrien held the pens, but our "editor-in-chief" (the PM, not me) spent a good deal of time honing the final text. The prime minister was an effective speaker. He could take a text and make it sing. But the cadence and rhythm that made a speech convincing were often the result of hard work by the prime minister himself and his speech writers. The substance was often supplied in drafts from officials, but the style and message was crafted in the PMO and personally by the prime minister.

When Parliament was in session, the days usually revolved around Question Period. Preparations within individual departments varied considerably. In my experience at External, especially when I was in the minister's office, the effort was often more extensive than useful. Hot issues of the day were usually determined by the media and the headlines that morning, but bureaucrats tended to err on the side of caution. Better to be over than under prepared. A point person in each minister's office monitored daily preparations, and these were coordinated somewhat loosely with the legislative aides in the PMO and the Deputy PMO. The deputy PM, Don Mazankowski, presided over a cabinet session from 1:00 p.m., which then led to a quick briefing for the prime minister alone at about five minutes to 2:00.

Monday mornings each week began with the Operations Committee, chaired by Mazankowski, attempting to sort and sift a variety of ministerial or departmental initiatives. The key cabinet committee, Priorities and Planning, met every Tuesday, after which the clerk, Tellier, Bernard Roy, the Principal Secretary, and I often joined the prime minister for lunch to reflect on the cabinet discussion and try to resolve topical issues.

Mulroney's style in presiding over cabinet undoubtedly reflected his experience as a board chairman, as well as his stature as prime minister and party leader. At Priorities and Planning, he moved ministers efficiently through the agenda and usually without extensive debate. Items were rarely brought forward without some degree of advance consensus. In instances where consensus was less apparent, the prime minister's position inevitably carried the day. He also used these meetings with his key cabinet colleagues to deliver a pre-caucus pep talk of sorts, one that he would repeat with even more flair the next day at caucus. My initial impression of cabinet was that the members were, for the most part, competent but dominated by the prime minister – not surprising, given the massive election victory of 1984. In an age of leadership politics, they (and caucus more generally) not only knew their place but also recognized clearly that their future clung to the fortunes, deserved or accidental, of their leader.

Cabinet changes can be delicate, especially when minsters are shuffled into assignments perceived to be a downgrade from where they have been. Brian Mulroney had been surprised when Davie Fulton (for whom he had worked as a young assistant in the 1960s) had agreed to accept a clear demotion from Prime Minister John Diefenbaker in 1962 to Public Works from Justice. In fact, Mulroney explained, that incident had taught him that "nothing in politics is a surprise. The only surprise is the lack of surprise!" While, from time to time, several ministers balked at proposed changes, I can recall no occasion when a direct proposal from the prime minister to change portfolios was refused.

Erik Nielson had reportedly unearthed a Liberal strategy in early 1985 recommending an all-out attack on the prime minister as the avenue back to power, no doubt the inspiration for the nefarious Rat Pack.* This "strategy" was cited from time to time in cabinet, especially when individual ministers basked in "good news" while negative fallout fell on the prime minister's shoulders. Electoral success in 1984 had been very much a personal triumph for Mulroney and against the initial odds. The drop

---

* Brian Tobin, Sheila Copps, Sergio Marchi, and Don Boudria, who assumed the appellation and played it to the hilt in Question Period and the scrums that followed.

in the polls was similarly personal, and so, presumably, would be any climb back.

The prime minister relied heavily on his deputy, Don Mazankowski, to drive the agenda and the cabinet secretary, Paul Tellier, to ensure that proper procedures were being followed. John Crosbie (Justice, Transport, and Trade during Mulroney's first mandate), Michael Wilson (Finance), Joe Clark (External Affairs), Lowell Murray (Federal-Provincial Relations), and Flora MacDonald (Communications) were among the more active contributors to cabinet discussion. Others usually confined their interventions to matters relating to their respective portfolios. The efficiency of these meetings owed a lot to the sorting and sifting done with similar dispatch at Monday morning meetings of the Operations Committee, chaired by the deputy prime minister.

Next to the prime minister himself, the most indispensable member of the Mulroney cabinet was Don Mazankowski or "Maz," as he was known by all. A veteran Parliamentarian, he virtually lived in the House of Commons. His office was open very late in the evening for "discussion," to deal with emergencies, to console disgruntled members from caucus, usually from western Canada and usually on issues like official language policy. He played a major role shaping and driving the government's legislative agenda. As the head of the Operations Committee of cabinet, Maz also controlled initiatives from individual ministers and/or their departments. As well, he supervised preparations for Question Period and directed traffic during the session itself. As part of this task, he had been asked to hold on to the bottom of the prime minister's jacket on occasion to restrain Mr Mulroney from rising hotly to the defence of his junior ministers. The prime minister was combative; Maz was more restrained and had very few enemies. Mulroney jabbed; Maz bobbed and weaved. Mr Outside and Mr Inside. They complemented each other, and the degree of trust and loyalty between the two was a stabilizing rudder for the government as a whole. As for me, I could not have survived without the steadfast support of Maz and his team during my Prime Minister's Office assignment!

A mystery for me on arrival was how I would connect with the party and how the preferences of the party – on policy, people, or whatever – would influence the Prime Minister's Office on a regular basis. In the event, there was very little interaction. Early on, the prime minister suggested that I meet with Senator Norman Atkins, the PC campaign chair. At last, I thought, I would receive some political marching orders. Instead, what the senator said simply was "I believe that good government is good politics. You look after the government part and I will handle the politics." In actual fact, the prime minister "looked after the politics." He was, as he had told me, *the* political strategist in the Prime Minister's Office, and he did not want or need help on the politics, least of all from the likes of me.

Meech Lake

The Meech Lake Accord occurred very early during my prime minister's Office assignment, but I was not directly involved. Preparations had been well advanced before my arrival. Bernard Roy was most active on behalf of the prime minister's Office, given the overriding significance of the file to Quebec. Lowell Murray, the government leader in the Senate, was the prime initiator in cabinet. Cabinet discussion, as I recall, was desultory. Very few, except perhaps the prime minister himself, expected a positive outcome from the meeting of First Ministers. Therefore, when it came together in a unanimous accord on 30 April 1987, it was a very pleasant surprise to all. The fact that few were prepared for success meant, however, that there was not really a game plan to explain what the accord was about and to gain broader support. Things happened on the fly and ultimately, of course, flew apart.

Following the surprise agreement, there was jubilation in cabinet and an immediate move to bring the accord to Parliament for approval. NDP leader Ed Broadbent leaped on board and brought his small band with him, despite concerns among some about the implications for social programs and the more entrenched skepticism of CAW leader Bob White. John Turner scrambled back from Montreal to endorse what had been agreed. Sharp divisions in Liberal ranks took time to surface. Special briefings were offered to Broadbent, Turner, and also Trudeau, who, at least initially and in what I believe was his only direct conversation with the prime minister, acknowledged that, while he might have done things differently, he did not want to "pee on the prime minister's parade." His bladder did not hold!

Meech Lake literally unraveled over time. It became the victim of time and a sequence of political hand grenades from players who were not involved initially. What began almost as a miracle to bring Quebec into the constitutional fold was slowly transformed by its critics into a "concession too far," favouring Quebec against all others. Pierre Trudeau wielded the heaviest axe, some contend purely out of spite, that is, to thwart a constitutional success that had eluded him. He, of course, registered more legalistic complaints but in a spiteful, personal manner. Newly elected premiers like Frank McKenna (New Brunswick) and Clyde Wells (Newfoundland) joined the critics' bandwagon, the latter irrevocably. Gary Filmon headed a minority government in Manitoba, which ultimately stymied passage within the time limit, but he did not really seem to have his heart in support of the accord either.

I do not propose to address the constitutional elements. I suspect these were secondary in any case. The debate became purely political on issues that have divided Canada before and since Confederation. The Meech compromise foundered on raw emotion and divisions reflecting competing interpretations of what was meant or intended and a fog of misperception of what had been agreed. For me personally, a crucial turning point had been Quebec premier Robert Bourassa's decision to invoke the "notwithstanding clause" of Trudeau's "flawed" compromise in order to overrule the Supreme Court on Bill 101, the Quebec law entrenching French language rights while denying equivalent rights for English, which the court had ruled unconstitutional. I compared it then to a referee in a hockey game declaring "no goal" when the spectators had clearly seen the puck go into the net.

Support for Meech eroded in part because its supporters failed to muster the same commitment in favour as those lined up against. Reason faced passion, and passion prevailed. The media thrived in the blood sport between Mulroney and a reincarnated Pierre Trudeau. Ironically, Mulroney, the Irish Canadian from Baie Comeau, was cast as "Quebec champion"; Trudeau led the charge outside Quebec, with Clyde Wells, Frank McKenna, and Sharon Carstairs (the Liberal leader of the Opposition in Manitoba) as his major outriders. The government was as ill-prepared to cope with the unravelling of Meech as it was for its initial success. After three years, the agreement expired under the single-feather dissent of Elijah Harper in the Manitoba legislature. This defeat, in turn, gave Clyde Wells an excuse to renege on his commitment to bring the matter to a vote in the Newfoundland legislature.

The effort to recognize Quebec as "a distinct society within Canada" became a distinct liability to the Mulroney government and to the prime minister personally. Ironically, he was criticized regionally for an agreement he saw as a unifying symbol for the country as a whole. What Meech Lake wrought, including ultimately the rupture with Lucien Bouchard (the prime minister's university classmate and Quebec lieutenant, brought in through a by-election to strengthen Quebec's voice in cabinet), the rise of the Bloc Québécois, and the futile rescue attempt at Charlottetown, culminated in the razor-thin referendum victory of 1995. The referendum was almost cathartic as the ghosts of Meech have been relatively invisible ever since.

One could argue that the collapse of Meech Lake contributed significantly to the rise of the Bloc in Quebec and the Reform Party in the West, both largely at the expense of the PCs. The net result was the creation of a virtual one-party state in Canada for a decade, with the Liberals dominating in government against splinters or fragments clumped loosely and non-threateningly in opposition.

Tax Reform

No sooner had the Meech Lake Accord been approved than cabinet attention turned to the massively complex and politically explosive tax reform package that Michael Wilson and his Finance team had been preparing since the previous fall. Wilson tried to establish a tight schedule for discussion, decision, and implementation, but politics inevitably worked at a slower pace.

There was a general consensus in favour of reform, but the prescriptions – business transfer tax (BTT), goods and service tax (GST), value-added tax – attracted competing volumes of opposition. The prime minister, no doubt influenced by the Peter Lougheed rule of successful government – "If it will get votes, do it. If not, do not" – was extremely cautious. With good reason, he was dubious about the politics. He was particularly leery of the public's readiness to accept any new type of tax, especially one on food. Wilson's preferred BTT had already been dubbed "Brian's Terrible Tax" by some and that had an ominous ring.

Wilson and his deputy, Stanley Hartt, were thorough and persistent. Cabinet watched carefully for a signal from the prime minister, who suggested "more study," including the need for a blue ribbon panel to try to de-politicize recommendations. Wilson contended that more study was not needed, but ultimately the timing of his initiative was postponed. The prime minister was particularly sensitive to the attitudes of small business. The last thing he wanted was a tax reform package that antagonized this group and endangered its strong support for free trade. As in most things, his sentiment prevailed.

"Pandemonium Is Paradise"

In July of 1987 I accompanied the prime minister, Mrs Mulroney, and the children on a political tour of British Columbia. We visited Quesnel, then Nanaimo to open the annual Bathtub Race, and finally back to White Rock to attend the Sandcastle Festival, another annual event in British Columbia. The first two stops were routine, but White Rock proved unforgettable.

Accompanied by two or three Mounties to provide security, we arrived in mid-afternoon by hovercraft, dressed more or less in business clothes. No one had pointed out that we were visiting a beach. And it was the peak of summer. More than 200,000 attended the festivities. Most were in bathing suits and well lubricated, outside and inside. There was no event as such, but some sandcastles scattered on the beach. We just moved into the crowd, accompanied by the local MP, Benno Friesen. Those at the beach were not shy. They were downright friendly, a slap-happy version of friendly.

A particular attraction was the Mulroneys' youngest child, Nicholas, who was then three years old. The problem was that many on the beach wanted a very close look. We were completely unready for any kind of crowd control, and even friendly crowds can have mob tendencies, especially when the beer has been flowing. Sensing danger, the Mounties and I formed a ring around Mrs Mulroney and Nicholas and began a slow retreat to the hovercraft. By the time we made it back on board, we were covered with wet sand, and I was genuinely frightened because of what might have happened. The prime minister was beaming. "What's the matter, Derek?" he shouted, grinning from ear to ear.

"We almost got killed out there," I muttered.

"You don't understand," he replied. "For a politician, pandemonium is paradise!" I did not understand but began to see that politics was indeed different, as were politicians. Mr Mulroney was on the top of his game and relished the beach event to the hilt.

In the journey back and forth, I also saw Brian Mulroney up close with his family. As well as prime minister, he was a devoted husband and father, an aspect the public never seemed to appreciate, and he devoted time and energy to all three. He had a young family and it was a big responsibility. Most of the children were old enough to know a little about his political life and were curious about why all, especially the media, did not share their enthusiasm for their father. On visits like this he was a husband one minute, a father the next, and from time to time, as prime minister, he conducted the business of government with me.

The British Columbia trip drove home to me just how much he enjoyed both his family and his position as prime minister. I also came away with a deep appreciation of just how daunting the combination can be for any man.

Mr Mulroney was, as is well known, a newsaholic. He read several newspapers, Canadian and international, every day, listened to radio news whenever he could, and watched television news live or on tape. It was impossible for anyone on his staff to keep up, and he always knew more about what was in the media than all of us combined. It was almost an obsession and he reacted to critical stories accordingly. It was not a habit he was prepared to change. Often on Saturdays he would call me at home to ask whether I had read a nasty article about him in the Toronto *Star* and I would reply, "No, Prime Minister, I don't read the Toronto *Star*.

"Why not?" he exclaimed.

"Because it only makes you angry."

"But you need to, in order to do your job," he implored. "We need to counter this stuff. It's a bunch of lies." We seldom did reply because, even if we did, it wouldn't change the next story.

In retrospect, he was probably right, but I still do not buy the Toronto *Star*. It remains, unfortunately, the most widely read and least balanced of Canada's major newspapers, its tendency to tilt in one direction not having been helped by its alliance with the CBC. If anything, the alliance has strengthened the worst aspects of both.

Mulroney did have a weakness for the media, and he did care too much about what they said. Sensing hostility, he was generally courteous but cautious in his dealings with the press. His attempts at candour sometimes backfired horribly, as in the "rolling the dice" comment during the crisis over Meech Lake. Trudeau, on the other hand, did not care about the media. He was generally unaware of daily events and often disdainful during his encounters with journalists. In fact, most in the Canadian media were intimidated by him. Given the difference in approach, it is ironic that the one who cared was given a rough ride, whereas the one who didn't care was treated mostly with kid gloves.

The Northwest Passage

In the summer of 1986, an American icebreaker, the *Polar Sea*, had ventured through the Northwest Passage, a body of water in the High Arctic that Canada regarded as "internal waters." The Americans were equally

adamant that it was "high seas" and therefore open to international traffic, particularly US Navy transit. It was well known that US, British, and
possibly Soviet submarines had used the passage at one time or another.
But, the *Polar Sea* had been visible to all and quickly generated a
firestorm of protest over the "invasion of Canadian sovereignty," all the
more fodder for the media because it happened, without notice, to a government that had been advocating closer relations with the United
States. A surface transit years earlier by the *Manhattan* had provoked a
similar outcry in Canada. The legal status of the Northwest Passage was,
in fact, an irritant, and sentiments in Canada are easily aroused around
irritants with the United States. They generally receive far more attention
than success does, as this incident would subsequently demonstrate.

The Northwest Passage persisted prominently on the "irritant list" so
much so that when President Reagan visited Ottawa in April 1987, it had
to feature on the agenda. The visit was short: a state dinner on the
evening of the president's arrival, a working session early the next day, a
more formal session with the cabinet, followed by a working lunch at 24
Sussex, and then the main event, a speech to Parliament by the president.

When a small group from each side gathered in the prime minister's
House of Commons office, Mr Mulroney showed the president an 1880s
vintage globe (a gift, I believe, from Paul Desmarais). He pointed out the
Northwest Passage, which on this particular globe looked more like the
St Lawrence River, and stressed how "internal" to Canada it really was.
"It is frozen 90 per cent of the time and Canadian Inuit live on the ice,"
he added for emphasis. The president was sympathetic but not persuad-
ed. "Well, Brian," he observed "it is not like the map they showed me on
Air Force One!"

At lunch, the conversation focused mainly on international affairs –
the Middle East and East-West (Soviet) relations – but towards the end
of lunch, the president declared that he wanted "to say something" in his
speech about "that issue Brian raised in his office" earlier that day. There
was silence on the American side of the table and not a few deadly
glares at their Canadian counterparts. Frank Carlucci, the US secretary
of defence, and I were dispatched to the sunroom to draft an appropriate paragraph for the president's speech. The task fell to Carlucci because
the US Navy was most adamant about preserving open access through
what it regarded as the "high seas." He did not relish the assignment but
knew very little about the issue, and we quickly arrived at a formula in
which the president announced in essence that the United States and
Canada had agreed to explore ways to resolve the dispute.

Adapting the process used to contain the acid rain dispute provided a model, and it was ultimately agreed to assign the Northwest Passage dispute to special envoys, in this case George Shultz's counsellor (or firefighter) at State, Ed Derwinski, and me. Derwinski was from Chicago and had served in Congress for more than twenty years before his State Department assignment. He had the full confidence of Shultz, and both were inclined to try to deliver on something in which the president had taken a personal interest. Loyalty was a virtue for all in this administration. Some were ideologically loyal; others pragmatically and personally. Shultz and Derwinski were in the latter category. But the opposition to any compromise was ideological and military. The Navy's view was supported initially by the National Security branch of the White House, then headed by Colin Powell. Ed Derwinski had an uphill challenge on his hands.*

The Canadian legal position was equally resolute. It was intrinsically legal, overlaid by "sovereignty," the most allergenic of all forces at play in diplomacy. Ever since Canada had been "short-changed" on the Alaska–British Columbia boundary dispute in 1903, disagreements over territorial waters involving the United States were hyper-sensitive in Ottawa. A standoff on principle was preferred by most to any notion of compromise. But the *Polar Sea* rankled and gnawed away at the prime minister's basic posture vis-à-vis the United States.

Closely advised and monitored by our lawyers, Derwinski and I tried various drafts in compromise language. Each version was rejected in turn either by the US Navy, which basically wanted the issue buried, or by my legal advisers from External, who did not want to undermine in any way the legal essentials of Canada's case should the dispute ever go to the World Court or some arbitration tribunal. The United States had no interest in any international arbitration.

Eventually, we settled on a solution that reflected more or less what neighbours might do: "I don't mind you cutting across my lawn to go to the corner store provided you ask first." So the agreement stipulated, in effect, that "without prejudice to either sides legal position," the United States would henceforth agree to seek permission for transit through the Northwest Passage. Canada agreed to answer such requests in the affirmative. This compromise removed the irritant. Although the legal positions remain entrenched and unresolved, the dispute disappeared from public attention.

---

* Ed Derwinski went on to serve as secretary of Veteran Affairs in the cabinet of George Bush the elder and was a valued interlocutor for me during my assignment in Washington.

Years later, as Joan and I were leaving Washington, Colin Powell, who was then chairman of the Joint Chiefs of Staff, spoke at a farewell lunch. He chided me for the "Rube Goldberg globe" that Mulroney had used to get the president's attention on the Northwest Passage. Powell added that, when he had served as national security adviser, he was always afraid of calls from two world leaders, Margaret Thatcher and Brian Mulroney, because, he said, they "could get the president to do anything they wanted."

Defence Policy

As with too many major cabinet items, the White Paper on Defence had been featured – that is, leaked – extensively in the media. The dispute between Defence Minister Perrin Beatty and Foreign Minister Joe Clark over nuclear-powered submarines was an open secret. Extensive discussion in the cabinet committee chaired by Clark failed to resolve the split. He was suspicious of defence policy planners, whose level of complexity exceeded deliberately, in his view, the grasp of most ministers. "How do we know whether what we are told is right or simply what they want us to believe?" Eventually, he seemed to fall in line, especially when he linked the issue to an assertion of sovereignty claims to the Arctic and the need for "Arctic-capable" vessels for the Canadian navy.

The decision, in principle, regarding nuclear-powered submarines aroused negligible fallout in Canada. The reaction from Washington was another matter. Canada's submarine option was seen more as a lever in favour of our claim to Arctic sovereignty – which it was – than as a bridge to more tangible North American maritime defence cooperation – which it also most certainly was.

Ignorance in Washington as to the full depth of Canadian plans and insensitivity to domestic political pressures were becoming unwelcome obstacles to the kind of relationship with the United States favoured by the Mulroney government. Never before had any Canadian government made so conscious an effort, with all the risks involved, of charting bold initiatives on trade, defence, and the environment with so little in the way of constructive response from the US administration. Positive rhetoric from President Reagan and Secretary Shultz was too often undermined by the actions of departments or wild cards in Congress. As the Administration became more beleaguered at home over the Iran-Contra kerfuffle, the prospect of real progress on the bilateral front seemed more elusive (and thankless) than ever. Most debilitating was the effect on free trade negotiations. But regarding nuclear submarines for Canada, the scarcity of financial resources and the sudden end of the Cold War eventually rendered the debate moot.

Social Issues

The two most contentious social policy issues during my time in the PMO were capital punishment and abortion. The first was a matter on which the government had promised a free vote in the House of Commons. The second arose unexpectedly when the Supreme Court ruled in January 1988 that Canada's existing abortion law (allowing only limited abortions) was unconstitutional and breached the Charter of Rights and Freedom.

The issue of capital punishment was a real time bomb. Although the polls showed decisively that the public strongly favoured a return of capital punishment, both the cabinet and the caucus were sharply divided. Many in cabinet did not want the opprobrium of being on the side of the "bad guys" (the "swingers," as they were called). Most simply wanted to get the issue behind them. The prime minister's personal position was clear: he was unequivocally opposed. He decided, however, to speak late in the debate so as not to over-influence (or agitate) his fractious caucus.

In fact, by speaking towards the end, he probably had much greater influence on both cabinet and caucus, especially on those who were anxious not to upset the government's relatively smooth ride in recent months. On 30 June 1987 the ultimate head count was tight, but the private member's motion to reinstate capital punishment was defeated – 148 to 127 – with the government's Quebec caucus proving decisive on the verdict.* A big sigh of relief in many quarters and one more election plank fulfilled.

On abortion, logic, common sense, and good politics dictated a measured response to the somewhat surprising decision by the Supreme Court to scrap the existing law. But for many in the Tory caucus, this was a call to arms. Compromise was not in vogue. For them, this was not politics, it was a moral or ethical issue with no room for compromise. John Crosbie stressed many times that the *only* politics was survival of the government – getting the matter dealt with expeditiously and with

* A similar free vote in 1976 had produced a similar result.

minimum damage. Easier said than done. Nonetheless, the court had encouraged the government to create new legislation on abortion, and the prime minister turned to the one person in cabinet whom he trusted as best able to bridge the unbridgeable – Lowell Murray. If only he had been elected!

In fact, Murray's relatively low public profile was probably his greatest asset and a major reason for the PM's full trust. Murray had a reservoir of patience and shrewd political instincts that paralleled Don Mazankowski's. His presentations were clear, forceful, and persuasive. He straddled a committee that was sharply divided on abortion (e.g., Jake Epp versus Barbara MacDougall) and spent hour after hour nurturing a solution that was more tactical than decisive. One year after the court decision, the government introduced legislation that provided some restraints and made doctors responsible for the determination of whether a woman's life was at risk. The bill passed the House of Commons but died in the Senate, and to this day, no further attempt has been made to legislate abortion in Canada.On these and other internally contentious topics, my job and that of my PMO colleagues was to be open to entreaties from the strong advocates on each side, many of whom wanted to be sure that the prime minister knew just how firm their conviction was.

South Moresby

One positive episode on the government's agenda involved the preservation of South Moresby as a national park. While the concept had strong support from major environmental groups, especially in British Columbia and Ontario, it was a complicated sell politically in British Columbia, notably with Premier Bill Van der Zalm. The logging interests in his province did not want to lose access to the area in the Queen Charlotte Islands.

I became involved on the prime minister's behalf and, with prompting from Dalton Camp (at that time, employed as one of the political operatives for the PMO although technically, and at his request, quartered in the PCO),* began to negotiate a package of benefits from the federal government to British Columbia in exchange for national park designation. After several discussions with Premier Van der Zalm and

---

* Judging from my PMO experience, Dalton Camp's reputation greatly exceeded his contribution. Although he sat in on most cabinet meetings, I can think of no issue, other than South Moresby, on which he played a significant role. He was presumably brought in for optical reasons and had insisted on being attached (at deputy minister level) to the PCO

his deputy, David Poole, we were able to strike a deal. The most memorable exchange came in an early conversation with the premier. Stressing the unique characteristics of the rainforest itself, I asked, "Did you know, Premier, that some of those trees (i.e., the ones that would be saved) are more than one hundred years old?" "Yes, Derek," he replied, "but if someone had cut them down seventy-five years ago, you wouldn't be asking." He certainly had me on that point, but in any event, we did secure his agreement, and the premier and the prime minister joined forces in a colourful signing ceremony in the British Columbia legislature a few months later. Typically, Mulroney received little credit for South Moresby. The environmental lobbyists celebrated it as a victory for goodness itself and accepted full credit.

Acid Rain

It was much the same on acid rain. The major differences on this issue between Canada and the United States were of long standing and had generated a lobbying industry of their own on the Canadian side. Trudeau and the Liberals had raised the question on several occasions with various US administrations, but to no avail. During President Reagan's visit to Parliament Hill in 1981, he had been greeted by hundreds of demonstrators calling for a halt to acid rain.

Reagan did have definite views on the subject. He was convinced that acid rain was a figment of someone's imagination. He had read an article somewhere (in the *Reader's Digest* perhaps) which convinced him on this point, and he would not be moved. Furthermore, several in his administration were even more rigid on the topic. While there were Americans, particularly in the border states, who were as concerned as their Canadian neighbours, acid rain was not a major topic in California. Voters there were more concerned about smog.

The Reagan administration was fundamentally pro-energy and whatever contributed to the steady flow of oil, coal, or nuclear energy to fuel the US economy. It (the administration) had support on this from both sides in Congress. Its paramount interest was the economy, not the environment, and Reagan officials were not receptive to measures they perceived as encroaching on US energy needs.

Mulroney, fully conscious of the lack of progress and of Reagan's deep-

---

rather than the "political" PMO. This resulted in a bizarre episode at a cabinet meeting in Edmonton. On a hotel telephone list distributed to cabinet attendees, Camp was described incorrectly as a PMO official. He took strong umbrage at this slight and remained in his hotel room for the duration.

seated position, decided to take a different tack. At the Shamrock Summit in March 1985, he floated the notion of special emissaries to study the problem. The US administration agreed, and former Ontario premier Bill Davis and former transport secretary Drew Lewis were designated to take up the task. Equally, Mulroney declared that Canada would come to the table "with clean hands" – with an action plan dedicated to reducing nitrogen oxide and sulphur dioxide emissions in Canada – the idea being to attract a matching program from the United States.

The emissary process bought time, and the two governments wrestled with the issue and their basic differences at every high-level meeting. Progress came very slowly and we never really succeeded in changing Reagan's mindset, although the prime minister was convinced that, if he ever could have taken the president to see a "dead lake" first-hand, it might have worked. Success would have to await a change at the top in Washington.

Ronald Reagan

Ronald Reagan's genius as a politician lay in his ability to project an image as a cheerful optimist in public and in private. He always appeared to believe that "there must be a pony" somewhere in any manure pile. His optimism was anchored in a few basic convictions that guided his approach to government, convictions from which he rarely wavered and which he communicated with great effect both to his colleagues and officials and to the public at large. The affection in which he was held was clearly in evidence during his funeral.

Reagan was the "Great Communicator" in public but rarely had much to say in private sessions. He had a penchant for anecdotes, some of which – notably his efforts to expel communist sympathizers from the executive of the Screen Actors Guild – served as anchors for his policy convictions. The only time he really engaged our prime minister on an issue relating to free trade was when he registered his concern about Canadian restrictions on the distribution of Hollywood movies in Canada. For the most part, he relied on his cabinet secretaries to carry the discussion during bilateral meetings. His comfort in delegating matters to his subordinates was critical to his success as president. With secretaries like George Shultz and Jim Baker, his trust was not misplaced, and they in turn proved fiercely loyal to him.

Reagan did like to tell Irish jokes, as did Mulroney, and this is how most sessions began. Reagan would also use a joke deftly to steer conversation away from policy when he wanted. He was very much at ease in meetings with Brian Mulroney; more guarded with Pierre Trudeau. Apart from the difference in personalities, I suspect that Reagan had been influenced on his views about Trudeau by less-than-sympathetic briefings provided by White House and State Department staff.*

Reagan had strong convictions on a few basic issues – defence, freedom, private enterprise – and rarely delved into complex policy terrain. I believe this characteristic really explains his enduring popularity in the United States. He looked and acted like a president, and even those who disagreed with his views respected the way he conducted himself. His optimism charmed even his fiercest opponents in Congress, including the speaker, Tip O'Neill, and enabled him to ride through serious crises (such as "Irangate") which would have jeopardized the careers of other presidents.

Ronald Reagan did not know a lot about Canada, but his affection for Brian Mulroney provided channels to others in the administration who had both knowledge and interest in Canadian affairs. This access gave us the opportunity for direct exchanges on bilateral and global issues and in a spirit of candour that a relationship based on trust will allow. Reagan also believed in free trade, even though the actions of his administration did not always sustain his rhetoric.

Loyalty was paramount in the Reagan White House. Just before the prime minister's Washington visit in April 1988, we were alerted to a *Washington Post* story of an interview with the PM which implied that the United States had broken promises on acid rain and that Governor Michael Dukakis of Massachusetts would likely be more amenable to Canada's position. While both points were probably accurate, they did not reflect what the prime minister had actually said. When George Shultz met us at Andrews Air Force Base to accompany us by helicopter to the White House, he was in a fury. He had been directed by the White House to complain forcefully about the press report. After hearing Shultz's tirade, the PM asked calmly what he (Shultz) might think if the report was a distortion. Shultz blanched. I handed him the transcript. As he pored over it, Shultz's demeanour changed markedly from anger to

---

* Shortly before a meeting with Reagan in Washington, Trudeau had been described as a "pot-smoking pipsqueak" by an unnamed State Department source widely presumed to have been Larry Eagleburger, a man of Rabelaisian appetites and views and briefly secretary of state in the closing months of George H.W. Bush's administration.

profound apology. In the transcript, Mulroney was, in fact, quite positive about President Reagan. Shultz continued to apologize throughout the balance of the Washington program, but it was clear from this episode just how fiercely loyal he was to the president. It was also, for us, a good lesson in the most fundamental rule of all in diplomacy – be prepared, well prepared, in advance.

Other Issues

Among the unexpected or unplanned events while I was in the PMO was the sudden arrival on the south shore of Nova Scotia in the summer of 1988 of more than a hundred Sri Lankan "refugees." While the newcomers were received warmly by the surprised Nova Scotians, the political reaction was less hospitable. Parliament was recalled for an emergency summer session, ostensibly to strengthen the government's capacity to cope with similar "visits" in future. Lengthy analysis and consultation proved relatively fruitless, however, as our legal advisers consistently pointed to the Charter of Rights and Freedoms and the extent to which it constrained almost any legislative move to curtail illegal entry into Canada, a problem that bedevils legal immigration to this day.

I was pitchforked, unexpectedly, into Aboriginal affairs when the prime minister, while travelling in the summer of 1988, delegated a representation to him by the chief of the Lubicon Cree to me personally, much to the relief of our then Minister of Indian and Northern Affairs, Bill McKnight. Bernard Ominayak was the chief in question. The Lubicon were a relatively small band of about four hundred Natives from Alberta who were without a settlement or reserve of their own and whose concerns had languished unresolved for most of the twentieth century. All efforts at resolution had failed, even though the Alberta government had offered land and the federal government had proposed varying amounts of cash over the years. This was by no means a topic on which I had either experience or knowledge. What I did learn, more than anything else, was just how unfortunate the plight of some in our Aboriginal community had become. On a different scale, I was dismayed to see the extent to which the fate of groups like the Lubicon had become an industry of sorts for the legal profession.

The first issue to be settled was the size of the Lubicon delegation and the time allowed in Ottawa for the meeting promised by the prime minister. On advice from his lawyers, Chief Ominayak requested authority for a six-week session involving more than two dozen from his group. He eventually settled for much less on each question.

After detailed consultations with Bill McKnight, his officials, and others from the Alberta government, we put together a package that we were convinced was generous and fair. It included some seventy square miles of land in Alberta and more than $100 million in grants to build a community, clinic, school, housing, and so on. The actual size of the Lubicon group was a matter of dispute, but even if the highest number were accepted, the total offer amounted to more than $500,000 per individual. Nevertheless, the proposal was rejected (as Bill McKnight had predicted), I suspect by the lawyers advising Chief Ominayak. The Lubicon are still without a settlement of their claim. Meanwhile, however, taxpayers continue to fund the advice they receive from lawyers – a sad commentary on a problem which, in broader form, chips away at the social fabric of Canada.

If my involvement in Don Jamieson's office had been my political baptism in Ottawa, life in the PMO constituted a full immersion. Even though the prime minister, true to his word, kept me out of direct activity with the party, the partisan tenor of the PMO was unavoidable. The unpredictability of events was beyond rational management, and the day-to-day pressure was physically, as well as mentally, draining. Time to think was scarce. The fundamental challenge was to ensure that the daily distractions did not undermine attention on what was clearly the government's most critical initiative, the free trade negotiations with the United States, which eventually became more partisan than anyone expected.

NINE

Free Trade: Getting It Done

Free trade became the paramount, as well as the defining, issue for the Mulroney government. Preparations had begun in earnest following the Shamrock Summit in March of 1985. Extensive consultations were conducted across Canada, sector by sector, and a team of Canada's best trade policy hands were assembled under Simon Reisman's lead in the Trade Negotiations Office (TNO).* Both ministers at External Affairs, along with the Minister of Finance, were fully involved, as of course was the prime minister himself. It was an issue that affected virtually all of cabinet. I kept my hand in initially from my senior position at External, where I was the departmental link to the Prime Minister's Office on US affairs more generally.

On 23 April 1986 a group of about twenty officials from the Prime Minister's Office, the Privy Council Office, the TNO, and External gathered in the Langevin boardroom to await the verdict from the US Senate Finance Committee on whether the administration would receive authority to begin negotiations with Canada. The atmosphere was upbeat and excited. Preparations were being made for a statement by the prime minister welcoming what was presumed would be a positive outcome.

By late morning the mood had become more subdued as word trickled in from our embassy in Washington that the vote was not a sure thing. Senator Daniel Patrick Moynihan had alerted our ambassador that games were being played. Some senators on the committee were, of course, opposed. The Democrats had the majority but were divided. The Republicans had been expected to be supportive, but some had

---

* Simon Reisman was a major force in convincing Brian Mulroney to launch negotiations, as well as the dominant Canadian negotiator. He had written a crisp summary of the rationale privately for the prime minister which proved, in effect, to be not only persuasive but also an unparalleled job application.

decided to use the vote to "send a message" to the administration on issues completely unrelated to Canada-US trade. Republican senator Malcolm Wallop of Wyoming, for instance, was going to vote no to register his concern about the lack of administration action against "slave labour in the Soviet Union." Such is the nature of politics in Washington. Clayton Yeutter, the US trade representative (USTR), had done little advance work, assuming, incorrectly, that the resolution would pass easily. Sensing failure at the last minute, our ambassador and Yeutter scrambled furiously to rally support. Senator Matsunaga was reminded pointedly about the importance of Canadian visitors to Hawaiian tourism. He decided to vote in favour.

By this time the mood in the Prime Minister's Office had become eerie. Most had left the boardroom, and only Don Campbell, who had replaced me as ADM for the US Branch at External, remained with me. "Don't you dare leave," I suggested. We began sombrely to prepare a draft statement for the prime minister in the event that the committee voted against the initiative. At about 4:00 p.m., the vote in Washington was concluded – a ten-to-ten tie. In the US Senate, a tie goes to the affirmative. It was a near-run victory at the very beginning, which served as an ominous prelude to the negotiations themselves. We now realized fully the extent to which the priority for free trade was vastly different in the two capitals. Free trade had become an all-consuming issue in Canada, debated intensely, heatedly, and in highly partisan fashion nationally, provincially, and even municipally. In Washington it barely raised a ripple. The biggest problem we had was trying to get the US administration to recognize the political priority of the issue for the Canadian government and to treat it accordingly.

The appointment of Peter Murphy as the US negotiator in January 1986 had not been encouraging. While a very able textile negotiator, Peter was a second-level USTR official. He was tall and Simon Reisman short; in every other sense, their stature was the reverse. Simon thought big and acted even bigger. He wanted a historic free trade agreement that would be a legacy for all time. He knew he had the full support and confidence of the prime minister in virtually all he did and said, although there were some exceptions on the latter, notably when he branded those he saw lying about free trade as "Nazis." He had negotiated multilateral trade rounds, as well as the Auto Pact, successfully with some of the best and best-known American trade negotiators. Peter Murphy, on the other hand, was not well known, even in Washington. He was not connected to the president or to anyone in the White House. He presided over an interdepartmental group of US officials who basically drew up a long list of trade irritants vis-à-vis Canada ("scalps," as Simon called them) on which he sought redress. Not much vision and even less clout. Simon Reisman had a full team of some of our very best trade officials dedicated exclusively to the negotiation, whereas Murphy drew his support primarily from many who had other day jobs. It was a high common denominator from Ottawa versus a low common denominator from Washington. Simon reported regularly to a special committee of cabinet on the progress (or lack thereof) of the negotiations.* I doubt that Peter Murphy ever met with a group from the US cabinet, except towards the very end. His manner and his authority were polar opposites to Reisman's.

Simon had a very short fuse. As a retired public servant, he was anything but retiring. Fiercely independent and firmly fixed in his opinions, he chafed at interdepartmental consultations, including, on occasion, with ministers. He once told trade minister Pat Carney to "go piss up a rope" when she pressed him for details on his negotiating position. Reisman had been involved with trade negotiations in a different age, when three or four senior officials from Finance, ITC, and External developed and implemented Canada's negotiation policy with minimal guidance from ministers. Their actions had served Canada well, and Simon could not fathom the need to consult officials and ministers who knew very little about how and why he was negotiating. After one lengthy wrangle in committee, I took him for a stroll on the Sparks Street Mall – to get some air. We came across a trio of Hare Krishna disciples, who were solemnly chanting in the usual manner. Simon rushed over to then and demanded, "And what is your view on US countervail?" They were nonplussed and simply resumed chanting. To Simon, however, they were about as helpful as his many interdepartmental colleagues.

There was clearly little appreciation in Washington of the enormous risk our prime minister had taken over free trade. Time and again, we tried to raise attention at the political level in the American capital. I wrote and spoke to the president's chief of staff, Howard Baker, and urged a higher priority to the negotiations. Our ambassador, Allan Gotlieb, was relentless in making similar efforts. On every possible occasion, the prime minister broached the issue with the president. His cabinet colleagues did the same in meetings with their US counterparts.

---

* Trade Minister Carney complained repeatedly about not seeing the details of what Simon was proposing to the Americans. This was partly because not much of substance had been exchanged, but it was also somewhat deliberate. We did not want to read details about our negotiating position filed by her friends in the Press Gallery, a tactic she indulged on other issues.

Same pitch, same sympathetic response, but little momentum at the negotiating table. Free trade with Canada was just not a priority in Washington. We lacked a political champion there, someone who would deliver for the president.

In fact, after sixteen months of palaver, very little tangible progress had been achieved by the negotiating teams. This was partly tactical. Both sides refrained from engaging on the major issues because both knew clearly from the beginning what those were – trade remedy and dispute settlement for Canada; investment restrictions for the United States. Equally, both sides understood that nothing would be agreed until as much as possible was agreed.

There were days of extreme frustration when the determination to move matters forward seemed thwarted on all sides. There were skeptics and critics and tepid supporters. It would have been easier on many occasions simply to pull back or, in bureaucratic parlance, "put down our pens." But on days like that, I could usually rely on the drive and commitment of my closest associates in the TNO – Michael Hart and Bill Dymond (who used the alias "Smith & Jones" in private memos to me) – to sustain the drive. On one such occasion, Bill Dymond sent me a quotation from Shakespeare's *Henry V*:

> We few, we happy few, we band of brothers
> For he to-day that sheds his blood with me
> Shall be my brother; be he ne'er so vile,
> This day shall gentle his condition:
> And gentlemen in England now a-bed
> Shall think themselves accurs'd they were not here,
> And hold their manhoods cheap whiles any speaks
> That fought with us upon Saint Crispin's day.

It made my day on that occasion and was a recurring tonic in the days and weeks that followed.

The US administration had until 4 October 1987 to signal to Congress its intention to conclude an agreement with Canada. As the deadline approached, we decided to make yet another overture at the political level. Having failed in our missives to the president's chief of staff, we acted on Allan Gotlieb's suggestion and asked for a meeting with Treasury Secretary James Baker on the eve of the IMF fall session, 19 September 1987 in Washington.

Accompanied by Finance Minister Mike Wilson and the ambassador, I met Secretary Baker and said, in effect, that it would be peculiar if the

United States could strike an arms reduction agreement with the USSR (as it was in the process of completing SALT II negotiations) but fail to conclude a trade agreement with its neighbour and close ally. Baker acknowledged that the trade agreement was more significant in legacy terms than the arms agreement but seemed otherwise unimpressed by our representation. He urged attention to "underbrush" issues (i.e., the list of irritants), leaving the major issues (Canada's priorities) "til the end." But for Canada, there was little distinction between his underbrush (investment) and our fundamentals (trade remedy). Even though Baker was seen by most as the man to go to in Washington in order to get things done, he was not really responsible for trade. However, investment was within his mandate and that was the United States' top priority.

Simon, meanwhile, had decided to make one last effort at a breakthrough on trade remedy at the negotiating table. Otherwise, it had been decided by the prime minister and cabinet in advance that he would walk away, that is, formally suspend the negotiations. On 23 September, Simon and his senior associates met their US counterparts in Washington. When nothing ensued, he walked. His action was inconsequential in political Washington, but was traumatic in Canada. Nevertheless, the prime minister and his cabinet had accepted the view that "no deal was better than a bad deal." Canada would not settle for something that fell short of the prime minister's basic instruction "to secure an agreement that made the trade relationship significantly better."

Many in Washington perceived the suspension as a bluff or a stunt by Canada. President Reagan's chief of staff, Howard Baker, called me and asked us to return to the table. I said that there was no point reconvening if there was nothing on the table that responded to our principal demands. I added that a call without substance "could be fatal." He quickly handed the reins to Jim Baker. At this point, in Ottawa, there was probably as much relief that the talks had failed as there was frustration, and little enthusiasm to try to re-engage. Certainly, those most closely involved, including me, were annoyed by the lack of priority and flexibility on the part of Washington. We sensed that the Americans had been convinced that Canada would accept virtually anything in order to proclaim success. Our immediate challenge was to disabuse them of that notion.

Intense efforts began, primarily in Washington, to restart the negotiations. In Ottawa our focus had shifted more to containing the fallout from a failed negotiation. New American proposals on trade remedy were examined carefully but rejected politely. Forging a consensus for our replies was rarely easy. By then, there were some on the Canadian side who would have preferred simply to stand down. Others, including notably our ambassador in Washington, were anxious to go "the extra mile" to try to secure an agreement. I was in the middle, struggling to keep our negotiating effort together but ready for either scenario. (At one point, my voice deserted me, no doubt from overuse!)

At the end of September, we really thought it was all over and on 1 October I was dispatched by the prime minister, along with Mike Wilson and Trade Minister Pat Carney, to confirm formal termination of the negotiations face to face at the political level in Washington. When the Americans first heard we were coming, they thought that we were resuming negotiations. Even ambassador Gotlieb was unaware of what was happening. The embassy had assembled a fleet of cars to transport our "delegation." However, when they saw us arrive without the negotiating team, they knew that one car would suffice.

The prime minister had instructed me to lead our trio, and I had rehearsed my message carefully with him at the airport before leaving. The Americans had proposed that we simply conclude a deal on tariff reductions and claim victory. What I said, in response, was that "the deal we wanted, we do not see; the one we see, we do not want." A deal on tariffs alone was not only lopsided (our tariffs being higher generally, we had more to give than to get), but it fell short of what we had set out to obtain in terms of relief from the application of US trade remedy laws or some form of "binding dispute settlement." We were more frustrated than bitter, but simply saw no acceptable basis for a resumption of negotiations.

From the outset, Canada's goal had been to increase and better secure access to our most important market. The basic economic rationale for free trade was significant in itself, but there was a need to improve and stabilize Canada's position as a magnet for investment on a footing at least equivalent to that of the United States. With increased investment would come increased production in Canada and, of course, jobs – good jobs based on market demand, not government pump-priming. In particular, we wanted security against capricious rulings by US trade agencies. Experiences with shakes and shingles, softwood lumber, and steel in the early 1980s had driven this lesson home in spades. Our exports to the United States were too vulnerable on too many fronts.

Improved productivity by Canadian firms was seen as a clear byproduct of trade liberalization, and there was confidence that Canadian industry and exporters could compete effectively in the US market, provided the ground rules were clear and fairly administered. Moreover, if

Canadian firms expected to succeed in global markets, it was essential that they be able to compete and win in the market next door. These had been the basic economic factors behind Canada's decision to enter negotiations.

For the Americans, the negotiations were much less vital and certainly less divisive, except for some in the border states. The Reagan administration and Republicans generally were free traders at heart, if not always in practice. Congress reflected many attitudes, most of them parochial, but was still inclined, at decisive moments, to tilt in favour of trade liberalization. American officials and politicians were frustrated by the lack of progress towards a new multilateral trade round and saw some strategic merit in moving regionally in order to kick-start global negotiations. In Washington, therefore, the motivation for free trade with Canada reflected some strategic global concerns, but a cluster of bilateral trade irritants underpinned most of the US negotiating position, reflecting the "all politics is local" tenor of the times.

The protection and preservation of Canadian culture – notably English Canada's culture and especially that of Ontario – was extremely sensitive in the context of free trade. Fear of assimilation by the United States was most acute among many of the cultural literati, mainly in and around Toronto. Many actors and performers shared this concern, even though a good number of them depended on the US market for much of their livelihood. Canada had a long list of protective measures in place in law, supporting Canadian magazines, Canadian films, and film distribution through restrictions and subsidies and, for Canadian broadcasting, through restrictions on ownership and on advertisements. All had been attacked in one way or another by US interests that regarded these as restrictions on commerce and were oblivious to concerns about Canadian culture. At one point during the negotiations Jim Baker retorted to me, "In Texas, Derek, sugar is culture." In retrospect, if we had defined our culture as a commodity like sugar, we might have had more impact on US attitudes.

Apart from the litany of US complaints and persistent media headlines, culture was never really a major issue for the negotiations. But given the sensitivities in Canada, it had to be contained visibly. The best tack was simply to remove culture from the negotiating agenda, and that is exactly what Simon and his team did. On every occasion, he stated solemnly that "culture" was not part of the negotiations, and he refused steadfastly to respond to US pressures. Equally, however, the Americans continued to press on magazine postage rates, restrictions on film distribution, and cable advertising, claiming these were trade-restrictive. The two sides talked past one another. Culture was removed from the Free Trade Agreement but the United States reserved its GATT rights to challenge any actions that "nullified or impaired" US access. Artful as the tactic may have been, it did little to assuage the angst of Canadian cultural nationalists, whose subsequent attacks on the government and the agreement played prominently in the media and in Parliament.

The interrelated issues of dispute settlement and trade remedy relief had been addressed many times by the negotiators and many formulas had been contemplated – for example, competition law to address antidumping rules and "safe harbour,"* "red light," "green light" codes to categorize acceptable, as opposed to unacceptable, subsidies, in an effort to defang countervail (duties). Apart from US reluctance to "surrender" any trade remedy leverage, the fundamental problem was that, because of the highly disproportionate weight of trade in the two economies, any imaginable formula on trade-distorting subsidies would result in more bite or political pain in Canada than on the United States. Canada was and is far more dependent on trade than the United States which relies for much of its economic growth on its own huge domestic market. Whereas virtually all Canadian government programs had a potential impact on our exports, the same was not the case for US programs. And, of course, national security provided a highly convenient umbrella for much subsidized research and development in the US, which indirectly supported exports but could not be captured under any "export" subsidy disciplines. With minimal defence expenditures, Canada did not have a similar shield.

Congressman Sam Gibbons, a Democrat from Florida and chairman of the House Trade Subcommittee, was an ardent free trader – unusually so for a Democrat. He was also well disposed towards Canada, as were most Florida representatives, and for good reason, given that some two million Canadians spent much of the winter in their state. Gibbons had suggested that the two countries simply develop a binational dispute settlement mechanism to oversee the implementation of each side's existing trade rules and ensure that the rules were being respected on their merits. It seemed simple enough, even though it fell short of the larger objective – agreed rules on competition and government subsidies that would obviate the need for the highly discriminatory and capricious trade remedy regime. And, of course, it had not yet been vetted by lawyers!

---

* In essence the US design of "safe harbours" for subsidies had no openings (no mouth) and no water inside. (The proposed limit of $10,000 per firm was derisory.)

Getting It Done

Ambassador Gotlieb proposed Sam Gibbons's idea to Secretary Baker, who then took a few soundings of his own on the Hill, including specifically with Dan Rostenkowski, Democratic chair of the powerful House Ways and Means Committee, which would ultimately have jurisdiction over any trade agreement, as well as with members of the Senate Finance Committee. We were finally getting the kind of political involvement in Washington needed to move the agenda forward. Baker then called me to say that the United States was prepared to consider "something like the Sam Gibbons formula" if that would help get us back to the table. He added that he would be directly involved. This was a critical move in itself. Jim Baker was known for his ability to deliver on key items of President Reagan's agenda. We knew that the president favoured a free trade agreement with Canada. We also knew that he needed someone like Baker to make it happen.

I spoke to the prime minister, and we went together into a cabinet session. He asked me to explain the US proposal and to summarize the pluses and minuses of the kind of agreement we now thought we might get. The ensuing cabinet debate was anything but unanimous. Even Trade Minister Pat Carney was among the most negative.* It was, in a sense, Lincoln-esque. Votes in Lincoln's cabinet were sometimes ten to one against, but the one prevailed because it was Lincoln's vote. After hearing a discordant mix of ministerial views, the prime minister concluded by saying, in effect, "Well, Derek, you know where matters stand."

I subsequently met privately with the ministers of Agriculture (John Wise), Fisheries (Tom Siddon), and of Communications (Flora Macdonald) because each had particular concerns about the impact of the negotiations on their portfolios and had become sensitive to the protectionist elements in their departments. I then went to a marathon session with Simon and his TNO team to obtain a detailed update on where matters stood on each segment of the negotiations. The next morning we were off again to Washington, this time with the full negotiating team. Again, the prime minister had instructed me to lead. I had asked him to explain this to the two ministers (who would be the public face of the Canadian team). Neither objected.

---

* In the negotiations themselves, Carney was also erratic. The only elements of real interest to her seemed to be those involving British Columbia, notably lumber, fish, and wine. I assigned Don Campbell the task of monitoring Carney carefully to prevent her from attempting to conclude side deals on each outside the plenary sessions.

Our negotiating team was stationed at the USTR office, but the core team – Wilson, Carney, Gotlieb, Reisman, Ritchie (Reisman's deputy), Hartt (Wilson's deputy), Campbell (from External), and I – were located in the Treasury building, on the other side of the White House complex. While the negotiations might be about trade, the responsibility of USTR, the final drama would take place in Secretary Baker's boardroom. To that end, we were allocated a small office right across from Baker's own office.

In addition to Reisman, Ritchie, and Hartt, I had added Don Campbell to our inside team deliberately. Campbell was the assistant deputy minister for US affairs at External (my old job) and one of my closest associates in that department. What you need most from colleagues in times of crisis management are trust and competence. Campbell consistently delivered both. He was steadfastly committed to the objective at hand, understood the political imperatives, and brought impressive knowledge, as well as balanced judgment, to our deliberations.

We met in plenary at the Treasury department and established basic rules of procedure. Representatives from each delegation reported jointly to the plenary sessions on the state of play for each segment of the potential agreement, summarizing what was agreed and what was not. As each reported, a determination would be made by the principals on how or whether to deal with outstanding elements. Some differences were simply set aside, and others resolved at the plenary table. Some were relegated to private sessions involving the key negotiators. We all knew what the crunch issues were. From time to time, there were also private sessions involving one or two principals from each side. The first plenary session was in fact quite stormy, reflecting the frustration and annoyance that had permeated both negotiating teams. We saw flashes of anger from Baker, directed crudely and personally at Mike Wilson over financial services. I returned the fire on intellectual property.

"Intellectual property" was somewhat new to trade negotiations, and the teams had made some headway but not enough for the Americans, who were determined to get more, especially on the protection of pharmaceutical patents. This was a long-standing grievance in which the Americans sought to preserve original patents for sixteen years, thereby restricting replication and lower-priced production by generic drug manufacturers. Canada had been "offside" on this one, in their view, for years, but the Mulroney government had already moved and had paid a hefty political price by bringing Canada closer to the OECD consensus. These proposals for change were already being resisted by the Liberal majority in the Senate, and it would have been politically impossible to try to make further changes at this delicate stage. Seemingly oblivious to all this, the Americans pressed for the promise of more patent protection. At this point, in Pat Carney's words, I "lost it," threw the draft chapter on the table, and said, "If that is your considered position, you can forget the whole chapter." I stomped out of the room, and the intellectual property chapter was in fact deleted from the agreement.* Ironically, an early draft of the negotiating team's summary report on this topic was subsequently leaked to the media prompting a mini-firestorm in Ottawa. All the more ludicrous, given what had actually taken place.

Despite the occasional theatrics at the plenary table, we made steady progress on most issues, and the elements of an agreement gradually began to take shape. But we had heard nothing specific on dispute settlement other than Baker's sketchy reference to Sam Gibbons's idea. Allegedly, the US legal team and possibly some in Congress were balking at the "compromise to US sovereignty" that any binational panel structure would entail. Given acute sensitivities in Canada to the erosion of "sovereignty" from free trade of any description, this US concern was more than ironic.

As with all the issues, once the principals had signaled the basic elements of agreement, the negotiators went to work to craft mutually acceptable language to go into the document, setting out what had been agreed. On trade remedies, two groups of lawyers and officials had been hard at work over at the Winder Building, the home of USTR, trying to put flesh on the Gibbons proposal. Unfortunately, US perceptions of that proposal differed markedly from Canadian perceptions, and even within delegations there were sharp differences on what would be involved in a fully articulated version of the Gibbons proposal. The Canadian team had brought in US counsel to help them through the maze, as both sides were forced to do staff work in a few hours that usually takes weeks or months.

In Secretary Baker's anteroom, we were given only occasional and somewhat sketchy reports on all this toing and froing. By early evening it was clear that the US side was distinctly uncomfortable with the full implications of the Gibbons proposal, particularly after some US lawyers had raised concerns about its "constitutionality," which we took to be code for concerns about sovereignty. Secretary Baker, for his part, found

---

* Theatrical outbursts of this kind are not unusual in major negotiations. A lack of sleep contributes to short tempers. Reisman was a legend in this regard, and I tried to be a good learner!

himself in the uncomfortable position of having authored a return to the negotiating table on the basis of a proposal that seemed politically acceptable on the Hill but was now running into trouble among the experts.

The principal legal adviser from the Department of Commerce, Jean Anderson, also found herself at a disadvantage because her political mentor, Commerce Secretary Mac Baldrige, had been killed in a tragic rodeo accident earlier that summer. She now had to deal with the formidable Baker on her own and carry the concerns and misgivings of the department with primary responsibility for trade remedies. In retrospect, it is not hard to appreciate why the trade remedy issue took so long to come together. At the time, however, it was nerve-racking and almost wrecked the negotiations as a whole.

I met Baker alone on Saturday morning, reviewed the balance sheet, and stressed the need for a more positive focus. I signalled our willingness to move on investment and financial services (Baker's priorities), but only if and when the dispute settlement issue – the deal-breaker for Canada – was resolved to our satisfaction. Time was running out. Over and over again during the course of Saturday's meetings, I emphasized to Baker that a binding dispute settlement provision on trade remedies was a *sine qua non* for Canada. When nothing had emerged by about 7:00 p.m. that evening, I telephoned the prime minister and advised him that we had still failed to get an agreement on this key point. "So be it," he replied. He then instructed me to tell Baker that he wanted to telephone the president to confirm that the negotiations were over. This decision was not intended to cajole the president at the last moment, though that may have been how it was interpreted. In any event, when I conveyed the message to Baker, he asked that we not disturb the president for a while (because, as he put it, Reagan was watching a movie at Camp David).

At about 8 p.m. I called the prime minister again, and he said he would leave Harrington Lake, proceed to the Langevin Building, and make a statement to the media announcing that the negotiations had failed. Everyone knew the deadline was imminent. Under the fast-track authority, the administration was obliged to report to Congress by midnight, 3 October, on its intent to conclude a trade agreement in order to subject such an agreement to fast-track procedures, that is, a straight yes or no vote, with no amendments, within prescribed time limits. We sat in our caucus room at Treasury, dejected and exhausted. At about 9 p.m. Secretary Baker burst in and flung a piece of paper on the table. "All right, you can have your goddam dispute settlement mechanism. Now can we send the report to Congress." Baker had finally knocked heads together on the United States' side and produced a text that met our fundamental needs.

We huddled together and I telephoned the prime minister urgently. "It seems like we may have a deal after all," I reported, "including binding dispute settlement." He was pleasantly surprised and no doubt profoundly relieved. He asked whether we all agreed that the agreement met his basic objective – that Canada would be "significantly better with it than without." I polled my group of eight and they were unanimous. Then Mr Mulroney stumped me: "So Derek," he asked "how will it play in Drumheller?" For a minute, I couldn't respond. Finally I said, "Well, it is very good for Canada on energy and red meat, so I assume it will go down well in Drumheller." (I really didn't have a clue.) "That's great," he said and then conveyed his thanks to each team member individually.

We were exhausted but elated, and slowly the historical significance of what was being achieved and the satisfaction of "getting it done" captured the mood. Mike Wilson went out and gave the Canadian media a thumbs-up through the Treasury office window. He also assembled the exhausted troops and thanked them for their magnificent performance in bringing the agreement together. Well after midnight, we adjourned to the embassy residence, where the ambassador's hospitality ran into the early hours of the morning.

But the struggle was far from over. We had very little on paper other than summary drafts on each chapter and a verbal commitment on dispute settlement. First thing the next morning, new problems arose. Don Campbell and I raced to USTR to resolve a dispute on lumber. Meanwhile, Konrad von Finckenstein, TNO's senior legal adviser, was reporting yet another deadlock on the dispute settlement mechanism. The American lawyers remained concerned about a potential constitutional challenge against what had been agreed. Specifically, they wondered what would happen if a panel member were found to have acted improperly. They insisted that there had to be an appeal body on top of the panels with authority to rule in such instances. Otherwise, the whole mechanism would, they claimed, be vulnerable to constitutional attack.

We were neither impressed nor amused by this last-minute wrinkle, but Konrad convinced us that the legal concern was justified. It elicited what became the "dead judges" provision of the agreement. A roster of US and Canadian judges was established to serve on appeals. No offence to the esteemed judges who were appointed, but we were assured by the US team that this appeal mechanism would never be invoked and was simply a "constitutional cover." – hence the appellation "dead judges."

Years later, during my tenure as Canada's ambassador to Washington, when the provision was invoked by the United States not once but twice, I complained to USTR Carla Hills and reminded her of the "negotiating history." She was not swayed. After all, she had not been involved in the "negotiating history." In both instances, however, rulings in Canada's favour were upheld by the "dead judges." We should have known that in the US political system, if there is an avenue for a further kick at the can, it will be used. On sensitive matters such as softwood lumber and pork and swine, as I learned then, matters are never over until they are over, and they are never over. There is always some wrinkle allowing for a new hearing or appeal. That is why Canada needs firm rules and credible procedures to address its interests in the United States.

Meanwhile, both teams were scrambling to get the pieces together for signatures and for a midday press conference. After that, we headed for home. Little did we know how much more remained to get done and how politically charged the whole issue would become in Canada. The hectic three days in Washington had been filled with emotional highs and lows, but the overall mood was decidedly upbeat. The prime minister, in particular, was rejuvenated and very appreciative.

What had made it happen was that political will ultimately galvanized both sides. There was push and pull on many issues and no shortage of acrimony. Tensions ran high between the delegations, and towards the end, the key players were tired and running on pure adrenaline. I had been adamant that no deal was preferable to a bad deal. Equally, I had insisted on unanimity within the Canadian team on approving or rejecting each key element. We all knew what was at stake. We had been given unusual latitude by the prime minister in arriving at decisions. We had been instructed to conclude a deal if it was good for Canada but otherwise to limit the damage of failed negotiations. In the end, it was a "near run" thing. For me personally, it was a singularly demanding experience, one that served as a benchmark of sorts for all subsequent career challenges, none of which matched the pressure, the stress, and the enormous responsibility of concluding that agreement.

But even with an agreement in place, there was still more to do. What we had concluded was, in business parlance, a "Term Sheet." It now needed a full legal text – in other words, the actual agreement. Over the course of the next twelve weeks, Konrad von Finckenstein for Canada and Chip Roh for the United States worked away with their legal colleagues to translate the term sheet into a legal text. Some of this was quite straightforward and built on the months of staff work and effort in the individual working groups. Other issues proved problematic and could not be resolved on the basis of legal drafting alone.

After several rounds of discussion between Reisman and Murphy, it became clear that concluding a final deal would again need intervention at the political level. This time it was held in Ottawa, in December, and we had all the TNO resources at our disposal. More importantly, the political imperative was by now actively driving both teams, not just one. Peter McPherson, Baker's deputy, and Alan Holmer, one of Yeutter's deputies, led the American team. I led the Canadian team – Simon, Gordon Ritchie, Gerry Shannon (our deputy minister of Trade), Don Campbell, and Konrad von Finckenstein, along with others. We worked our way through each chapter following a similar routine to the one adopted in Washington.

Never before was the adage "The devil is in the details" more apt, and the brittle emotions between the two negotiating teams – the aftereffects of eighteen months of deadlock – did not help. While there was a clear determination at the top to "get it done," some were still anxious to renegotiate. Simon was more than ready to start all over if necessary, and his admiration for the US team had not improved since early October. Gordon Ritchie did much of the heavy lifting, along with Alan Holmer on the US side. I dealt primarily with Peter McPherson. Though new to the negotiation in October, he had brought a much-needed element of balance and calm deliberation to issues on which positions were rigid and emotions raw. He played a key role in moving towards a mutually acceptable result. Particularly in the December negotiations, MacPerson injected an element of constructive civility into the process, working systematically to reduce and resolve sticking points. His demeanour prompted a similar response from me, and we worked together to "get it done" in the manner we both knew that our political leaders wanted. McPherson and I established a degree of professional and personal respect that has enriched our association.

The toughest nettles I recall during the "legal text" phase involved North American content provisions on autos, complicated provisions on sugar-containing food products, and the issue of simulcasted TV signals, notably the advertising restrictions applied by Canada to ensure local Canadian ads on programs being simulcast from US networks via cable to Canadian audiences. There were moments of high tension even within the Canadian delegation, as Gordon Ritchie's memoir, *Wrestling with the Elephant*, illustrates. Simon was never far below the boiling point, and his wrath was not directed exclusively at the Americans.

There were lighter moments, too. The Americans were customarily in direct contact with industry representatives for advice, and this was specifically the case on autos. They were in hourly contact with Detroit and were pressing for a higher percentage on content – 60 per cent rather than the 50 per cent that had been agreed. We resisted primarily because the issue had already been settled but also to keep open the possibility of increased Japanese investment in the Canadian auto industry. At one point I asked "Why aren't we consulting anyone?" "Because," replied Gerry Shannon, "the guys they are consulting [i.e., the Big Three auto manufacturers] in Detroit, are our guys!" The "rule-of-origin" language enshrining the percentage was drafted in haste and was less than precise. As a result, a few years later, we faced a major hassle with the Americans on the content of Honda Civics assembled in Canada. In NAFTA the Americans did get the higher content percentage and the ambiguous FTA treaty language was clarified.

One issue in particular sparked another row with Pat Carney. On both coasts, Canadian provinces had restrictions on the sale of unprocessed fish, for example, salmon. These had been in place for some time on the East Coast and were enshrined in provincial law, but had only recently been initiated in British Columbia. The Americans had challenged the West Coast restrictions at the GATT before the legislation was adopted by British Columbia. We had succeeded in preserving or grandfathering the East Coast restrictions in the negotiations but could not move the United States away from its existing GATT challenge to the British Columbia measures. Our choice, therefore, was to accept half (the East) or none. We settled for half, but this did not sit well with Carney. At Christmas, she actually sent me a small salmon "for all those you failed to protect."

Ultimately, the legal documents were finalized, and on 2 January 1988 the prime minister and the president officially signed the agreement. There was no elaborate ceremony. The prime minister signed in his House of Commons office, and the president separately at his ranch near Santa Barbara, California. They spoke briefly by phone. It was a high point for all concerned, but in Canada the real battle had only just begun.

My capsule assessment of the key players involved is as follows. On the Canadian team, the prime minister became a believer in time and saw the agreement as good for Canada's future and the key to his attempt to refurbish relations with the United States. It also carried a political dividend for his caucus, heavily represented by Quebec and the West, the two regions most favourable to free trade. As prime minister, he took a huge risk and gave full authority to his negotiating team, including me personally, never second-guessed any of us, and never pushed for "any" result. Mulroney was remarkably sanguine, on the surface at least, about the prospect of failure, but his confidence and conviction provided an essential rudder throughout the ups and downs of the negotiation.

Simon Reisman was a true believer, one who would tackle and berate anyone, including his allies, if he thought they were obstructing his effort. Wily and vexatious to some, he could be a charmer when he chose. He never lacked self-esteem and was knowledgeable and highly skilled at negotiation but difficult with people. Simon became a genuine celebrity in Canada – respected as a tough little guy who stood toe-to-toe with the Yanks (every Canadian's dream) – and gave FTA critics much more than the back of his hand. Gordon Ritchie was very solid throughout, highly organized, almost dictatorial in disciplining his troops. He had a delicate, sometimes fractious, relationship with Simon but an impressive grasp of all elements in the agreement and was particularly helpful in explaining the agreement in both official languages and in all forums.

Michael Wilson was cool, dependable, and unflappable. A genuine team player, he showed good judgment on the issues as well as a strong grasp of details. He was not as tough as some, perhaps, but credible in the truest sense. Pat Carney was the polar opposite. Mercurial and moody, she could be excellent, even charming, when she chose, but was impossible to predict or comprehend.

Allan Gotlieb has a brilliant policy mind. He was determined and irrepressible on tactics, more anxious than any for success, and the recipient of withering attacks by Reisman and others for his perennial optimism – a real contributor of ideas and judgment. Stanley Hartt was a veritable idea factory, a deal-maker at heart constantly prodding with initiatives and enthusiasm to keep matters moving, and a genuine asset. Don Campbell was, and is, always reliable. Dependable, discreet, and industrious, he filled the gaps and covered the angles. He proved an ideal colleague in the crunch.

As for the United States team, Jim Baker, secretary of the Treasury, was tough, single-minded, even crude on occasion, especially when badgering Mike Wilson on financial services. We nicknamed him "Texas Crude." Baker knew how to get things done when it was a priority for the president. A highly skilled negotiator, he was very much at ease representing the raw power of the United States, well connected, and determined to succeed for the president.

Clayton Yeutter (USTR) was ebullient and relentlessly friendly on all occasions, but his effectiveness was not certain. At one point, he declared that he knew about Canadian culture since he had gone to Niagara Falls for his honeymoon! Peter Murphy was almost absent during the final negotiating rounds, confirming just how distant he had been from the power centre during the lengthy preamble. Peter McPherson was a superb complement to Baker. He kept his cool throughout (much like Mike Wilson), patiently working for compromise and conciliation in the face of entrenched views. A good American.

Throughout the negotiations, the prime minister, along with his ministers and the senior TNO team, had arranged regular briefings with the provinces, whose leaders were sharply divided over this initiative. It was done in the spirit of consensus–building but without compromising the federal government's explicit constitutional authority for trade policy. There were elements of the agreement, nonetheless, that fell within provincial jurisdiction, such as beer. So the consultations required a delicate balancing act. The premiers from the West, except Howard Pawley of Manitoba, and the premiers for Atlantic Canada, except Joe Ghiz of Prince Edward Island, were in favour. Premier Robert Bourassa of Quebec was strongly supportive; Premier David Peterson of Ontario was lukewarm and occasionally negative. At one session, I asked him directly to explain what he had problems with, so that we might try to address them. "I can't," he replied, "but it just doesn't feel right in my tummy." Not much I can do about that, I thought.

Mr Mulroney was at his best in these sessions: patient in the extreme, careful never to isolate or embarrass one of the critics, while mustering the support of his allies selectively in order to sustain a generally positive atmosphere. At the federal level, the two opposition leaders – Turner and Broadbent – were firmly opposed. They both adopted a "nationalist" stance and decried the agreement as a "sellout" of all that was sacred in Canada. Within Liberal ranks, opinions were more mixed or nuanced, but publicly they supported their leader. The Rat Pack – Brian Tobin, Sheila Copps, Sergio Marchi, and Don Boudria – all newly elected Liberal MPs who had made a reputation for themselves as aggressive critics of the government during Question Period, were unleashed and used every possible pretext in the House of Commons to lambaste the government and the agreement. It was hard not to take some of it personally. In Parliament the attacks seemed more theatrical than genuine, but with a Liberal majority in the Senate, the theatrics had real blocking potential.

John Crosbie replaced Pat Carney as trade minister in order to pilot the legislation through Parliament and to convey a stronger, more confident, public voice in defending the agreement. It helped that he not only understood the agreement but also was fully committed to its implementation. His oratorical skills were second to none, whether in the House of Commons or on the stump. Crosbie was a happy warrior whose intelligence was complemented by his distinctive wit. He was ably assisted throughout by Simon Reisman on the public platform and by Gordon Ritchie in parliamentary committees. "Gordon," as the prime minister often stated "speaks in paragraphs."

Quite apart from the debates in Parliament and the national media focus on free trade, we also had an international audience to contend with. The G7 Summit in the summer of 1988 was hosted by Canada in Toronto, and the prime minister wanted an endorsement from his G7 colleagues for the free trade initiative. It almost didn't happen. While all the leaders were inclined to be supportive, some of their officials were less so. There was, for some, a concern that the regionalization of trade negotiations might undermine the success of the new multilateral round launched in Punta del Este, Uruguay, in September 1986 (Canada would host a "mid-term review" ministerial conference in December). The effect, and the American intent, was just the reverse. Japanese officials, sensing isolation, worried about the "exclusionary" or preferential nature of the Canada-US agreement. While it was not intended to be exclusionary (and would evolve into NAFTA), it was preferential by its very nature.

Whatever the reason, the phrase in an early draft communiqué endorsing the free trade initiative was deleted during the all-night sherpa session before the final summit day. I was informed about this unwelcome development during an early morning staff session at the summit in Toronto. Our sherpa, Sylvia Ostry, was not in attendance. I asked someone to bring her to the meeting, and when she arrived, I told her that it was imperative that this endorsement be put back in. After all, Mulroney was the host and we did not need a last-minute about-face among officials on a topic so vital to the prime minister and the president of the United States. Miraculously, the endorsement was reinserted in the communiqué. Several of the leaders reinforced the message in their subsequent press conferences.

During the same summit session, our former ambassador to France, Lucien Bouchard, won a by-election in Lac Saint-Jean. It was hoped that he would add stature and stability to the Quebec contingent in the Mulroney cabinet. He generated the former briefly but definitely not the latter.

By the end of the summer, the prime minister seemed more comfortably in charge of his government as well as his party. He had learned that you do not have to please all the people all the time and that you cannot lead through committees. Leadership involves choices and decisions – decisions with which some will agree and others inevitably, will not. Little crises stayed little. Even the cynics acknowledged that the FTA, Meech Lake, and the prospective tax reform involved courage as well as substance.

Meanwhile, the polls during the summer of 1988 brought unexpectedly good news for the government. For the first time since late 1986, the prospect of another majority win was a reality or in the realm of reality. (The biggest shift was in Quebec. Ontario and British Columbia were problematic.) The economy was humming. Jobs were expanding, and scandals abating. Attention was turning to the prospect of an election. Lowell Murray was put in charge of election strategy. Senator Norm Atkins was assigned campaign organization.

Opposition Leader John Turner seemed more desperate by the day. Liberal knives were turning inward. However, Turner called for "the people to decide" on free trade, and the wily Senator MacEachen, who lead the Liberal majority in the Senate, stonewalled deliberations on the agreement. As August loomed, the opponents of free trade found something other than the agreement itself on which to fasten. The combination of democracy ("Let the people decide") and nationalism posed a new threat and gave Turner and the Liberals new life. It also foreclosed some options on election timing. The government could not postpone matters to 1989 if free trade was to be implemented on schedule in January. The election call was probably one of the toughest decisions of Mulroney's political life. History has more lessons of how not to, rather than how to, make the right choice. And John A. Macdonald was the last Tory to win back-to-back victories.

The free trade debate in Parliament in September was illustrative of what might be expected in an election campaign. The prime minister was forthright and non-partisan. He sought to persuade through analysis and think-tank endorsements. The Opposition used every emotion possible, bombast and flags included, a precursor of what was to come. On 30 September the prime minister called on the governor-general and proposed an election for 21 November.

The 1988 election campaign started slowly and uneventfully. If anything, Turner seemed to stumble out of the gate. Earlier signs of internal dissent among the Liberals (featured in reporter Greg Weston's book

Reign of Error) had not dissipated, and there was not much from the Opposition in terms of issues or focus. The Progressive Conservative campaign got off to a relatively smooth start and the polls were in the government's favour.

Morning meetings with the Ottawa-based campaign strategy group, chaired by Senator Lowell Murray, focused inordinately, in my view, on the Atlantic region, where there were clear signs that a number of seats held by the PC's were in jeopardy. In frustration over this concentration, I asked that we delete the "A" word from future discussion.*

The televised debate in French went smoothly. Lucien Bouchard and I were involved in the preparations, but this was the prime minister's milieu. He was relaxed and confident. Turner was neither. The next evening, the debate in English started in similar form. Turner seemed to be suffering from severe back pain but took a hard line on free trade, claiming that the agreement was a "sellout" of Canadian interests in much the same way as he had during Question Period and parliamentary debate. The prime minister dismissed the allegations and referred to the impressive list of third-party endorsements – premiers, economists, and the like. To those attending the debate, Turner's attack had a familiar ring, but to thousands watching and hearing for the first time, it proved to be electric.

The first indication I received that a shift had occurred was when I arrived home and my son Alex asked why the prime minister seemed to distance himself from the agreement by referring constantly to others who endorsed it. The overnight polls delivered a harsher, more troubling verdict. The fat was in the fire. The media thrived on the prospect of a real race, not a cakewalk. The allegations and fears promulgated about free trade became more outrageous by the hour, and the Progressive Conservative campaign was caught flat-footed.

The days immediately following the 25 October debate were negative on all fronts. The polls tumbled quickly, as did the tenacity of the Progressive Conservative campaign's senior organizers. At one point, Senator Atkins and two cohorts trooped into my office to offer urgent advice. "We want you to advise the prime minister to announce that he will hold a referendum on free trade," they counselled. "Are you crazy?" I asked. After a few moments of silence and an attempt to discuss the "merits" of their proposal, I said I would convey their view to the prime minister but was confident it would be rejected. It was, without a blink,

---

* For more on this and the election as a whole, read Graham Fraser's account in *Playing for Keeps: The Making of the Prime Minister* (McClelland & Stewart, 1989).

and I do not recall receiving any additional advice for the prime minister from those campaign advisers.

The attacks on the agreement became more outlandish during the campaign. Allegedly, according to Maude Barlow and others, we had agreed to sell our fresh water to the United States. Try as we did to point out that no such provision existed and that no trade agreement obliged any country to sell something it did not wish to sell, the attacks persisted and the media thrived on the differences. (Simon had been involved previously as a consultant on a water-diversion scheme that never went anywhere, but this gave only the slightest credence to the canard.)

Most vexatious of all were the allegations that this agreement had sacrificed all of Canada's social programs – health care, pensions, unemployment insurance, and welfare. The rational argument that a country needs a strong economy in order to initiate and support social programs, let alone sovereignty, was not an effective antidote to the fear-mongering. A fourteen-page tract by Marjorie Bowker, a family court judge in Alberta, ignited fears about the loss of social programs and, once transformed into a book with the help of some shrewd nationalists and an enterprising publisher, sold like hotcakes.

We had heard all the allegations in Parliament, and we actually thought that, by the fall of 1988, the tone of the debate had mellowed somewhat. What we did not realize was just how lethal these attacks could be when featured in a nationally televised election debate. Emotions out-raced logic in a highly uneven contest. After all, it was extremely difficult to counter charges of "sellout" or "traitor" with David Ricardo's theory on comparative advantage or Adam Smith's views on the societal benefits of wealth generation through liberalized trade. While I understood the historic allergy to free trade in Canada, I could never really appreciate why the prospect of more-open trade aroused greater nationalist passion than the extent to which our national security or monetary policies were so closely linked to those of the United States. It was a bruising affair.

Some of the zanier attacks against the agreement had nothing to do with what had been negotiated. Mel Hurtig proclaimed that there had been a "secret agreement" in which Canada had pledged to match our dollar to the US dollar within five years. This was a reach even for a trade negotiator like Simon Reisman. We often wondered what the governor of the Bank of Canada thought about it. In years since, the claim has become even more ludicrous, but the media revelled in it at the time. The wilder the charge, the more it played.

The prime minister rose to the challenge. He took ownership of the agreement, brandishing it at each campaign event and defending it vigorously. At one point, to silence hecklers in Victoria, he offered to answer any questions they had about the agreement if they would first give him the courtesy of being able to finish his speech. They did, and at the conclusion of his speech, two of the hecklers sat at a table with the prime minister under the glare of television cameras from all the networks. The agreement was on the table. "All right," said Mr Mulroney. "Please ask me anything you want about the agreement."

"Well," said one tentatively, "it will ruin our social programs."

"Show me exactly how and where it says that," countered the prime minister. "Show me the section."

"Well, it may not say it, but that's what it will do" was the reply.

"That, sir, is the problem with your question. It is not based on anything in the agreement."

Another electrifying moment in the campaign was when Mike Wilson stood at a microphone in Ottawa and called John Turner "a liar." The Peace Tower clock almost stopped. This was Mike Wilson, after all, the quintessential Toronto example of all things proper.

Within a week, the polls started to come around, notably in the Toronto suburbs, at almost 1 per cent per day and on 21 November, Mulroney recorded his second straight majority victory. Not as large as 1984 but a clear majority and with representation from all regions. (There were notably fewer seats from the "A" region, on which so much time of the campaign committee of advisers had been spent.) It had been one of the rare elections in Canada actually fought on a major issue. The principal parties had reversed roles: the party of Macdonald championed free trade; the party of Laurier opposed it. It was also, I believe, the only time in Canadian history that the ruling party moved down and then up in the polls during a campaign and went on to win.

An election campaign that I had expected to be a quiet, pre-posting period of cleaning out my PMO desk became a nerve-racking, up-and-down battle where my knowledge of free trade became critically relevant. I received advice from many quarters. Neighbours and football coaches came to my door at home with inspirational messages and slogans urging, in essence, that we stress our ability to "compete and win" under free trade. Others were equally passionate on the other side. Both my mother and the prime minister's mother were, in their respective nursing homes, warned by Liberal and NDP candidates that they would be thrown out if free trade was approved. It is remarkable that the politics of fear did not prevail.

The business community rallied in unprecedented fashion to demonstrate support for the agreement and confidence in its ability to compete successfully. Tom d'Aquino, in his capacity as president of the Business Council on National Issues, not only galvanized substantial support for free trade from key elements of the community, but, along with former Alberta premier Peter Lougheed, was a key participant in public debates – a true road warrior in every sense and indispensable to the positive outcome in Canada.

In retrospect, if there are lessons about what might have been done differently on the FTA, the obvious one is that a greater attempt should have been made to gain broader support across the political parties. Donald Macdonald's royal commission had provided a catalyst, and Robert Bourassa's support in Quebec was crucial. But opposition to the FTA was about the only thing that John Turner and the Liberals had going for them in 1988, and they made the most of it. The fact that many of the fiercest opponents ultimately became advocates once in government – some, like Brian Tobin and Sergio Marchi, openly acknowledging they had been wrong – was some consolation, as well as the best form of approval.

More time could also have been spent establishing adjustment measures. The de Grandpré report commissioned for this purpose (chaired by Bell Canada Enterprises CEO Jean de Grandpré) offered a veneer of sorts, but more tangible measures might have been contemplated to address genuine concerns about industries that would be affected. The merit of such a strategy, is evident from what happened to the wine industries of British Columbia and the Niagara Peninsula. Although many had predicted that they would be "paved over" following free trade, they have flourished on the basis of initial government assistance, which enabled them to convert from production of protected "plonk" to competitive, high-quality vintages, including the now famous ice wines of Ontario. I suspect that more targeted support programs for other sectors facing adjustment might have had similarly positive results and could have attenuated some of the opposition. This is probably what Ontario should have demanded.

The free trade initiative was an act of political courage by a prime minister who refused to be hobbled by history and was emboldened by his confidence in Canada's future. He demonstrated tenacity of purpose in pursuing the initiative, despite prolonged indifference from the US administration and furiously partisan, often irrational attacks on the home front. He was particularly fond of the great historian Lord Macaulay, who observed in 1824: "Free trade, one of the greatest blessings which a government can confer on a people, is in almost every country unpopular."

Elections in Canada revolve almost exclusively around leaders, and as a result, this was very much a personal victory for Brian Mulroney. To paraphrase Vince Lombardi, winning in politics is not everything; it is the only thing. Mulroney had experienced a roller-coaster ride in the polls from the days of his first victory, including during the six-week election campaign in 1988, and he came out on top. It was a very sweet personal victory. Back-to-back majority wins are something few political leaders in Canada have savoured.

The day before he called the election, the prime minister had said he wanted to make good on his commitment prior to the election to confirm a posting for me. He asked where I wanted to go. I replied, "Japan," which I had mentioned as a possibility to him when I was appointed to the PMO. "Well, I want you to go to Washington," he responded. I had never really expected to go to Washington, but I certainly did not object and neither did my wife. And with the election over, I could now prepare in earnest to go to Washington, not Pyongyang.

TEN

Washington: The Best Job in the Foreign Service

I arrived in Washington in January 1989 with many of the absolutes most Canadians hold about the United States and about our bilateral relations. I learned very quickly that those absolutes – and that certainty – had enormous scope for enrichment. I had a lot to learn, including many things I was never taught by my mother. But the experience was as exhilarating as it was satisfying, and here are some of the reasons why.

I have often said that being ambassador in Washington is "the best job in the Canadian foreign service," and in my experience, 1989 to 1993, it was certainly that. Washington is the apex of global power in the broadest sense. The adrenalin for diplomacy is access; the lifeblood is relevance. Canada had both in Washington at a time of major convulsion in world events and significant achievement in bilateral relations. It was not all roses, however. There were persistent problems on trade and differences to be bridged on the environment. The unravelling of the Meech Lake Accord, together with the 1990–91 recession, generated bitterness on the home front that was difficult to ignore, particularly in Washington. But the sense of involvement was acute, and the measure of achievement was real.

The initial highlight was the opening of our new embassy in May 1989 on Pennsylvania Avenue, a powerful, even majestic symbol of our presence in Washington and of Canada's significance to the United States. The embassy quickly became a magnet of attention in Washington and a showcase for much of our best in the heart of American democracy. We used it representationally and functionally to bolster all of our diplomatic activity – to feature Canadian artists and artworks, to support medical research and charities, and to attract a network of contacts from all branches of the US government.

My four-year tour coincided with the single four-year term of

President George Bush the elder. If the embassy serves as a symbol of our relationship, the leaders of our respective governments set the tone for the relationship. As ambassador, I was fortunate in that the personal relationship between President Bush and Prime Minister Mulroney was open, direct, and very positive. The frequency, the scope, and the quality of their contact was unprecedented.

Their families were also close. As a result, the doors to the White House and the key departments were open to Canada and to me personally. Mr Mulroney was determined to be a player in major world events as they unfolded. He had cultivated George Bush systematically (and given him "an earful on free trade" on one occasion) when Bush was vice-president, and they got along well. He also knew Jim Baker, the new secretary of state, and many others in the administration and Congress on a first-name basis. Above all, the prime minister wanted Canada to be involved on global issues. He saw our proximity to the United States and his personal relationships as a means to register our views and influence key Washington players. He also knew several of the other major world leaders (Mitterrand, Kohl, and Thatcher), and his views on how to deal effectively with each were sought by the newly elected American president.

The role of Canada's ambassador in Washington involves differing elements of diplomacy, politics, and high-class saloon keeping. As the main spokesman for "all the Canadas," it can be, at times, a high-wire act, successful in so far as it is in perfect synch with the prevailing views of the government in Ottawa but usually only "news" or worthy of attention when there is some deviation from the standard line.

The power of the position depends heavily on the individual's relationship with the prime minister, as well as the tone or relevance of bilateral relations at the time. When the chemistry between the prime minister and the ambassador is positive, and known to be positive, the ambassador's position can be significant and powerful, especially when and where it counts in Ottawa. When the mood is similarly positive between Ottawa and Washington at the most senior level, access to the power circles in Washington is definitely easier to obtain. I experienced the latter combination during my stint as ambassador, but I had witnessed chillier times on both counts during earlier assignments in Ottawa.

The ambassador's job is, in essence, to represent publicly, privately, and systematically the key areas of interest and concern in the bilateral relationship, reinforce Canada's priorities, and explain carefully but firmly why any of this should matter to Americans. It is not an easy challenge, even in good times, because Canada is rarely a top-of-mind concern for Americans. I often used humour to leaven my message:

> Americans believe anything worth doing must be worth overdoing. Canadians believe anything worth doing must be worth a government grant!
> Americans are proud of what they are – Americans. Canadians are proud of what they are not – Americans.

The three-hundred member embassy was organized around three major functions: trade and economic affairs; general relations (including environment, transboundary issues, global political reporting, and congressional relations) and military, both the standard monitoring of defence relations and the day-to-day administration of almost one thousand members of the Canadian Armed Forces serving on secondment with their American counterparts. A public affairs section (media, academic and cultural relations) along with an administrative group, supported the embassy's operations as a whole. Washington also had a small immigration and consular unit, which primarily provided screening of third-country visa applicants as well as normal immigration advice and procedures. A similarly small unit served as liaison for the RCMP and CSIS with their American counterparts.

As virtually every department of the Canadian government has interests of some kind in the United States, or is influenced by what happens there, the embassy's primary role is to monitor developments thoroughly, alert Ottawa as to what is happening or about to happen, and register Canadian concerns, differences, or desires as appropriate. These activities constituted the day-to-day grunt work of many in the trade and general relations sections of the embassy. A fundamental rule of thumb for all in the embassy was that it was easier to prevent or amend potentially damaging action by Congress than it was to undo it after the fact.

As well, the political officers engaged in a regular dialogue with various branches of the State Department on major or topical global issues, reporting American views to Ottawa and to our major embassies (or those directly affected) and, where appropriate and available, transmitting Canadian views on a given topic. These duties also involved seeking US support for Canadian positions, for example, at the United Nations, or in other multilateral forums, and for Canadian nominees to international agencies. The key rule here was to try to separate what was important to Canadian interests from the seemingly urgent. Weekly meetings with senior embassy officers provided opportunities for regular updates and to determine on which issues or topics the ambassador's direct involvement would be useful. These meetings were used to set priorities more generally for embassy activity and to resolve differences between or among embassy sections.

Because Washington had the highest contingent of Canadian media representatives anywhere outside Canada, as well as a smaller group of US journalists representing newspapers along the border, media relations were of particular importance to the embassy and the ambassador personally. Although the ambassador's position had never been filled by a political appointee, the head of public affairs often has and usually by an individual with a strong media or public relations background, such as Richard O'Hagan and Pat Gossage during the Trudeau years and Bruce Phillips, Jock Osler, and L. Ian MacDonald during the Mulroney tenure. The latter two were in Washington with me. Their political judgment was a decided asset, as was their nose for news and their suggested response tactics. These are not tasks for which bureaucrats have much experience.

Networking: The Washington Game

Networking is the key to success in Washington, including for diplomats, and arriving at the beginning of a new administration was a great way to start. Many members of the Bush administration were in the same boat. Some, like Baker, were not really new. Others, like Carla Hills at USTR, Bill Reilly at the Environmental Protection Agency, and Dick Cheney at Defense were.* The first priority for me was to get to know each of them early so that, as events or issues evolved, contact had already been established. Congress required special attention not just because of the distinct separation of powers in the US system but also because both the House and the Senate were controlled by the Democrats. Each contained allies and opponents on many issues critical to Canada.

Within the administration, my most regular contacts involved the national security adviser, Brent Scowcroft, and various members of his team: Jim Baker, Bob Zoellick, Bob Kimmitt, and Larry Eagleburger at the State Department; Carla Hills and Jules Katz at USTR; Bill Reilly at the Environmental Protection Agency; and John Robson, deputy secretary of Treasury. Baker had a different style from George Shultz and, after

* Cheney was not really new. He had served as President Ford's chief of staff and, for many years, as a Congressman from Wyoming. But he was new to Canada.

the free trade negotiations, was less involved in the bilateral relations. This was no doubt in part because, in Baker's time at State, the prime minister had an active and continuing dialogue with President Bush on bilateral as well as international issues. Relations generally were much smoother. Hence there was less need for the quarterly reviews of the Reagan era. And Jim Baker clearly had other priorities during his tenure at State. He never seemed to understand why a regular review with his Canadian counterpart – who was only a phone call away – was needed.

Nonetheless, the quarterly process was maintained at least for a while. At one session in Bermuda in 1990, the two ministers spent most of the day ticking off a laundry list of bilateral topics (lumber, beer, auto parts) and then moved to global issues – the Middle East, East-West relations, and such. At one point, Joe Clark said he wanted to discuss "Northeast Asia security." Essentially, he was seeking to extend some of the principles from the Conference on Security and Cooperation in Europe to a region seen as containing one of the last remaining flashpoints from the Cold War – Korea. Baker was puzzled as to why this was a topic of priority for Canada. "What exactly are Canada's security interests in Northeast Asia?" he asked meaning, implicitly, "How many troops do you have in that region?"

This Canadian initiative did not generate much enthusiasm at the table, and when I accompanied Baker on the return trip to Washington, he asked what had prompted it. In return, I asked if he had ever thought what it must be like to be Canada's foreign minister. "Every day you look out your window and all you can see is a big elephant or the long shadow of an elephant obscuring almost all you can see." He had not thought about it in that manner. I asked whether he had a younger brother. He did not. I explained that younger brothers are often frustrated by references others constantly make to the older brother. Similarly, when Canada's foreign minister travels abroad, he or she is usually asked about US views or actions, seldom about Canada's. As a result of the elephant's shadow or the older brother phenomenon, I suggested, he should not be surprised when Canada made a special effort to find a place or a position in global affairs not already dominated by the United States. We crave distinction from our neighbour in many ways, and this is one. I don't pretend that this explanation registered with Jim Baker. He concentrated on other priorities, notably the Gulf War, and American interests were always central to his view on the world. Quarterly meetings with Canada at his level were not central and gradually disappeared, as did their original purpose.

Largely because of the chemistry between our two leaders, Brent Scowcroft, Bush's National Security adviser, was remarkably accessible on both global and bilateral issues. Although he was distinctly uncomfortable hearing my complaints about trade irritants, he always listened patiently and directed his economic assistants to do what they could to stimulate a more positive response from others in the administration. Scowcroft also ensured easy direct access for me with his NSC associates, including his deputy, Robert Gates, his Soviet adviser, Condoleezza Rice, and his Middle East expert, Richard Haass. (It may have helped that I usually brought along handmade Belgian chocolates from our chef for Scowcroft and his secretary – the "social" side of diplomacy.) Brent Scowcroft was an indispensable, calm adviser to the president during turbulent times. He received well-earned respect at all levels in Washington.

Larry Eagleburger, the deputy secretary of State, was not a fan of Belgian chocolate. Instead, he savoured hamburgers and onion rings, something rarely, if ever, presented at diplomatic functions. But that became our fare for regular one-on-one luncheons at the embassy prepared exquisitely by our Belgian chef, Christian Le Pièce. Eagleburger also carried an inhaler to counter his other habit, tobacco. He was genuinely curious about Canada's national unity debate. His views on global issues of the day were often as colourful as his culinary preference.

Baker's other two deputies, Bob Kimmitt on political affairs and Bob Zoellick on economic issues, were invaluable interlocutors. Primarily because of the positive chemistry at the top, each made a special effort to keep me informed on breaking issues and were promptly receptive to my representations on behalf of Canada. I served jointly with Zoellick as G7 sherpa for the London (1991) and Munich (1992) summits. We compared notes and positions candidly and systematically before, during, and after each event. Zoellick was clearly the dominant player among sherpas, as the US sherpa often is, but he used his intellect and his formidable grasp of the issues rather than the raw power or status of his country to drive consensus. He displayed impressive abilities for analysis, negotiation, and communications which later enabled him, almost single-handedly, to restore momentum to the Doha Round of global trade negotiations.* He was unfailingly receptive to explanations of our concerns about ongoing trade disputes, and even when our positions were different, the exchange was candid, civil, and informative.

The Gulf War brought me into direct dialogue on various occasions

---

* Zoellick's principal interlocutor on Doha was the EU's trade commissioner, Pascal Lamy, who also had been the EU sherpa in London and Munich.

with the chairman of the Joint Chiefs of Staff, Colin Powell, resuming a relationship that had started when he served as Reagan's national security adviser and I was the prime minister's chief of staff. More selectively, I met other members of the administration as issues or events demanded. I had occasional meetings with the chairman of the Federal Reserve, Alan Greenspan, the chairman of the Council of Economic Advisors, Michael Boskin, and Roger Porter in the White House, primarily to elicit their views on the condition of the US economy and on global economic trends. I would use these sessions, as well, to register particular points regarding Canada, ranging from our concern about US protectionism to their concern about national unity in Canada, a topic that perplexed Americans generally and contrasted with their image of Canada as "the peaceable kingdom."

Congressional contacts required a similar routine of regular calls on key figures, notably the chairman of the House Ways and Means Committee, Dan Rostenkowski of Illinois, the chairman of the Senate Finance Committee, Senator Lloyd Bentsen of Texas, and either supporters or opponents of key issues (acid rain, ANWR, softwood lumber, etc.) on our bilateral agenda. In all cases, my calls reinforced the pattern of contact and dialogue established at other levels by my colleagues in the Embassy.

My most valuable interlocutor from the House of Representatives was Republican Bill Frenzel of Minnesota, who was the ranking minority member of the Ways and Means Committee. Frenzel was unusually well informed and supportive and, at the same time, pragmatic on trade issues. He also had a remarkably open view of global affairs. After his retirement from Congress, an event in Minneapolis at which I was privileged to speak, Frenzel was recruited by President Bill Clinton to muster support for NAFTA among Republican House members. His efforts were singularly successful. Bill and his vivacious wife, Ruthy, were frequent guests at our social events in Washington and remain close friends.

Several Washington "pundits" were also valuable sources of information on the political dynamics of Washington. Charles Cook (author of the Cook report) had encyclopedic knowledge of all electoral contests, including topical data on polling results between and in the run-up to elections. Kevin Phillips offered a more detached policy critique of the domestic priorities of each major party. Although a Republican, he is the author of numerous books written, in large part, to counter much of what passes for conventional policy wisdom in Washington, and he offered, more often than not, quite critical opinions of Republican positions in Washington.

The Embassy

I was very fortunate to be in Washington for the official opening, in May 1989, of our new embassy on Pennsylvania Avenue, proof of the importance of the Canada-US relationship and a powerful draw for the social or representational side of diplomacy in Washington. The ambassador's office – "the half oval" – looks out directly at the Capitol building over a sixth-floor terrace, large enough to host one thousand people at an outdoor reception. It was also a superb vantage point for Fourth of July fireworks displays at the Washington Monument and we invited Washington families to attend an American-style picnic each year. It proved to be a very popular event.

The embassy has a theatre and an art gallery, as well as a spectacular dining facility. All were essential parts of Canada's showcase. Added to the facility was a first-class staff of more than three hundred, Canadians and Americans, covering virtually every topic imaginable on the bilateral side as well as global economic, political, and security affairs. It was hard not to smile each day that I walked into the embassy – and it was certainly a long way from Thunder Bay. Not surprisingly, visitors to Washington from Thunder Bay assumed that they were on a first-name basis with the ambassador, even though I had left my hometown in 1958, and regularly told the embassy receptionist that I would certainly be available to meet and greet. I did so proudly, as often as I could.

Len Legault was my first deputy head of mission in Washington. A top legal officer in External Affairs, Legault managed the trade and economic branch of the embassy and brought his formidable skills to bear in implementing the FTA, negotiating NAFTA, and riding herd on groups of US lawyers engaged for various trade disputes. He also had a flare for speech writing and humour. Both were highly desirable commodities. Paul Heinbecker was the head of the embassy's smaller, political section when I arrived. Like Legault, he had extensive knowledge and experience on the issues, bilateral and multilateral, as well as a particular gift for speech writing. The prime minister was the principal beneficiary of the latter as Heinbecker went on to serve almost exclusively in that capacity on his return to Ottawa in 1990.

Legault was replaced at the embassy by Marc Brault, who came from the Trade Commissioner Service and had served as head of post in his own right in Africa. He brought a strong francophone fact and face to the embassy in a period of constitutional turbulence on the home front. Mike Kergin replaced Heinbecker ably as head of the Political Section in 1990 after serving as our ambassador in Havana. He eventually returned to Washington as ambassador in 2000, following his assignment as Jean Chrétien's foreign policy adviser in the PCO. Mike is, much like Si Taylor, in the mould of the quintessential Canadian diplomat, one who has quickly mastered the blend of politics and diplomacy. Washington usually attracted the very best from all branches of the Canadian government, and I was fortunate to have first-class talent available at all levels. General George Kells was the head of our military section and, during the tense build up to the Gulf War, proved to be a solid, stabilizing source of information and advice

During most of my assignment, Jon Fried was the congressional liaison officer who, along with his own dedicated staff, skilfully steered me through an extensive but selective range of meetings with senators and congressmen, all with a specific purpose or message for Canada. He now (2004) has a major role in the PCO as a manager of Canada-US relations and as a top foreign policy adviser to the prime minister.

For my summit sherpa role, I was supported by two senior officials in Ottawa, David Dodge from Finance and Louise Fréchette from External. Both went on to much greater fame, but from 1990 to 1992, they gave Canada strong representation in their respective G7 forums. They were as delightful on a personal level as they were professional in their functions. Phillip Somerville, from the embassy's economic section, performed yeoman service for me on summitry, successfully straddling various elements of the Ottawa bureaucracy from the distance of Washington.*

Consulates General

The consulates general provide service, such as trade promotion, tourism, and immigration, as well as general information on Canada. They sponsor cultural events and support to universities specializing in Canadian studies. In effect, they "show the flag" or represent Canada to the United States and, as well, offer the Canadian government a series of windows on the US extending well beyond the Washington beltway. This can be particularly useful in countries as diverse as the United States, or Brazil, Australia, and India, less so in countries where the

---

* While my special relationship to the prime minister made the sherpa function work, it was unusual to have it performed by someone outside the capital.

capital is the financial and media centre as well as the capital, such as France. A by-product of consulate activity is the "care and feeding" of visiting citizens and the more traditional consular role of rendering advice and assistance to Canadians who find themselves, for a variety of reasons, in need of such support.

As we know only too well, "consular cases" can quickly become the front window for the government as a whole and for individual ministers, especially when things go wrong. The media thrives on instances when Canadian officials are unable to rectify the incarceration, or worse, of travelling Canadians who have run afoul of local laws or practices. Consular assistance is just that, not an automatic exit card or a basis for overturning actions of other governments, no matter how dubious they may seem through a Canadian lens.

I made a point of getting out of Washington as regularly as possible using our twelve consulates and consulates general in the United States as the focal points. Visits were organized essentially with a speech or two ("showing the flag") together with a mixture of business-related, media, academic, or cultural events as part of the schedule. The farther away from our border, the more general the message was likely to be. Occasionally, Joan would suggest that I "start with a map."

Public diplomacy by the ambassador is very much the order of the day not only in Washington but also in regions outside the capital. Speeches and messages for Cleveland or Seattle are crafted and honed in a vein similar to those prepared for calls on Congress. Environmental issues loomed large, especially along the border. Trade disputes were usually concentrated in specific regions (lobster in Maine, lumber in the Pacific Northwest). Global issues have broader appeal to more specialized audiences, such as the Councils on Foreign Relations in New York and Chicago or the World Affairs Council in Boston. Purely domestic topics – like the collapse of Meech Lake – were of interest to similar groups.

New York, Los Angeles, and Chicago were visited at least once per year. Others, like Atlanta, Boston, Seattle, and San Francisco, were visited less often but targeted to specific events, such as the prime minister's speech at Stanford University's 100th anniversary. A favourite for me was Cleveland, in large part because of the creative energy and enthusiasm of our one-man consul, Larry Lederman. His territory included Cincinnati and Louisville, Kentucky. He organized everything from fashion and food shows featuring Canadian products to a ceremonial pitch (for which I practised) at a Cleveland Indians – Blue Jays baseball game.

Our consular offices are rarely involved with policy issues, except to explain Canadian government positions, and as a result, they are managed more or less on their own without regular embassy oversight. Because of its size and the importance of the financial market, New York operates at a higher and broader level. Our consul general in New York at the time was Tony Eyton, who, with his wife June, provided stellar representation for Canada, drawing on his extensive experience as a senior trade commissioner and his impressive network of business contacts in Canada and New York.

Time and again, efforts are made to upgrade or enhance Canada's image in the United States through our diplomatic offices, especially our office in New York. Personalities can help, as Ken Taylor, in particular, demonstrated, and we should maintain the effort, but Canada will always struggle to gain attention at the core of American opinion. The priority, nonetheless, should always be on managing the basic elements of our relationship properly, to enable our image ultimately to flow from the substance and the relevance of our relations. It may well be that, as concerns about terrorism and border security increase, the role of our consular offices will have to change and their links to the embassy be coordinated more systematically.

Social Diplomacy

The social side of diplomacy – receptions, luncheons, and dinners – is intended for pure representation (showing the flag, supporting Canada's image on culture, trade and politics) and for networking. In Washington we had a full plate (!), including the famous "Power Breakfasts." But what distinguished Washington from other capitals was that virtually all representational activity was bilateral in nature, meaning that the focus was on American guests from all walks of Washington life. At other embassies around the world, social events would usually include other diplomats, who were often good sources of intelligence as well as amenable guests. This was rarely the case in Washington. It was definitely hard on the waistline, but the impact was positive, and the variety of guests was, for the most part, stimulating.

Joan really came into her own in Washington and was an incredible asset to me and to Canada. She managed the Residence staff, juggled the entertainment side both for the Residence and the embassy, and, most importantly, cultivated her own network of contacts, which in some ways was much better than mine.

Since the post-war days when Washington was inundated with hundreds of new diplomats, many of them from brand new countries, a network of international clubs had been developed by the administration to help ensure contact for senior embassy spouses with those of administration, congressional, and media personalities. Joan was recruited for International Neighbours Club No. 1, whose members included the wives of the chief justice and other justices of the Supreme Court, the White House chief of staff, the chairman of the Joint Chiefs of Staff, the secretary of Energy, several prominent senators, including Lloyd Bentsen of Texas and Mark Hatfield of Oregon, the director of NASA, Admiral Dick Truly, and CBS's chief Washington correspondent, Bob Schieffer. These couples became the nucleus for many of our social events at the Residence and, on more than one occasion, a channel for me on business. Joan eventually became president of the club.

One of her best friends in Washington and, like Joan, an avid folk art collector was Martha Bartlett. They met in a change room at Loehman's discount clothing store! Martha's husband, Charlie, was a semi-retired newspaper columnist for the *Washington Star* who wrote a weekly report, "The Coleman-Bartlett Report," and arranged quarterly briefings in Washington for business executives from various parts of the United States. Charlie was also known as the man who had introduced Jacqueline Bouvier to Jack Kennedy. Charlie and Martha were also close personal friends of George and Barbara Bush.

In April of 1990 we received an invitation to brunch at the Bartletts' and happily accepted. What we did not know was that the Bushes were the guests of honour and that the others in attendance (about twenty) were mainly family and very close friends of George and Barbara Bush. We were the only non-Americans. Nonetheless, Martha sat Joan right next to the president in one of three rooms used for a quite casual brunch. Talk about proximity! When Joan attempted diplomatically to move after the first course, the president objected. "You stay right here. I'd rather talk about the Skydome and baseball." He had recently visited Toronto. Eventually, they both wondered about coffee. Martha, being Martha, had not planned to serve coffee. The president dispatched a Secret Service agent to the kitchen. The agent returned with a cup of Sanka – one cup. The president quickly offered to share, saying, "It's OK. I just had my medical. So what would you like in your half?"

Later the same day, Joan and I were invited to a private dinner with Chief Justice Bill Rehnquist and his wife, Nan. Joan had become a very close friend of Nan's through their involvement with International

Neighbours Club No. 1. The dinner was a simple affair, just the four of us, and Joan helped Nan put it together in the kitchen. Because it was Palm Sunday, conversation turned on the number of times Jesus had entered the gates of Jerusalem. Efforts throughout dinner to research the answer were futile but engrossing. The day as a whole left an indelible impression of just how remarkable our assignment to Washington was becoming.

The next year we were invited again to a similar brunch by the Bartletts. Martha knew that we had been having problems on trade with the United States – lumber and beer, as I recall. This time she decided to seat me next to the president, and with some advance notice. "You sit right there, Derek, and you give him hell for the way we are treating you," she urged. The president was a bit startled, but he listened patiently as I did my diplomatic best to deliver on Martha's candid invitation.

One highlight of our years in Washington was a dinner attended by the president and Mrs Bush during a visit by the prime minister and Mrs Mulroney. I took particular pleasure in escorting the president to "the half oval" counterpart to his "full oval." He was suitably impressed. The prime minister was at his best that evening, mentioning by first name almost every American guest at the dinner with after-dinner remarks that prompted guests at my table to speculate about "what a terrific candidate he would be for president if he lived in the USA." More ominously, that same evening, the chief justice and two other Supreme Court justices left the dinner to preside over a last-minute appeal against a death sentence. They returned, after rejecting the appeal.

The social side of diplomacy had other moments of drama. During a visit to Washington of the Cirque du Soleil, we combined a reception at the embassy in support of a DC charity with tickets to the performance for about one hundred VIP guests; families included. At the top of our list was Colin Powell, who arrived in civilian clothes and sat proudly with his son and grandson a few rows ahead of us and near the very front of the theatre. He was accompanied by several heavy-set bodyguards, also in civilian clothes.

Much to our combined surprise, one of the star performers, a pantomime clown from rural Quebec, targeted General Powell for one of his routines involving audience participation. He climbed onto Powell's lap and deftly cut his tie with a pair of scissors. The bodyguards flinched but made no overt move. Powell, meanwhile, turned and glared ominously at me, certain that this had been a set-up. Try as I might to assure him that I had nothing to do with the episode, Powell remained dubious. Nonetheless, he and his family enjoyed the show. When it was over and I explained to the clown just who and what his target had been – and what might have happened to him – he was, well, true to form, speechless.

Joan sat on the boards of the Columbia Lighthouse for the Blind and the Arena Stage Theatre and was active in numerous other charitable causes. Each activity was satisfying in itself, and each also broadened our network of people in Washington. More than anything else, Washington is a city of prominent people, some of whom had been involved as far back as the Truman administration. I could have had lunch and dinner with someone different each day of our four years in Washington and would never have run out of interesting people. It was the best possible stimulant for my job.

We mixed socially with prominent Democrats as well as Republicans. One evening in 1991, we were at a small dinner hosted by a Democratic couple where the guests, apart from Joan and me, were all Democrats. The conversation turned to the choice of a candidate to run against President Bush in 1992. Our host had been linked to the young governor of Arkansas, Bill Clinton, who at that time was not well known in Washington. When I asked what sort of candidate he would be, I received an unexpected response. "Well," said our host, "he is extremely bright, a terrific communicator and an excellent politician. There's only one problem," he added. "He's carrying too much fuckage!" The conversation stopped abruptly at that point, but the message came back vividly to me years later.

Jack Kent Cooke was one of Washington's more intriguing characters. A former Canadian who became a US citizen by act of Congress, he was best known as the owner of the Washington Redskins. Allegedly, he had left Canada in a huff during the 1950s when his bid for what became the CTV private television network was rejected by the Board of Broadcast Governors. Cooke moved to California, where he built a highly lucrative cable TV network and the Los Angeles Forum, home of the Lakers (basketball) and the Los Angeles Kings (hockey). He moved to Virginia in the 1980s and gradually gained ownership of Washington's football team, the Redskins.

Cooke was fascinated to learn from Joan that she had been born in Rainy River and had also lived in Dryden before moving to Port Arthur. These venues had been part of his sales region in the 1930s when he covered most of northwestern Ontario for Colgate-Palmolive. Meeting Joan obviously brought back memories, and as a result, we became regular invitees to his special box at RFK stadium, where he presided over sixty-five hand-picked guests ranging from the vice-president and various cabinet secretaries to media luminaries like George Will, Larry King, and Leslie Stahl. It was called "the best ticket in town." Also in regular attendance were former politicians such as Senators Eugene MacCarthy and George McGovern. Quite a network and a very friendly ambience, especially as the Redskins usually won in those years.

When the team went to the Super Bowl in Minneapolis in January 1991 – and won – Cooke brought the entourage from his special box with him, as well as the players' families, in a rented Boeing 747. He was a complicated, some would say irascible, fellow but certainly gave us important access to Washington personalities and many good times. Cooke seemed proud of his Canadian roots. He had played in Percy Faith's band and was very fond of all literature. We introduced him to the works of Wallace Stegner, including *Wolf Willow*, which describes life along the Prairie border at the turn of the twentieth century, and Cooke enjoyed it as much as we did.

We reciprocated Cooke's hospitality with some of our own, but it was not without challenges. He could be a very "physical" table companion, reinforcing his strong opinions with wrist clutches and elbows – so much so that I had to be very selective in choosing female guests to sit beside him. At one dinner Andrea Mitchell, an NBC correspondent who subsequently married Alan Greenspan, complained that she had drawn the honour "yet again." "I've still got bruises from the last one," she lamented. I apologized but added, "You are the toughest one of the group, Andrea." Cooke remained true to form.

We also enjoyed a close friendship with Abe Pollin, the owner of the Washington Capitals and the basketball Bullets, and his wife Irene. Abe explained to me that he had obtained the NHL franchise for Washington before he had seen his first hockey game. He needed it to help fill the sports complex he owned in Landover, Maryland (a Washington suburb). The embassy maintained close contact with the hockey team – "our team" – and when Ottawa joined the NHL in 1991–92, we initiated a "Capital City" event involving the two teams. Hockey also served as an entrée for an albeit smaller (than football) network of Washington movers and shakers, but some significant ones like Bob Kimmitt, who was undersecretary of state for Political Affairs, and Reagan's former chief of staff, Ken Duberstein. We were pleased to celebrate the Canadian game in Washington any way we could.

In a more serious vein, I also tried to meet regularly with several Washington media personalities – David Broder, Jim Hoagland, and

Haynes Johnson of the *Washington Post*, Rowlie Evans of Evans and Novak, Chris Matthews, then of the *San Francisco Chronicle*, and Strobe Talbot of *Time* magazine – in one-on-one sessions over breakfast or lunch to glean their views on domestic and international affairs. I also established contacts with key Democrats who had served previous administrations and were always potentially eligible for future duty. Among these were Madeleine Albright, Ron Brown, and Stu Eizenstadt, all of whom assumed senior roles in the Clinton administration.

The give and take of these and other exchanges with Washington personalities was the most invigorating and satisfying part of my ambassadorial duties. What I appreciated most was the level and tone of the dialogue. My interlocutors were knowledgeable and had definite views. Occasionally, they also had a sincere curiosity about events in Canada. But they were professional to the core. The journalists, for instance, were obviously interested in a potential story but were not seeking to play a "gotcha!" game in order to get one. In that sense, they were a sharp contrast to some of their Canadian counterparts.

One of the most endearing journalists was Allan Emory, Washington correspondent for the *Daily News* of Watertown, New York . Emory was an elegant, old-school journalist with neither bile nor bite. He hosted regular breakfast briefings for me with the "border journalists," all journalists in Washington representing US newspapers along our border. More importantly, he was my host for the annual "Gridiron dinner," one of Washington's most prestigious annual events, in which the media come together in white tie with the key players in Washington for an evening of speeches and skits roasting ("The Gridiron singes but never burns") luminaries from both parties. Keynote speakers for each party, usually including the president, try to outdo one another with barbs and wit. The skits are semi-professional in manner, and many Washington media personalities, including my host, played major parts on or behind the stage. We were usually joined by Emory's publisher from Watertown and a senior New York congressional figure, such as Senator Moynihan.

We had a steady influx of distinguished Canadian visitors to Washington: cabinet ministers, provincial leaders, opposition leaders, business executives, and cultural lions. Among my favourites in the last group were Robertson Davies, who gave a delightful reading to several hundred fans followed by a buffet reception at the Embassy, Norman Jewison, who brought Gregory Peck for the premiere in our embassy theatre of his film *Other Peoples Money*, and Mordecai Richler, who came primarily to complain about being slighted by the embassy but who seemed to accept my explanation that no slight had been intended.* Richler had been one of the few English writers in Canada to support free trade and that did register with me.

I had an even more awkward moment receiving Jacques Parizeau, who was then leader of the Opposition in Quebec's National Assembly. He was entirely civil throughout our discussion, but when I took him to the Rotunda of the Provinces at the front of the embassy, a monument held up by ten pillars representing each of the provinces, and asked cheekily whether he intended to remove one "like Samson," our rapport deteriorated. When Parizeau became premier, I was criticized by his New York representative at public functions where I was the guest speaker in Washington. So I guess it may have been a payback of sorts.

I would acknowledge readily that, on the question of national unity, I had trouble keeping my emotions in check and said more to American and Canadian audiences on this topic than some would have regarded as appropriately diplomatic. It was not easy, at times, representing a country that seemed intent on unravelling. I genuinely believed that the country was stronger than the forces attempting to pull it apart, but in explaining our dilemma to Americans, I chose offence as the best defence. I was definitely uncomfortable with what I saw as timid attempts to placate, rather than confront, separatist threats. The national unity issue proved to be a worrisome, even debilitating, part of our representative life in the United States. It perplexed more than troubled Americans, who, for the most part, neither understood nor wanted to understand what we seemed to be doing to ourselves.

Retail Politics: Public Diplomacy

Retail politics is what prevails in Washington, and it has become an essential element of diplomacy. In the past, diplomats concentrated exclusively on the State Department for all their representations, including on bilateral trade issues. But that approach would simply not cut it today. Regular calls on Congress and explicit efforts to rally support or refute misleading impressions were as significant, if not more so, than calls on the administration. A full-court press was often what was required, carefully planned and selectively implemented. It was general-

---

* Richler had expected the embassy to host a reception for him. He concluded wrongly, that we had not done so because of an article ("Oh Canada! Oh Quebec") he had written for the *New York Times*.

ly easier to allay or modify measures in the making than after the fact. Therefore our embassy had to be vigilant and constantly on the alert to head off actions that might damage Canadian interests. It is no exaggeration to say that these activities were closer to hand-to-hand combat or blocking and tackling in football than to textbook descriptions of diplomacy. But in Washington that was how the game was played. Above all else, we were determined to be alert and aware at all times, in order to defend and advance tangible Canadian interests across the full spectrum of our bilateral relationship, especially on trade and environmental issues, where differences were significant.

In the Washington diplomatic pecking order, the Israeli ambassador occupied the most powerful position reflecting the scope and intensity of his country's economic and security relations with the United States, as well as the importance of Israel to US domestic politics. Ambassadors from the Soviet Union (before it imploded), Britain, Germany, and Japan were next in line, followed closely by China, Canada, and possibly France. Italy, Greece, and Ireland ranked next, more because of the size of their respective communities in the United States than because of the scale of their contribution. Especially with NAFTA under negotiation and with the growing Hispanic population in the United States, Mexico's ambassador also figured prominently. Similarly, during the Gulf War, the Kuwaiti and Saudi Arabian ambassadors rapidly rose to the top. (The latter, Prince Bandar, became a prominent and sometimes controversial fixture on the diplomatic scene for many years thereafter, serving continuously from Bush to Clinton and to Bush again.) These were, in my view, the most active and, for differing reasons, the most relevant ambassadors in the Washington game during my assignment.

With Joan and "Maz,"
January 1989

Presenting credentials at the White House, January 1989: Alex Burney, Jeff Burney, Joan Burney, George Bush senior, Barbara Bush, Derek H. Burney, Ian Burney, and Derek J. Burney ("Sonny Bono")

Full-court press at 24 Sussex, the first post-election visit by President Bush, February 1989: *left to right*, Chief of Staff John Sununu, Ambassador Tom Niles, President Bush, Secretary of State Jim Baker, National Security Advisor Brent Scowcroft; on right, *left to right*, Secretary of State for External Affairs Joe Clark, Prime Minister Mulroney, Ambassador Derek Burney, Chief of Staff Stanley Hartt, Assistant Deputy Minister External Affairs Don Campbell

The Iron Lady smiles! Margaret Thatcher and Derek H. Burney at the Houston Summit,
July 1990, with Mrs Mulroney in foreground

Relaxing at Kennebunkport, August 1990, before the Gulf War: Derek H. Burney and President George Bush

En famille in Washington, December 1990: Ian, Derek J., Derek H., Joan, Alex, and Jeff Burney

Diplomatic telethon at Kennebunkport following the attempted coup against
Mikhail Gorbachev, August 1991

Engine trouble at Kennebunkport, August 1991: note who is most concerned!
(A Secret Service agent is holding the president.) Also note the press in an
adjacent boat.

The president comes to dinner
at the Canadian Embassy,
Washington, May 1992 (a "first")

After-dinner entertainment at the embassy: *from left*, Mr and Mrs Jack Kent Cooke,
Speaker of the House Tom Foley, Chief Justice Bill Renquist, Joan Burney, Prime
Minister Mulroney, Mrs Bush, President Bush, Mila Mulroney, Derek H. Burney,
Susan and Jim Baker

To my friend Derek Burney,
With fond memories of all we've been
through together. You've been great.

Farewell call on Colin Powell in Washington, January 1993

Meeting with President Kim Dae-jung on my return to Seoul as chairman and
CEO of Bell Canada International, April 1998

ELEVEN

Washington: The Issues

Trade Disputes

We had differences – significant differences – with US authorities during my time in Washington, and trade disputes were the most aggravating as well as the most time-consuming. Differences over softwood lumber were never-ending. Less visible but similarly frustrating were battles over pork, meat inspection, steel, potatoes, beer, the size of lobsters, and the North American content requirements affecting Honda vehicles assembled in Canada. Some, like pork, were resolved satisfactorily through the dispute settlement provisions of the FTA. Others, like Honda, were eventually clarified, if not resolved, by NAFTA. (Part of the problem with the Honda dispute had been clumsy drafting in the FTA, wording that was ambiguous enough to give credence to differing interpretations.) Problems over beer stemmed from age-old provincial restrictions on beer not bottled in the province of sale, restrictions that came under attack as Canadian brewers gained more and more US market share.

Our prime concern was protectionist measures or "trade remedy" actions targeted directly at Canada. Occasionally, however, as on steel, we were sideswiped by measures intended more for others. Either way it hurt, and it was small comfort for those directly affected to be told that their exports represented only a small portion of total trade, the vast bulk of which moves unimpeded both ways across our border.

The most nefarious trade remedy in the US arsenal – the "nuclear bomb" of what we called their "weapons of mass disruption" – is section 301 of the 1974 Trade Act. This allows the president to impose "temporary" trade barriers when he concludes that an increase in imports is hurting US industry. The most recent example of its use was the restrictions imposed in 2002 against steel imports. When the WTO declared these measures to be illegal, the United States relented.

The US Congress is extremely sensitive to any loss of autonomy in negotiating trade remedy measures – countervail, anti-dumping duties, and 301 restrictions. It is very much a "sovereignty" issue. American negotiators must be able to convince Congress that any loss of autonomy is worth enduring for the sake of the greater good of expanding worldwide trade. The difficulty experienced recently by the US administration in gaining fast-track negotiating authority for global trade negotiations underscored these sensitivities, as well as the increasingly protectionist mindsets of many in Congress.

It is never easy to pin down the locus of power in Washington. The separation of powers can, in some circumstances, become a convenient excuse. The administration can blame Congress. Congress, meanwhile, can always blame the administration. It can be frustrating when you are looking for solutions, particularly in a system where the scope for restrictions is much broader than the avenues for redress. Individual congressmen can wield unusual authority, especially when initiating action against those who do not vote for them, and even those who may object in principle are not anxious to support non-Americans. The objective for us, nonetheless, was to try to find some constituents in the United States who would suffer specifically from US restrictions on Canadian products and build a coalition for redress. On softwood lumber, this meant rallying the US National Association of Home Builders. On wheat, we turned to processed food (i.e., pasta) manufacturers. On some, such as lobsters and potatoes, we had no ready support base, and for those, our only recourse was to confront the attacks overtly.

Retaliation was always tempting, but when you are one-tenth the size, it can be as short-sighted as it is short-lived and ineffective. Linkage is another temptation. "You hit our softwood. We will curtail energy exports" was (and is) a popular political posture for some on the home front, but one that was never seriously contemplated. Our objective was to curtail or at least contain damage, not to allow matters to evolve into an all-out trade war, one we knew we could never sustain, let alone win.

We clung fiercely to the rule of law and to the dispute settlement measures of the Free Trade Agreement. More often than not, the latter prevailed in Canada's favour. This is not to say that Canadians were without sin when it came to trade restrictions. Occasionally, the Americans had legitimate complaints. On these, our first inclination was not to amend our practice but rather to buy time and seek an honest compromise, provided there was the will in Canada to reach a settlement.

No one should assume that positive chemistry between the prime minister and the president and the conclusion of the Free Trade Agreement made the challenge of managing day-to-day trade relations easy. There are enormous linkages between our two countries, spanning every facet of government activity, and these inevitably generate differences and disputes. The embassy's fundamental task was to contain the differences whenever possible and to seek persistently to resolve issues, large and small. Invoking the close relationship at the very top helped open doors and get us a hearing. It could not guarantee a result.

On more than one occasion, I raised our trade disputes with the national security adviser, General Brent Scowcroft, stressing to him, selectively but deliberately, the importance of a timely resolution for our prime minister and his government. Scowcroft tried to deliver, even though he was clearly uncomfortable dealing with trade issues. For him, throw weights, missile defence, and East-West strategic issues were much more familiar territory. This was not a channel that could be used for all grievances; otherwise the effect would be diluted. The fact that I was able to see Scowcroft regularly reflected the importance the White House attached to relations with our prime minister. The trade issues also involved frequent sessions with USTR, Treasury, and others in the administration, as well as with key members of Congress and their assistants. The 1991–92 recession increased the significance and the political heat on trade issues on both sides of the border, and the tendency in Canada to "blame every sparrow that falls" on the FTA did not make matters any easier.

The range of issues can be diverse: representations to the Treasury department about confusing and inconsistent interpretations by US Customs of North American content rules for automobiles (e.g., Honda), debates with US senators over the relative merits of Canadian versus US restrictions on the size of lobsters or the "threat" posed by traces of blight in PEI potatoes. You need to be agile and assertive but, of course, diplomatic in such discussions. You need, as well, to be able to absorb briefs quickly and turn them effectively and efficiently into messages for various kinds of recipients. It takes careful staff work in advance. Getting the facts right makes the argument more compelling, if not more convincing. I was fortunate to have support on many fronts from my staff in Washington. They earned the respect of their counterparts in Congress and the administration. We did not win on every dispute or difference, but we rarely missed getting an opportunity to register the Canadian point of view.

The issues were usually of greater significance to Canadian than to American interests. That did not make it easier, however, because any

American interest or stake, no matter how small or local, always counted for more with Congress or the administration than those from anywhere else. Where we could identify a real parallel interest (a US constituency) in the United States, it made our task more one of reinforcement rather than of "special pleading." The former were clearly preferable and easier.

No trade issue between Canada and the United States has been as persistently quarrelsome, costly, or counterproductive as the long-running
dispute over softwood lumber. Disputes over lumber actually predate
Confederation, but during the 1980s and 1990s, three separate battles
dominated the agenda and almost overwhelmed the free trade initiative.
Setting aside the volumes of claims and counterclaims, the issue is primarily about market share. Canada exports about $7 to $9 billion of
softwood lumber to the United States, which represents 30–35 per cent
of the total US market. Lumber competitors in the United States resent
this share and have done everything possible to contain or reduce it. Tens
of millions of dollars have been spent by the Canadian industry, provincial governments, and the federal government to defend us against US
allegations that our lumber is being either subsidized or "dumped" onto
the US market, thereby causing "injury" to the US industry. If confirmed
by US trade tribunals, these charges would trigger a countervailing or
anti-dumping duty, the amount of the duty being determined by the
extent of the "injury."

At the root of the hassle are Canadian stumpage practices, the manner in which provincial governments charge lumber companies for the
right to cut wood on Crown (government) lands. Most of Canada's lumber comes from Crown lands, for which lumber firms are assessed a
stumpage fee. Most US lumber comes from private land, and cutting
rights are auctioned annually to logging companies at a "market price."
While the stumpage fee system varies somewhat from province to
province in Canada, and the revenues are used to build roads and support silviculture, the American industry contends essentially that it is
not "market-based" and, as a result, constitutes a subsidy. The sagging
Canadian dollar in the early 1990s only intensified matters. Canada
argued that the stumpage system is both conservation and market-based
and has provided a better and more consistent yield than the US system,
where the price and the harvest fluctuate according to demand.

In Lumber 1 (1982–83), Canada's position prevailed before the US
Department of Commerce, which ruled that the subsidies (stumpage-
based cutting rights) available to the lumber industry were not specific,

that is, were generally available to a number of industries. The US industry returned to the charge in 1985–86, banking on a change in the senior administrator at Commerce and the impact of a number of court rulings about the interpretation of the "specificity" rule, particularly one involving "carbon black" from Mexico. That case turned on very similar considerations to the lumber issue. This time (Lumber II), confronted with the dead certainty of a ruling favouring the US industry, Canada agreed to impose a 15 per cent export tax on its lumber going to the United States, on the theory that, if a tax was to be applied, it was preferable to have it collected by Canada.

It needs to be noted that the federal government's role in all of these disputes was to try, in the first instance, to gain a consensus among the provinces and to be guided significantly by the wishes of key provinces. Lumber is of crucial importance to British Columbia but of significance to others as well, notably Quebec, Ontario, and Alberta. It is significant to New Brunswick and the other Maritime provinces too, but because much of their lumber comes from private land, they have been more or less exempt from US penalties.

British Columbia usually had a mind of its own on lumber and, on at least one occasion, tried to negotiate a side deal with the Americans, an initiative that did little to strengthen Canada's overall negotiating position. Hence the nefarious export tax, or "managed trade" solution, in 1986 represented a "least worst" solution but was favoured, in particular, by the industry in British Columbia and, of course, our minister of Trade, Pat Carney, who came from that province.

Lumber II was a five-year agreement, and during the fifth year (1991), pressures mounted on both sides of the border to determine "what next." Because of the number of lawyers involved representing all involved, we had to hold our meetings in the embassy's theatre!* In the spirit of free trade, we were determined to let the five-year agreement expire.† There was strong support for this approach from the provinces at least up until the last moment, and though we hinted strongly to USTR officials that this would be our position, they did not really believe we would simply terminate the agreement.

* That was on the Canadian side alone. US interests were equally well represented, led by Alan Wolff, the formidable lead trade lawyer for Dewey Ballantyne, whose experience included a period as Bob Strauss's deputy at USTR.
† Because the softwood lumber agreement of 1986 was preserved under the Free Trade Agreement, some have contended, incorrectly, that softwood was exempted from the agreement. That is simply not true. Once the five-year agreement expired, lumber fell under the fundamental provisions of the FTA and eventually NAFTA.

In September 1991, that is exactly what we did. Don Mazankowski, as acting prime minister, announced our decision, and we put on our hard hats to await the firestorm in Washington. USTR officials were upset and bitter, claiming they had been blindsided. The US Coalition for Fair Trade in Lumber – an oxymoron if ever there were one – launched a furious broadside. We had prepared factual summaries for key senators, congressmen, and the media in an effort to hold the line. We knew that the worst that could happen would be another countervail challenge by the US coalition. That is exactly what happened, and when Canada appealed the initial US ruling, the binational dispute settlement panel ruled in our favour, albeit on national grounds: three Canadians versus two Americans. An appeal to the "dead judges" was also upheld, again on national grounds: two Canadians in favour, one US judge against. This was a sweet victory on softwood lumber and a clear vindication of the FTA's special trade remedy dispute settlement mechanism (chapter 19).

It was, nonetheless, too good to last. A few years later, in 1996, the US coalition mounted yet another assault through US trade tribunals, and once again the Canadian government yielded to the wishes of the industry and key provinces by concluding a new five-year "managed trade" solution (Lumber III), this time agreeing to limit Canadian exports to a predetermined percentage annually; any shipments in excess were subject to duty.

In a sombre repeat of history, Canada let this agreement expire on its due date in the summer of 2001, and the US coalition launched yet another trade remedy action (Lumber IV and obtained both a countervail and an anti-dumping duty against Canadian lumber, the penalties of which remain in effect but are being challenged through the WTO and NAFTA. Once again, however, some in the industry, notably from British Columbia, are urging a "managed trade" solution.

Despite the never-ending hassle over softwood lumber, Canada has been reasonably successful in obtaining redress through the dispute settlement panels. In nine of fourteen cases up to 2003, Canadian exporters gained a reduction or elimination of duties as the result of a successful challenge; one involving pork exports was upheld unanimously by an extraordinary appeal tribunal. Even lumber shows spasmodic success, but the political pressure and stonewalling in the Unites States is unrelenting and retards enthusiasm for new economic agreements with the Americans.

Canada and the United States also battle from time to time over the lobster fishery on our respective east coasts. Essentially, the United States argues that Canada catches lobsters too small in size, thereby creating unfair competition. Canada contends that size limitations are more valid in terms of preserving the lobster stock than the more arbitrary volume limitations set by the United States. In reality, it is a contest about market share and market price. Each side would prefer more of both for itself. At dinner on one occasion, in response to my complaints about this dispute, John Sununu, President Bush's chief of staff, presented me with a giant US lobster. In fact, it was the shell of a giant lobster, which enabled me to quip that it had as much substance as the US position in the dispute.

In an even lighter vein, one potential trade problem did get resolved in a timely, if unusual, manner. A Manitoba printer of lottery tickets had won a significant order in Mexico and planned to ship the tickets by truck through the United States. Unfortunately, this shipment would have run counter to a nineteenth-century piece of US legislation prohibiting the shipment of "gambling devices" through the United States. The company had appealed to the embassy for help, and I was advised that we might try to enlist the support of a friendly senator to request a waiver of the restriction from the Senate. This approach, in turn, would work if there was no dissent.

A few weeks earlier, Joan and I had accompanied Senator Bob Dole and his wife on a semi-official visit to Ottawa. That acquaintance was sufficient for me to call the senator (the minority leader at the time) to see whether he might help get the necessary waiver. After all, the sale was not jeopardizing any US economic interest. Senator Dole was more than happy to oblige and asked me to fax him the particulars. I did so and, shortly after, watched on TV as Senator Dole read the request on the Senate floor. He then handed it to a Senate page. To my surprise, a Democrat in the Senate at the time casually scanned the resolution and rose on a point of order declaring that the top of the page said clearly "Fax Canadian Embassy." "Exactly who is the honourable gentleman from Kansas representing in making this request?" he asked. A somewhat sheepish Senator Dole acknowledged quickly that he was indeed making the request on behalf of "our friends and neighbours to the north." And the waiver went through unopposed. I often thought, however, that if something similar had happened in the Canadian Parliament – a government minister acting on the basis of a fax from the US embassy – there would have been cries of interference galore and some genuine fireworks. I have often used this incident to illustrate the intrinsic value of goodwill in diplomacy (and from senatorial visits).

Canadians have no monopoly on sanctimonious or self-righteous positions. The US Senate can be a sanctuary for both. The separation of powers in the US system provides a lot of latitude for such indulgence. Senators, after all, do not represent the government, and the administration is not responsible for actions by individual senators or congressmen, even those from their own party. Sometimes Canadians fail to appreciate these distinctions and regard senatorial or congressional posturing as "the American position." No one played into this more actively and successfully than Senator Max Baucus of Montana, our *bête noire* on softwood lumber and on many agricultural disputes. Baucus would issue a press release denouncing Canada for our actions on lumber or whatever, and it would play strongly in Canada, usually inflated by a television or radio interview on the CBC or another Canadian network. This exposure in turn would play well for Baucus in Montana, which was, of course, what it was really all about. I once told Senator Baucus that he was the envy of every Canadian cabinet minister. Puzzled, he asked, "Why?" "Because," I responded, "you get more coverage on Canadian television than any of them."

What made matters worse was that attempts by the embassy to rebut with facts some of the most outlandish senatorial changes against Canada received little notice from our media. As the adage goes, "Don't confuse me with facts. I'm onto a good story."

The North American Free Trade Agreement

Canada came very close to not participating in NAFTA. The Mexicans wanted very much to learn from our FTA negotiating experience but, at least initially, were not sure about having us at their table. Mexico's minister of commerce, Jaime Serra Puche, did make some preliminary soundings with Canadian ministers, as did some of his officials, but they concluded that Canada was not keen to participate and might constitute a drag on the negotiations. The Americans, possibly because of the FTA experience, did not really want us either. Each had a bilateral agenda, and neither saw the need or advantage of a role for Canada. On the home front in Canada, there was little enthusiasm, including at the cabinet table. The country was in the throes of a major recession. Support for the FTA had waned sharply, and there was little appetite for "more" free trade. Besides, and despite the FTA, we still had a host of trade irritants with the United States.

Views in Canada were, in fact, more negative than positive. There was, in a sense, a free trade fatigue at the political level and little enthusiasm at the bureaucratic level. Nonetheless, some of us were convinced that Canada had to be at the table primarily to preserve what we had negotiated in the FTA and to prevent the United States from implementing a "hub and spoke" approach of different preferential agreements throughout the hemisphere. That could have undercut our desire to maintain a competitively, attractive platform for investment in Canada as well as an open environment for trade. The prime minister and his key economic ministers – Mike Wilson and eventually John Crosbie – were of the same view, but we had to lobby hard in Washington to secure a seat and an equal voice in the negotiations.

I had several sessions with Jim Baker's economic deputy, Bob Zoellick, as well as with Baker himself and several White House aides to make our case as firmly as I could. The prime minister raised our desire to participate both with President Bush and Mexican president Carlos Salinas de Gortari. This personal appeal made it difficult for either to resist. But the American administration was under pressure from key senators, like Lloyd Bentsen of Texas, who wanted a negotiation exclusively with Mexico for political as well as economic reasons and did not want matters "complicated" by Canada. I met Bentsen and other concerned senators, as well as key congressmen, to reinforce our wish to participate. The US administration was concerned that we would not only complicate the negotiations by reopening issues left over from the FTA but also delay ratification beyond the point of no return. It was mindful belatedly of the enormous political challenge the FTA had posed for Canada and may have been worried that we would face more of the same. By then the polls were not favourable to the Canadian government, and the Liberals were openly opposed to NAFTA.

In the event, after giving solemn pledges that we would neither complicate nor delay proceedings, Canada was invited to join the negotiations and, in due course, according to both Mexican and American negotiators, played a constructive role throughout under the able leadership of our chief negotiator, John Weekes. It was, in fact, the Americans who ultimately delayed ratification. Despite campaigning fiercely against the agreement during the negotiations, the Liberal government of Jean Chrétien approved it quietly shortly after the 1993 election.

NAFTA proved almost as controversial for Americans as the FTA had been for Canadians. Organized labour was firmly opposed, as were many influential senators and congressmen. The political parties themselves were divided. More Democrats were opposed than supportive, whereas most Republicans were in favour. Ross Perot campaigned vigorously against NAFTA. President Clinton had to rely ultimately on strong Republican support in Congress to get the agreement approved. Such bipartisan spirit did not emerge in Canada, at least not until the Liberals moved from opposition into government.

On balance, and despite the difficulties of the 1990–91 recession, I believe we made progress on the trade agenda. Some disputes will never die, but the FTA and subsequently NAFTA have served Canadian interests well. As both the United States and Canadian economies recovered in the mid-1990s, the greater, more secure access generated unprecedented growth in bilateral trade – so much so that some of the fiercest opponents of the agreements became their strongest champions. NAFTA also gave rise to the notion of free trade for the Americas, still more a concept than a reality but nonetheless a positive reflection on the success experienced under more liberalized trade by Canada, the United States, and Mexico.

Health Care

Canadian health care aroused persistent interest as well as criticism in Congress and in the US media. The embassy and I responded with factual presentations to clarify the debate and to counter unfounded criticism, primarily from the *Wall Street Journal*. We arranged visits and seminars by knowledgable Canadian officials and health-care practitioners. On each occasion we stressed that we were not trying to "promote" Canadian policy to Americans, but at the same time, we were obliged to defend our system against unwarranted attacks. The debate in the United States was, and is, highly polarized. Apart from labels about "socialized" or "state-run" medicine, which triggered reflex allergic reactions in the United States, there were also charges that were more difficult to refute; that Canada benefited indirectly from the larger research and development expenditures and technological advances stimulated by the private sector in the United States. The fact that many Canadian doctors had moved south added credibility to this type of allegation.

It is true that some Americans do indeed get the "best health care money can buy." It is also true that 44 million of Americans have no health-care insurance, except Medicare and Medicaid for the lower-income and elderly members of their society. I was more than ready to defend the advantages of a taxpayer-funded, universal system. At a very early age, I had been told how my father needed to get a mortgage on our house in order to pay for his mother's long-term hospital care in the 1930s. Besides, from the limited personal experience of my own family with health care while in Canada, I had no reason for complaint. On returning to Canada in 1993, however, I quickly discovered the extent to which health care – in Montreal, at least – had deteriorated to deplorable levels. Overuse and abuse, a lack of accountability, and a similar lack of investment have meant that the balance between supply and demand is badly distorted. Despite numerous special studies and recommendations for reform, very little has changed. While the fundamental principles of universality and portability remain compellingly favourable over the US system, the lowest-common-denominator nature of delivery in Canada tends to undermine some of our bragging rights.

Acid Rain

Throughout much of the late 1970s and the early 1980s acid rain was a running sore in the Canada-US relationship. Canadians were alarmed by increasing amounts of nitrogen oxide and sulphur dioxide ("nox and sox") being generated primarily by coal-fired power plants and steel foundries, which were literally killing lakes and rivers on both sides of the border. Both countries were contributing to the problem, but given the disproportionate size of the two economies (and populations), it was obvious that the United States was doing more damage to Canada than vice versa.

The two countries had a long history of relatively successful steward-ship of our common environment, on matters such as water levels in the Great Lakes and more isolated border issues such as the Garrison Diversion project involving Manitoba and North Dakota. The International Joint Commission had, since 1909, overseen the resolution of various issues in a largely uncontentious and unheralded manner. But acid rain did not fit into the mould of prudent management. There were strong disagreements about the scientific basis for concern (not unlike the debate today about climate change) as well as about the extent (cause and effect) of the damage. These differences were accentuated by environmentalists, who lobbied vocally and vigorously for action by government and were as vigilant in denouncing any attempts at compromise.

Governments in Canada – federal and provincial – were more or less united on the need for action, and there was little political opposition to moves that would reduce the volume of "nox and sox" emanating from Canadian sources. (There were, of course, different views about who should pay and how much or how fast.) Above all, there was concern that no matter what Canada did on its own, it would not be sufficient. Comparable action was needed by the United States, which, it was estimated, generated as much as 50 per cent of the acid rain falling on Canada.

Opinions in the United States were sharply divided, politically and regionally. The Canadian view had support along the northern border and through New England. But opposition was strong in the coal states (West Virginia and Pennsylvania) and, more generally, the industrial centre and the Midwest. These regions were, of course, the source of much of the pollution. The issue of acid rain barely registered on the radar screen in the South and the Southwest.

The basic Canadian tactic was to build coalitions of support for action in the United States while educating the public generally about the cause-and-effect relationship between the noxious gases being emitted and the damage to formerly pristine lakes and rivers which no longer supported life of any kind. Support for a common action plan, one involving agreed overall targets for reduction and a flexible means of implementation, were being discussed but were repeatedly blocked or stonewalled by key congressional figures such as Senator Robert Byrd of West Virginia or Congressman John Dingle of Michigan, both very powerful in their own right, and by the Reagan administration, whose attitude on this issue ranged from dubious to negative. (The Carter administration had been more positively inclined, as on many issues, but held little sway even with senior Democrats in Congress.) The move to establish emissaries on acid rain at the Shamrock Summit had been intended to defuse the angry headlines highlighting differences and try to establish a more rational basis for dialogue and, ultimately, a common action plan. We had made very little progress with the Reagan administration but saw President Bush as a potential ally.

We knew that President George Bush was more sensitive on the subject, if for no other reason than, as a summer resident of Maine, he was fully aware of the acid rain problem. We also had considerable support from another powerful resident of Maine, Senator George Mitchell, who had become the majority leader in the Senate (a position that gave him significant control of the Senate agenda) and was determined to get congressional approval for an action plan. George Bush's director of the

Environmental Protection Agency, Bill Reilly, also became a champion for action in Washington. It was not an easy position for a Republican, but he manoeuvred skilfully, with the endorsement of Bush's legal counsel, C. Boyden Gray, and the tacit encouragement of the president. I have to believe that having a chief of staff from New Hampshire (John Sununu) may also have helped, although his strong political differences with Senator Mitchell on most other issues may have neutralized his position on acid rain.

When I presented my credentials to the newly elected president in January 1989, I stressed the importance of reaching early agreement on a common action plan to combat acid rain. Ultimately, the changes at the top in the administration and the leadership of George Mitchell in the Senate, along with others in the House, gave the necessary impetus to officials on both sides. On 31 March, 1991 in Ottawa, Prime Minister Mulroney and President Bush signed the Canada-US Air Quality Agreement, establishing reduction targets and commitments for both countries. After years of frustration and disappointment, it was a very sweet victory. The acid rain issue literally disappeared from the bilateral agenda as a result, and the agreement has become a model for progress on other environmental issues in North America. It was a very positive outcome. Through sheer perseverance and tangible commitment ("clean hands"), Mr Mulroney put to rest a major irritant that had bedevilled bilateral relationships for more than a decade. Nevertheless, he got very little personal credit for the success.

In the spring of 1990, our minister of the Environment, Lucien Bouchard, came to Washington to meet his American counterpart, Bill Reilly. A few days before his visit I had appeared on a US cable television show to answer questions spontaneously from American callers. I had been asked at one point to explain Quebec's language laws and, in ambassadorial fashion, had defended them to the best of my ability while at the same time encouraging the caller to come for a visit and see the charm of Canada's bilingual character. This response had been picked up and featured by *La Presse* and *Le Devoir* in Montreal and was very much in Bouchard's mind when he arrived.

I had, of course, known Lucien Bouchard both from my time at External, when he served as our Ambassador to France, and from my time in the PMO. I had helped brief him on free trade for the 1988 campaign and had participated with him in preparing the prime minister for the French-language TV debate during the campaign. He was as talented as he was complex.

Bouchard waved the Montreal newspaper articles at me and asked, "You said this?" When I acknowledged that I had indeed defended Bill 101, he said, "But you don't believe that?" "What I believe is not important," I replied. "As ambassador of Canada, I am obliged to defend the laws of our land, whatever they are." Bouchard was surprised. "I could never do that," he stated solemnly. "But," I continued, "as a member of cabinet, you may have to defend positions you do not fully endorse." He shook his head. "No, I could not."

Bouchard also expressed some concern about how he was perceived in "English Canada." "They all think I am a separatist," he complained. I told him pointedly that, as the minister responsible for Canada's national parks, he was uniquely placed to win the hearts of English Canadians. (He had rarely visited western Canada and knew very little about that region.) I suggested that if he went to Banff and declared that he was "proud to be the minister responsible for this magnificent park," I was sure those attitudes would change. Bouchard shook his head again, saying, "I could not do that either."

Over dinner that evening at the residence, Bouchard was seated beside my wife, who had Senator Jim Jeffords of Vermont, an ardent environmentalist, as her other table companion. For whatever reason, Jeffords continually asked my wife to repeat to him what Bouchard was saying. He may have thought Bouchard was speaking French. He may have also simply had difficulty hearing. I am not sure. At one point, however, Bouchard observed, "You know, Senator, we Québécois feel closer to you Americans than we do to English Canadians." When Jeffords asked my wife to repeat the message, she declined and glared undiplomatically at Canada's environment minister.

Not too long after, Bouchard resigned from cabinet and launched the Bloc Québécois. Of all the things that frustrated Brian Mulroney's time in office, I don't think anything impacted more negatively and painfully on him personally and professionally than the actions of his former Laval classmate. It is often said that Mulroney was hurt most by those closest to him or by those for whom he did the most. Lucien Bouchard would certainly top that list.

The Arctic National Wildlife Refuge

While acid rain dominated our environmental agenda, it was by no means the only issue. The prospect of drilling for oil in the Arctic National Wildlife Refuge (ANWR), an area of 19.5 million acres that straddles the Alaska-Yukon border, was and is a persistent matter of concern to Canada. Efforts to drill have been successfully thwarted by US domestic concerns, supported vigorously by Canada and specifically by our embassy in Washington. The issue flared up in the early 1990s and because of our open opposition, I came under strong personal attack by influential members of the Bush administration.

Canada and the United States share treaty rights to protect the porcupine caribou herd, which migrates annually from our Arctic region some six thousand miles south into the United States. The herd supports the livelihood of the Inuit, and ANWR is the major calving area for the herd. Concern about the potential impact of drilling on the calving is the basis for Canadian opposition. Democrats on the Hill generally shared these concerns and were able to stymie efforts by the administration to open ANWR for drilling. Republicans, especially those in Alaska, favoured drilling for economic reasons and as a means for reducing US dependence on foreign oil supply, including that from Canada. This aspect has caused some to suggest that Canada's motives were more than environmental.

As the Bush administration, led by Chief of Staff John Sununu and Energy Secretary James Watkins, initiated legislative moves to open ANWR for drilling, the Democrats rallied opposition forces on and off the Hill. Consistent with Canada's fundamental position and our treaty rights, I joined in with letters to Congress and public reinforcement of Canada's position. A visit at the time by the Yukon government leader provided an additional spotlight on our opposition.

The Bush administration was furious and cried foul, claiming that this was "interference in domestic affairs," a pretty serious allegation in any diplomatic dispute. The anger took a bizarre twist when the deputy secretary of energy, Henson Moore, called my social secretary, ostensibly to cancel his attendance at an embassy dinner but primarily to hector her about my behaviour on ANWR. I told him emphatically that if he had concerns about my behaviour, he should deal with me personally and not take it out on my secretary. He went further and announced a ban for the whole Energy department on accepting hospitality from the Canadian embassy! (His ban was more honoured in the breach than the observance.)

Meanwhile, I was being urged by friends at the White House to meet personally with and explain our position to Secretary Watkins. I did so and also met with the secretary of the Interior and John Sununu to try to contain the damage. They saw little merit in the substance of our opposition. What I tried to explain was that we had a shared responsibility and mutual treaty rights to protect the caribou herd, thereby rejecting the "interference in domestic affairs" allegation. I stated further that my actions had been consistent with that of the Canadian government well before my time in Washington. Ultimately, the effort to drill in ANWR was defeated by a healthy margin in the House and the Senate. I no longer received "chitlins" from Henson Moore at Christmas, but in time, emotions returned more or less to normal. The issue, of course, has flared up again under the current President Bush, but to date it remains unresolved in the face of strong opposition.

There was always a risk of becoming embroiled in ideological domestic politics, most notably on environmental issues like ANWR and acid rain. But it was a risk we could not avoid. One thing that is understood, if not always appreciated, in the United States is frankness or candour, along with a modicum of fairness in hearing an alternative point of view. So, while the engagement could be tense and even fractious at times, it could also be invigorating, adding spice as well as substance to the diplomatic chore.

G7 Summitry

Although bilateral issues – the meat and potatoes of our relationship – dominated the embassy's and my agenda, there were momentous developments on the international scene during the Bush presidency (Bush senior), most notably the implosion of the Soviet Union, the unification of the two Germanies, and the Gulf War, each of which required regular attention and reporting by the embassy. My dual position as ambassador and the prime minister's personal representative, or sherpa, for the Houston (1990), London (1991), and Munich (1992) G7 Summits gave me unusual exposure and involvement with each of these events.

The annual G7, now G8, Summits are the high point of global diplomacy for Canada, if not for all other participants. Despite the turgid communiqués, the non-decisive nature, and increasingly, the "showcase" veneer of these annual sessions, they represent the least formal and most restricted get-together of senior world leaders. While it would be difficult to list major achievements, these summits do help focus attention on key issues of the day, and on occasion, they can help to influence consensus or direction on macro-economic policy (giving collective support for tough individual action) and on major multilateral initiatives, such as trade and the environment. Inevitably, the leaders are more comfortable discussing the "hot" political issues of the moment than more complex economic questions, but here again, results stem more from the candour of the gathering than from decisions or directions taken. The rapport developed at summits among leaders, ministers, and senior officials can pay dividends between sessions and is probably the most tangible benefit of these annual events. It is the ultimate global network and, for Canada, an annual opportunity to play in the premiere diplomatic league. Canada was added to the group after the first summit in 1975 at Rambouillet. When the Europeans pressed to add Italy, the United States insisted on including Canada, no doubt with strong encouragement from Ottawa. We may be "a country without a region," but we should never discount the advantage of our North American position as a neighbour to the United States.

George Bush senior was not a fan of G7 summitry. For one thing, it involved, for him, too many Europeans. More fundamentally, it was usually a forum in which the United States found itself on the defensive and where, only with the greatest difficulty, did it gain support for what it deemed important. This was partly the burden of being a superpower and, since 1989, the world's only superpower. It was easier and more effective to convey US positions in bilateral, as opposed to multilateral, settings. Like his father, the current president Bush has found summitry with the Europeans a trying and generally unrewarding experience.

Bush's concern about the European presence at summits had some basis in fact. Not only did Europe have four of the seven traditional summit seats, but the European Commission president also participated, as, on occasion, did the president of the European Council (the rotating member-state president). Though summits were scheduled as often as possible when Britain, France, Germany, or Italy held the council presidency, this was not always possible. That made, on occasion, six Europeans at a table of nine. Bush was particularly peeved by the attendance of the "unelected" European Commission president. Coincidentally, Jacques Delors' role at the summits grew significantly as the launch of the new trade round became more prominent on the summit agenda, trade policy being within the exclusive purview of the commission, as opposed to the member states. Besides being non-elected, Delors was a socialist. Neither qualification appealed to George Bush.

At Houston in 1990, and partly because of their frustration at being outnumbered and relatively isolated, the Americans suggested that the summits be scheduled every two years instead of annually. The suggestion received no support. After all, despite a record of limited achievement, the G7 Summits were the pinnacle of global councils. And despite increased advance orchestration for each event, G7 Summits were the most intimate and relatively informal gathering for a select group of world leaders.

The focus of summitry was intended to be economic, but inevitably, political issues of the day dominated discussion. In 1990–92 the leaders grappled with a global recession, the promise of successfully concluding the Uruguay Round of trade negotiations, and the need for consensus on the global environment in the run-up to Rio de Janeiro. But from the collapse of the Berlin Wall in 1989 to the collapse of the former Soviet Union two years later, the overwhelming issue was how the West should respond and establish what George Bush's administration had labelled a "new world order."

At Houston, opinions were decidedly mixed. The Europeans were understandably worried about the growing instability so near to them. The Germans were thinking the unthinkable – unification – and wondering how, not whether, it would evolve. The Americans were mainly concerned with the huge nuclear arsenal in the Soviet Union and the continuing threat it posed. They were not convinced that Mikhail Gorbachev was, as Margaret Thatcher had declared, "someone we can do business with." Brian Mulroney shared Mrs Thatcher's view and encouraged the president to keep an open mind. Whatever their real views, the Americans preferred, as always, to deal with the Soviet Union bilaterally and not through a council of leaders where their voice was one of seven or eight or nine!

Nonetheless, one major outcome was an invitation to Gorbachev to attend the London Summit the following summer. His participation in London was memorable in several respects. He spoke eloquently, passionately, and at length about wanting a constructive engagement with the West and about his hopes for perestroika. He was proud but pragmatic. His western counterparts were receptive but guarded. Mr Mulroney saw the meeting as "the end of the Cold War," and in that sense alone it proved to be the most dramatic aspect of any summit then or since. The extraordinary performance by Gorbachev in London did not, however, prevent the coup attempt against him in Moscow a few weeks later.

Following the attempted coup in Moscow during the summer of 1991, President Bush immediately invited Mr Mulroney to Kennebunkport to assess the situation and to determine how the G7 should respond. I accompanied the prime minister and, together with National Security adviser Brent Scowcroft, sat in on an unusual round of telephone calls the president and prime minister made to their G7 counterparts in an effort to develop a common response. It was an extraordinary time and a remarkable example of the intangibles and the personal, networking capability of summitry.

In between calls, there was the opportunity for candour on related topics. During one of these interludes, the usefulness of summitry itself came up. Knowing the president's reservations, I asked whether he had ever considered how important the annual get-together was for Japan. After all, even though Japan was the number two economic power globally, it did not have a commensurate stature on the world stage. This lack of status was partly self-imposed. Japanese leaders changed almost annually and rarely left significant footprints, Yasuhiro Nakasone being a singular exception. It helped that he spoke English. (Helmut Kohl had an unfortunate habit of removing his headphones when the Japanese prime minister spoke at summits.) But Japan lacked a permanent seat on the Security Council and was not involved in a security alliance like NATO or in any regional group of significance. The G7 Summit was the only world council where its participation reflected its economic power and global significance. I cannot say this information changed Mr Bush's mind, but he did listen.

During this Kennebunkport get-together, the prime minister decided, unexpectedly, that Canada should recognize Ukraine as an independent country. He called me very early one morning to ask what I thought and instructed me to take a sounding with Ottawa. I asked him whether he had discussed this idea with President Bush, who, I presumed, would not want to be surprised by such an announcement coming on his front lawn at Kennebunkport. The prime minister said he would but asked me to check, as well, with Brent Scowcroft when I arrived at the Bush compound later in the morning.

External Affairs was alerted and started to work on a press release. As I recall, the president did not object, though he and Scowcroft were, I suspect, puzzled about the venue selected for this Canadian initiative. With all the bases covered, the announcement was made by the prime minister during a joint press conference with the president, and that is how Canada was one of the very first countries to officially recognize Ukraine.

Participation in these annual summits gives Canada a position of privilege and relevance that others envy. Our involvement has provided successive prime ministers, as well as our Finance and Foreign Affairs ministers, with unique and regular access to their counterparts in G7 (now G8) countries and the opportunity to help shape the direction of policy responses on major global issues. It has given us relevance and recognition globally on a level we did not receive at the end of World War II, even though our credentials then were as worthy as that which enabled us to join the G7. The summit is not a table of equals and each participant knows that. Power or weight do count, but the network is real and, depending on the inclination and capability of the individual, can be used selectively to advance Canadian interests. It is the pinnacle of global diplomacy, one in which we do have the opportunity, from time to time, to punch above our weight if we have representatives and views enabling us to do just that.

When it comes to punching above one's weight, however, no one can match the French. They are masterful at getting a lot with a little, and that skill goes back at least to the years following World War II. After fighting poorly for about six weeks and being occupied for the next four years, France emerged as a "victor," became one of the four occupying powers in Germany, and received a permanent seat on the Security Council. French officials have consistently outmanoeuvred all others since, gaining leadership positions in multilateral institutions – the IMF, the OECD, the EBRD, the European Bank – and by being more offside than on, have gained special attention, if not consideration, within the Western alliance, notably, if sometimes irritably, from the United States. It is an enviable record, one that extends to trade policy as well. Whenever we wanted to retaliate pointedly in a given dispute, we would ponder among ourselves "What would the French do?" When battling Japan on one occasion, the French adopted an unusual tactic. They declared that all Japanese VCRs would henceforth have to be shipped through Poitiers, where normal French customs procedures would be able to approve no more than four per day! It worked. The Japanese settled quickly, albeit unhappily. We might learn a great deal from the French!

Several of my sherpa colleagues went on to greater fame: Jacques Attali of France became the first head of the European Bank of Reconstruction and Development (EBRD) and served until he was forced out because of allegations about excessive personal expenditures. Pascal Lamy, the EC sherpa, became the EC's commissioner for external relations (trade policy) in 2000. Horst Kohler, the German sherpa, succeeded Attali at the EBRD and then became managing director of the IMF. He is now (2004) president of Germany. Bob Zoellick of the United States became USTR under the second George Bush and worked closely with Pascal Lamy at Doha in November 2001 to launch the next multilateral trade round. Umberto Vattani became Italy's deputy foreign minister.

German Reunification

Canada was caught off guard by the sudden "two plus four" agreement*
on German reunification, key elements of which were concluded privately during a NATO ministerial hosted by Canada's secretary of state for
External Affairs, Joe Clark, in Ottawa. Although Canada had no legitimate claim to be directly involved, I thought that, as host, we should
have been, as a matter of courtesy, entitled to some advance notice of
arrangements being discussed in our capital. I complained to Brent
Scowcroft in more pungent terms, saying, "Even the piano player in a
whore house knows what is going on upstairs!" He winced but clearly
saw larger priorities than the perennial lament about Canadian "sensitivities." The reality was that events on the ground in the two Germanies
rapidly superseded the plans of outside powers. In a bold stroke by
Chancellor Kohl, the two entities merged, warts and all, at a pace no one
could have predicted or planned. It happened almost as suddenly as the
collapse of the Berlin Wall – without the benefit of piano players or
detailed alliance consultation.

The Gulf War

In July of 1990, I was invited to the Canadian Armed Forces fishing camp
at Eagle River in Labrador, along with US Defense Secretary Dick
Cheney, my American counterpart, Ambassador Ed Ney, and several top
US and Canadian military officers. Our minds were distracted from the
prospects of salmon by the threat of war in the Middle East. We were
there when the US ambassador in Baghdad, April Glaspie, called on
Saddam Hussein to seek reassurances about Saddam's intentions regarding Kuwait. Secretary Cheney received a report on this meeting via secure
radiophone sitting on a large rock at the edge of Eagle River. On taking
the call, he cut short the fishing and returned promptly to Washington,
along with his military entourage. Later that summer, Saddam Hussein
invaded Kuwait triggering what became the "Gulf War."

During August of 1990, while I was vacationing in New Brunswick
(with Opposition Leader Jean Chrétien as my next-door neighbour), I
was summoned back to Washington to attend a dinner with the president and the prime minister and their advisers. I did not make the din-

---

* The two Germanies and the four occupying powers: the United States, the United Kingdom,
  the Soviet Union, and France.

ner on time but returned to Ottawa that evening and received a full briefing from the prime minister en route. As he would emphasize repeatedly during the run up to war, the prime minister had emphasized to the president the importance of responding to Iraq's invasion of Kuwait with a broad-based coalition, preferably under United Nations auspices. Canada would support fully a military engagement as part of such a coalition, once the requirements of Parliament had been respected. President Bush was more than receptive to the notion of a coalition and proved himself to be especially adroit at moulding and sustaining a strong coalition, acting on the basis of explicit United Nations resolutions. No doubt his experience as US ambassador to the United Nations gave him a realistic sense of both the utility and the limits of such diplomacy. It also helped that Canada held a seat at the time on the Security Council. Our advice regarding a role for the United Nations was all the more relevant.

The prime minister was consulted frequently and closely by the president as plans for military action evolved. At one point at Kennebunkport, and when much of the advice to Bush involved a "surgical strike," Mr Mulroney cautioned against such, saying in football parlance that, when you are up 70-0 (on the strength of the coalition being assembled), there is no need for a "long bomb." Mr Mulroney faced a different battle on the home front, where the Opposition came out firmly against Canadian involvement in the Gulf War. Mr Chrétien's position was curious. He advocated that Canada be involved, but only until the shooting started. At that point, he suggested, the Canadian troops should be brought home. Following the appropriate debate in Parliament, Canada dispatched a CF-18 squadron, several ships, and an army field hospital to participate actively in the war from day one. The prime minister was advised regularly by the president and Secretary of State Baker as plans evolved, including the ultimate decision to evict Iraq's forces from Kuwait.

George H.W. Bush

George Bush the elder was very personable and clearly relished the task of being president. He was highly experienced; having served as a congressman, CIA director, ambassador, and eight years as vice-president, he was certainly well-groomed for the office. He was more comfortable and more confident dealing with foreign, as opposed to domestic, policy, and that is what ultimately cost him the 1992 election. The 1991 recession ("It's the economy, stupid") and his change of heart on tax increases also contributed to his defeat. Bush never saw Bill Clinton as a real threat until it was too late. He could not imagine Americans electing a young governor from Arkansas, especially one who carried a lot of personal baggage. But they did, twice!

Bush was not really a main-street politician and was never at ease speaking in public. He was much more focused, precise, and personable in private. Although he had distinct views on policy, especially foreign policy, he was not really ideological, much to the consternation of the right wing in his own party. Bush believed in things like honour, duty, and service and, above all else, wanted to do what he considered to be the right or prudent thing. Though Texas became his home, he was really a New Englander, a Yalie, in manner and attitude. His Republicanism retained that eastern flavour, while that of his son is much more Texan in tone and substance.

The Gulf War was the apex of George Bush's presidency and his popularity. He led a multinational coalition and rallied the support of the American public (and Congress) for this intervention with a combination of confidence and diplomacy. Best of all, he achieved the basic objective with minimal US casualties. If the election had been held in the fall of 1991, Bush would have won in a landslide. His unprecedented popularity at the time was, in fact, what kept many prominent Democrats like Mario Cuomo, the popular governor of New York, out of the 1992 race.

Bush knew Canada and was familiar with the major bilateral issues on our agenda. He had a very close relationship, personal and professional, with Brian Mulroney, and this gave me an enormous advantage in terms of direct access to White House officials. It did not mean that our position or representations regularly won the day, but it meant that we had an opportunity to register our view and to elicit assessments on key global issues from White House officials. More importantly, it was evident that President Bush trusted our prime minister and welcomed his judgment on such matters as coalition-building for the Gulf War. His memoirs illustrate the extent of this trust.

Washington revels in what are described as "defining moments" in global affairs, and the Bush administration was quick to adopt this description for its response to Saddam Hussein's invasion of Kuwait. President Bush chose to "take a stand" or "draw a line in the sand" against this invasion, and the world was put on notice that this would be a "defining moment" for others to do the same. Americans rally best around calls to patriotism and morality, and the Gulf War engagement played fervently to both. There was little room for shading or nuance. Iraq had violated fundamental international law, and its actions could not be allowed to stand. While concern about Middle East oil, in general, and Saudi Arabia, in particular, were never far below the surface, Jim Baker knew that "oil" was not much of a rallying cry. He translated it into "jobs," American jobs, but this appeal did not really register either. Once the United States committed its military might, it became a much simpler cause of good against evil. Its allies had an equally simple choice: get onside or stand on the sidelines. For Americans, it became a call to patriotism, the roots of which run deep throughout the United States.

For Canada, morality and human rights usually figure prominently in foreign policy choices. Except on some occasions, patriotism is a harder sell. Joining a US-led coalition against Iraq, endorsed by the UN Security Council, was not a difficult choice for the Canadian government, although the Liberal opposition in Parliament chose a much more tentative, if not ambivalent, stance. By joining more forthrightly, Canada became part of the core group influencing policy before, during, and after the Gulf War, a position that generated dividends in terms of briefings and consultations at the highest level. I also suspect that both Secretary Baker and President Bush appreciated Prime Minister Mulroney's perspective because Mr Mulroney had a deep appreciation of the US domestic scene as well as of the sensitivities of other coalition players.

George Bush faced a twin challenge in confronting the Iraqi invasion of Kuwait. He had to build and maintain a solid international coalition involving close allies and key regional players. But even more crucially, he had to build support for potential military action with a Congress in which the Democrats had a majority in both houses and were not inclined to do favours for a Republican president. The strategy and tactics for the latter did not always strengthen the former. At one point, Prime Minister Thatcher cautioned the president not to "go wobbly" vis-à-vis Saddam Hussein, when what he was really trying to do was to demonstrate carefully but deliberately to Congress that all diplomatic efforts ("going the extra mile") were being utilized prior to military engagement.

Following Jim Baker's last-ditch meeting with Tariq Aziz, Iraq's foreign minister, in Geneva, President Bush won the day in Congress with a narrow 52-47 vote in the Senate. Shortly after, the United States and its allies moved against the Iraqis in Kuwait. Desert Storm was initially as successful in terms of domestic politics as it was militarily. But the glow of success faded not long after both in the United States for George Bush and in the Mideast.

One episode during the war itself stands out in my memory. American fighter jets bombed what turned out to be a hospital in Baghdad, and this incident caused an uproar in the House of Commons. The prime minister undertook to register his concern with the United States, and I became the designated messenger. I called on General Colin Powell, then chairman of the Joint Chiefs of Staff, and diplomatically explained the purpose of my visit. If looks could have killed, I would have been a dead messenger. Powell exploded, flinging a file at me. "Do you and your prime minister want to help me pinpoint targets? Go ahead," he shouted. I quickly moved the conversation away from the bombing incident to Powell's assessment of the war itself. Subsequently, I reported to Ottawa that I had registered the concern of our government with the chairman of the Joint Chiefs and that he had "taken note."

The Organization of American States

There was one issue on which the prime minister and I were in disagreement – the question of Canada joining the Organization of American States. Mr Mulroney believed that Canada should join, essentially to reinforce our position in the Western Hemisphere. I was opposed, as were most in External Affairs, because the OAS was regarded as a somewhat moribund organization, one in which the risks of Canada joining were seen as outweighing any perceived advantages. The biggest risk was that, on any given issue, we would have to take sides between the United States and many Latin American members of the OAS. These concerns had kept this issue "on the back burner" at External for decades. We had opted instead for "observer" status, a quintessentially non-controversial, Canadian position from which we could listen but not speak and never have to "take sides." (It is sometimes said that foreign policy for Canada means having no policy.)

The prime minister saw things differently, and needless to say, his position prevailed. He proved me to be dead wrong. Not that our full participation increased the stature of the organization, but it did allow Canada to become more involved in its own hemisphere, and the perceived risk of being the "ham in the sandwich" never really materialized.

NAFTA was an even more tangible step in this direction and, together with our OAS membership, prompted Canada to take a lead role in promoting the concept of free trade for the Americas. I would go farther to suggest that, particularly as the European countries draw closer together, our links to Europe become more historical, whereas our geographic proximity to the Latin American and Caribbean countries in our own backyard becomes more relevant. We should give higher priority to issues concerning our own hemisphere.

Haiti

Prime Minister Mulroney also had a strong interest in Haiti, and as the situation there deteriorated in September 1991, his concern was manifested in a succession of conversations with President Bush. Reaction to the coup that overthrew President Jean-Bertrand Aristide became a major topic bilaterally and in the United States. The State Department was somewhat perplexed by the strength of Canada's interest in Haiti until I pointed out that the "desk officer" for Haiti was none other than the prime minister himself – just as, at the time, George Bush was seen by many in Washington as the "desk officer" for China. Mr Mulroney was determined to see the victor of a democratic election restored in Haiti, and he went to some lengths to enlist President Bush's support and US involvement in the process. Ultimately, that is what happened, but Haiti being Haiti, it did not make much of a difference.

As we began our fourth year in Washington, Joan and I both decided that it would be our last. Our departure would coincide with the presidential election and that, as we had learned, would be a good time for change. Besides, my waistline could not be indulged much more. I could have stayed longer in government but chose instead to look in a different direction. After the pressure-cooker atmosphere of the Prime Minister's Office and the persistent public glare of Washington, I was ready for something different, preferably in the private sector. In January 1993, as Bill Clinton moved into the White House, Joan and I left for Montreal, where I became executive vice-president (International) at Bell Canada Enterprises.

TWELVE

Managing Canada–US Relations: A Matter of Choice

Most Canadians may want to have a good relationship with the United States, but the definition of "good" is often open to lively debate. Many recognize the importance of the United States to Canada in virtually all fields of endeavour, but some resent the country's significance even if they understand it. This attitude can present a real challenge for diplomats trying to manage the relationship, and even more so for our political leaders.

Canadians, notably English-speaking Canadians, have complicated views about the United States in general and about relations with the United States in particular. These run the gamut from envy to admiration, from a sense of inferiority to one of moral superiority, and from concern to compassion. French Canadians tend to have fewer hang-ups, in part because they have a distinct culture and language that provides for real difference, but they have a strong aversion to the United States' use of its military power. English Canadians have been known to dwell on the ways in which to define how we differ, but to an extent that diminishes rather than enhances how Canadians actually see themselves.*

There is an enormous power difference between our two countries which complicates the relationship. The Americans are singularly powerful – number one in many ways. They know it and act accordingly. Canadians know that they are *not* number one and, in that sense alone, are very unlike Americans. But Canadians also seem less certain about what or who they are, other than "not American." Being genuinely concerned about what the United States may do with its awesome power contributes not only to unease but also, on occasion, to outbursts of

---

* Joe Clark, while minister of External Affairs, kept a scorecard on the number of times Canada voted differently at the UN, precisely for this reason.

moral superiority by Canadians.* They can also be very sensitive to a lack of attention or perceived slights by the United States about things Canadian (Bush's failure to mention Canada after 9/11 is one example) and yet equally sensitive when the attention becomes overt or critical. When we capture the spotlight in Washington, it is not always positive, but Canada would like to be known as something more than the source of "cold fronts moving south."

Canadians can be both attracted to and repelled by the immense magnetic force of the United States. They want maximum benefit from a productive partnership and, at the same time, a certain space for themselves. That can be a delicate balancing act for any Canadian politician or diplomat. The basic challenge for Canadians is to reconcile the advantage of their proximity with the risk of close co-operation. For Americans, the challenge is proportionately much less. They can measure the real value of their proximity to Canada against the risk of indifference.

There are definitely streaks of anti-Americanism in Canada, reflecting the concern, distaste, and discomfort of living alongside the only global superpower. These sentiments are stimulated not just by what Americans and their government do but by the intense influence of the United States on the lives of most Canadians – from television to books, from films to popular music and sports, from what Canadians eat and what they watch to what they hear and what they read. It is not surprising that they relentlessly define themselves in reaction to this pervasive influence.

As seen from the United States' perspective, this mix of Canadian attitudes about its neighbour can be baffling. Canadians may appear friendly but prickly and, at times, sanctimonious or smug in their efforts to proclaim their difference. The fact is that very few Americans spend much time concerning themselves about Canada, a more-or-less benign indifference that only aggravates Canadian sensitivities. We tend to see one another through opposite ends of a telescope.

What is particularly troublesome is the extent to which the inferior or junior-partner image that Canadians have of themselves reflects a lack of self-confidence or an inability to see full value in their own status. Canadians fear they can never truly measure up to an American standard, but they seem reluctant to celebrate a standard of their very own because, as seen through an American filter, any other standard will always be secondary. Yet in the 2002 Winter Olympics, for example, Canadians proved that they, men and women, could beat the Americans

---

* One of Canada's premiere diplomats, John Holmes, put it this way: "We find security in the Americans' power and insecurity in considering what wild things they might do with it."

at Canada's own game, hockey, something many believe is the most defining characteristic of all for Canadians.

I would argue that we have been least effective in foreign affairs when we have tried to separate or distance ourselves from the challenge of this primordial relationship in the name of "sovereignty," "counterweights," or "soft power," labels that are more rhetorical than meaningful. Differentiation and detachment risk making Canada irrelevant where our interests are paramount. Conversely, by earning and nurturing the trust and respect of the world's greatest power, we have, on occasion, been able to assert and protect our vital national affairs while enhancing our effectiveness in the resolution and advancement of multilateral matters. The two are not mutually exclusive. But once lost, such hard-earned trust is not easily regained. After almost a decade of distance and differentiation, we find ourselves now with a diminished capacity to defend our national interests in the United States and a shrinking relevance in world affairs. What is troubling to me is that anti-Americanism is becoming more popular in Canada. When ads featuring the president of the United States are used in a Canadian election, it is not difficult to understand the motive. Tweaking the eagle's feathers makes for good politics in central Canada, and in 2004 it had the intended effect.

The reality is that Canadians and Americans are very much alike, and on fundamental issues of peace, freedom, and prosperity, their values and their instincts are closely entwined. Canadians' self-confidence or sense of self need not be defined by the magnitude of difference but rather by what they choose to make of the relationship for their own purposes. More troubling is the ambivalence or apprehension of Canadians combined with indifference or, worse, annoyance among Americans. The hardest reality for Canadians to stomach is that they have more at risk and more to lose when things go off track than do the Americans. But if, in their desire for distinction or difference, they neglect to engage consistly with the United States, they will undoubtedly pay a disproportionate price.

That is also why managing the US relationship can be frustrating and difficult. The locus of power in Washington can be elusive, depending on the issue. The president does have an awesome amount of military power at his disposal, but the distinctive American system of checks and balances helps to decentralize or fragment much political power. Even if the White House wants to resolve a particular problem, it cannot always get its way. Moreover, Americans can be tough to deal with, whether in Congress, in the administration, or at the state level. They play hardball, serving their own priorities, their own concerns, and, especially these days, their own view of the world. A Canadian prime minister has real political power, day in day out, even without much of the military variety. He or she can make decisions and set directions for domestic or foreign policy if and when choosing to do so. The prime minister can also set the tone for managing our most vital foreign relationship.

Managing relations with the United States should be a primary concern for all Canadian prime ministers, but it rarely is and for many reasons. It can be a tough business and is seldom rewarding in popularity terms – tough because the relationship itself and the risks involved are enormously lopsided. Any wisp of smoke from the Americans can become a three-alarm fire in Canada under an unrelenting media spotlight (witness, for example, the Arar case in 2004). This is particularly true when there is a credible opposition in Ottawa, one that favours distance and differentiation vis-à-vis the United States, rather than engagement. For the Americans, issues directly involving Canada seldom generate attention from Congress or from the media or elsewhere. American hostages from Iran. That event resonated strongly and positively throughout the United States – even more so when it was portrayed in a movie.

Managing Canada-US relations can be tough too because the Americans no longer need much alliance solidarity, a trump card that many lesser powers, including Canada, used with effect during the Cold War. The aura of American power can be daunting for some. I have seen more than one Canadian politician cringe at the prospect of delivering a difficult or contrary message to his or her American counterpart. Much easier to convey that critical view to the Canadian media – easier but with no practical effect. My meetings with congressmen or administration officials who were staunchly opposed to Canadian practices, whether on trade, energy or the environment, were tough but essential parts of my Washington agenda.

Washington is a very busy global capital; Ottawa is not. In Washington, serious problems get serious attention, but it is much harder to attract time and effort toward solutions for lesser problems, even if tangible US interests are at stake. And the separation of powers in Washington can be a useful defence mechanism for the administration. "We would be happy to help resolve this for you, but unfortunately, the senator from North Dakota is adamant" was a refrain encountered in various forms time and again as we attempted to build coalitions to resolve bilateral disputes.

The United States does share tangible economic, environmental, and security interests with Canada, but it also does so and more, on a global scale. US officials tend to see major global issues in black or white terms.

Defining moments become matters for fundamental choice: "You are either with us or against us." There is no room for nuance or middle ground, and the positions taken by other countries on what US officials see as "defining" global issues can influence the tone and the priority they attach to bilateral issues with those countries.

Virtually all aspects of Canadian public policy are affected by our relationship with the United States. The fact that the same is not the case for the United States only compounds the challenge for Canadians involved in managing this relationship. When Canadians act as if the US factor is not consequential, we inevitably pay a heavy price. Three examples bear this out – the GST, the Kyoto Protocol, and, most recently, the Iraq War. One can argue that Canada's action in each case was sound and in its best interests, but by failing to take into account the very different position of the United States on each, Canada created additional burdens for itself.

With the GST, and despite thorough analysis, the government underestimated or ignored what Canadians would do initially to avoid paying the new tax. They shopped in droves across the border, spending billions of retail dollars in the United States rather than in Canada and making the 1990–1991 recession more severe here than in the United States. They were "saved," if that is the right term, prolonged negative effect only by the fact that their dollar eroded in value to the point where cross-border shopping, even without the tax, was no longer advantageous. (Incidentally, the Americans are now doing much the same in reverse, albeit on a much smaller scale, to purchase less-expensive Canadian pharmaceuticals.)

The GST was an excellent tax initiative for Canada. It was consumption-based, the fairest form of taxation, replacing a hidden sales tax that had discriminated against Canadian manufacturers and exporters, and it greatly enhanced the subsequent Liberal government's effort to transform the deficit into a surplus. The fact that Canadians rebelled against the tax by shopping in the United States simply proved that Canadian policies do not operate in a vacuum and that "sovereignty" has its limitations, even for Canadians! With the Canadian dollar again on the rise and the American dollar weakening, cross-border buying may intensify.

The different position of the two countries on the Kyoto Protocol has a potentially more damaging effect. Canada chose to ratify it with the best of intentions, wanting to be in the vanguard of countries supporting action against global warming, even if its contribution will be marginal at best and even though the government has no real idea of the costs of implementation. Canada does not, as yet, have a plan. More ominously, the Americans (and the Mexicans) have chosen not to ratify the protocol, thereby giving themselves an automatic perceived advantage over Canada concerning decisions on investment and expansion for our two economies. Every advantage given the Americans has to find an offset somewhere – in productivity, tax rates, or exchange rates – and it is a fight Canada is not winning.

What would have been a more practical and more effective course of action for Canada on climate change would have been a call for a North American accord, challenging and engaging the United States in the spirit of Kyoto to negotiate commitments to a mutually agreed amount of reductions in greenhouse gas emissions for our shared environment, much as we did in the early 1990s to combat acid rain. This would have been a tougher approach, certainly, than solemn declarations relatively free of substance, but unquestionably better in the long term for our economy and our environment – better overall but less compelling politically and difficult to achieve, which is probably why it was not contemplated.

The American objections to Kyoto are based essentially on their view that the obligations would have been more onerous for them (and for Canada, incidentally) than those negotiated by the Europeans. There is a sound basis for this concern, which only makes the notion of a North American solution as a step towards Kyoto more practical all around. But as committed multilateralists, we chose the "high road" before we knew the price or the means to meet our obligation.

On Iraq we chose, in the name of "sovereignty," not to join the United States and the "coalition of the willing," but it was the manner more than the substance of our disagreement that the Americans found offensive. Undisciplined anti-American remarks by government members of Parliament, including one cabinet minister, did not help. Although our preference for a "united" United Nations position was widely known, the Americans had expected that, in the end, Canada would be supportive or, at least, not overtly opposed. For one thing, we already had more troops providing indirect support in the region than many in the coalition. We also provisionally had troops in Florida training directly with the US invasion force. (Our decision to send troops, instead, to Afghanistan was a last-minute diversion taken with minimal planning and was never fully explained to the Americans as an alternative to Iraq.) Instead, we chose to oppose action by our closest friends, and in an abrasive manner that undermined their position at a delicate time.

In hindsight, Canada may have made the right decision, but our reasoning at the time was flimsy, and our failure to give the United States proper notice, let alone a clear explanation, is not how relations between allies should be conducted. Combined with the public slights against the president by government officials, this breakdown in normal diplomacy further strained already troubled relations between Washington and Ottawa.

American leaders often use moral and idealistic language to rally support and simplify their intentions to foes as well as friends, but first and foremost, for home consumption. This language does not distill smoothly in the halls of diplomacy and often provokes quibbling if not outright condemnation from erstwhile allies. But the more powerful the United States becomes, the less it cares about sensitivities outside the country. The war on terrorism has heightened this tendency. The president reduces the issue to basics: you are either "with us or with them." This tactic plays well on the home front but resonates less well with US allies. The overwhelming dominance of the United States in the world, in terms of economics, military might, technology leadership, and even culture, is upsetting conventional concepts of balance and counterweights in foreign policy. The real choices and room for manoeuvre for its allies are now more limited than ever.

Canada does have the luxury of choice. We can decide to either harness advantage from our proximity or seek to distance and differentiate ourselves from the United States. Throughout history, we have tried both distance and proximity as the basis for managing our relations. John Diefenbaker sought to divert 15 per cent of our trade to Britain and disagreed sharply with the Americans on the issue of arming BOMARC missiles based in Canada. Pierre Trudeau's Third Option and the NEP evoked similar sentiments, as, most recently, did manifestations of "soft power" and, of course, Canada's decision to oppose the US-led invasion of Iraq. The Auto Pact, free trade, and moves towards a more secure perimeter reflect conscious efforts to derive advantage or value from our proximity.

The choice can be blurred by simplistic references to "sovereignty" or "nationalism" or "independence" in foreign policy. Agreements between nations can easily be misconstrued as compromises of sovereignty, but if they are intended to serve the interests of those agreeing, they should be seen instead as assertions of sovereignty that strengthen both the sense of nationhood and the capability for more independent action. Moreover, when you are one-tenth the size of your neighbour, agreements based on the rule of law constitute the best antidote to the power imbalance. Indeed, it is ironic that those who champion the virtues of multilateralism ignore the fact that multilateral agreements (as opposed to process) also involve compromises of sovereignty – less independence – and yet are intended to provide a stronger bedrock of international law.

During ten years' stewardship of Canada-US relations, I experienced both trends of management and spent a good deal of time analyzing the factors influencing Canadian approaches, as well as the results. My preferences relate to that experience. It is not difficult to play the differentiation game. In fact, assertions of difference are almost certain to ignite headlines and will have some popular appeal in Canada. But we should not confuse difference for the sake of being different with significance, influence, or even independence. I have often thought it would have been easier, much easier, to sit on the sidelines and gripe about positions taken by the United States. The Canadian media thrive on this kind of differentiation. It does, in fact, get headlines – in Canada – but public critiques from the sidelines tend to reveal more about motive than policy objective and are often seen by American officials as grandstanding at best or cheap shots at worst. Either way, it becomes more difficult to register genuine concern about US actions or pronouncements. If we criticize the Americans from the sidelines in high moral tones, invoking our role as what former secretary of state Dean Acheson once described as "the stern daughter of the voice of God," we may receive much worse than benign neglect by way of response. And if we choose, as we did on Iraq, to be openly opposed on an issue that the United States regards as fundamental to its well-being, we should not be unduly surprised if our expressions of concern on bilateral issues (mad cow disease, softwood lumber, etc.) fall on deaf ears.

A further misunderstanding harboured by Canadians complicates relations – that we do better with Democrats than with Republicans – and we end up cheering for the former, with even ministers and government representatives expressing preferences. The reality is that we need to work with whoever is in the White House or the Congress. Rather than expressing political preferences, Canadians would be better off devoting more energy to gaining a clear sense of American priorities and how best to influence them, no matter who is in power. George W. Bush's re-election poses exactly that challenge for Canada. It is time, in my view, for a more mature approach by Canada and a better appreciation of what drives American policy preferences, rather than juvenile whining from the sidelines.

If we really want to engage the Americans on issues or positions of concern to us, we need to be ready to pay more than lip service to their concerns. We have been freeloaders on defence, contributing less than half the average of all NATO countries, and the Americans know this. You have to pay to play the ultimate power game, and because we pay very little, our ability to influence Washington and others is at a very low ebb. For the United States, concern about its own security is more fundamental today than any other national interest. By ignoring that basic consideration, we risk marginalizing our influence in Washington and our place in the world.

Continued neglect of our military creates a similar degree of detachment from American priorities and actually makes Canada more vulnerable and more dependent on the United States in securing our own territory – the essence of sovereignty. We have vacillated for years on the issue of ballistic missile defence, leaving the field of public opinion open to advocacy groups, most of whom are predisposed to oppose the preferences and policies of the current US administration. This absence of leadership by government confines us to a position of increasing irrelevance in terms of North American security. Whatever legitimate concerns Canadians may have about missile defence are better registered from a position of mutual respect than from one of marginal significance.

The real danger with distance is that it can breed neglect. Nothing, in my view, could be more damaging to Canadian interests in the United States than the absence of engagement. To defend and advance our interests, we need access and relevance in Washington, and we have to work at them consistently and coherently so that they can deliver dividends when needed. This does not mean that we are obliged to "go along" at all times in order to "get along." Our relationship is too complex and too sophisticated to lend itself to simple slogans. But I also believe that our distinct sense of being Canadian should be defined by more than a catalogue of differences or by rhetorical claims of "independence" in foreign policy. Some believe we can do more in world affairs by choosing to distance ourselves from the United States and US positions; I do not. Distance and differentiation are not an end in themselves; nor are they substitutes for engagement. It is, in fact, ironic that, while most countries search constantly for ways to get closer to the United States, Canada often strives for distance.

A long-standing objective of Canadian foreign policy has been to keep the United States constructively engaged in the multilateral system. At a time when world trade negotiations are drifting, when the UN struggles for legitimacy and NATO searches for relevance, this objective – and Canada's potential leverage – is more important than ever.

The fact is that we can walk and chew gum simultaneously on the world stage, provided we have a confident view of what interests and values we wish to advance.

To be significant or influential, points of difference need to serve distinct interests or relate to fundamental foreign policy objectives. We also need the capacity and the will to act or contribute tangibly to a global objective. Otherwise our motives could be dismissed as merely avoiding the cost and controversy of involvement. When we do choose to differ with the United States, we need to convey our differences in a manner that respects honest differences between allies. We can "disagree without being disagreeable." Above all, we should measure our significance, our "independence," by the ultimate effect of what we can do or by what we actually achieve.

It is also true that our ability to hold influence in Washington (or anywhere else) will increase if and as we develop a more confident sense of self and purpose as Canadians. There were days during my assignment in Washington when the unravelling of the Meech Lake Accord and the defeat of the Charlottetown Accord added unwelcome baggage to my assertions of Canadian purpose and raised questions, if not concerns, in Washington about our future as a unified partner on the northern US border.

For the most part, my years in Washington constituted a high point in mutual trust and influence between the two countries. That is not to say we had no differences. We fought hard over bilateral environmental and trade issues, and we worked diligently to find solutions. Differences on global issues were also exchanged in a manner that was as spirited as it was civil. Engagement is better, in my view, than irrelevance! Unless I was confronting a hog farmer in South Dakota or a timber baron in Georgia, I found American attitudes towards Canada to be generally benign. Introducing myself as the ambassador of Canada would elicit a warm smile virtually anywhere, even if discussion of Canadian concerns frequently prompted a blank stare. When I called on members of Congress, I customarily brought a one- or two-page fact sheet on the issue or issues of the moment in the hope that it would register in some way at least with a staff member.

The fact that Canadian issues did not capture much priority in Washington also meant that administration representatives had little appreciation of the political importance of these issues to their Canadian counterparts. This was most evident on free trade. It did not help that senior administration officials were not elected and therefore had little direct sense of political pressures. Their sole political focus was on the president. Our biggest challenge was to attract and sustain the attention of a champion in Washington for any major issue – from the administration or Congress, preferably both – and channel our representations accordingly.

A solution to a bilateral dispute or irritant requires a degree of give and take by both sides, but virtually any compromise with the United States also risks being perceived in Canada as a "sellout" or worse. That is why, if Canada genuinely wants to engage the United States to resolve an issue, perseverance, patience, delicate manoeuvring, and a lot of homework are required. Those involved also know that success is unlikely to garner much in the way of popular appeal. Ultimately, it is a question of leadership, a clear priority determined at the top political level in Canada, and a sustained commitment of time and intellectual energy with little guarantee of political reward.

It is frequently asked whether personalities can make a difference in diplomacy. The "correct" answer quotes Lord Palmerston to the effect that countries have permanent interests, not permanent friends, and as diplomats, we would faithfully argue that the management of issues, especially with the United States, reflects the importance of the issues rather than the power of personalities. We would say so whether relations were good or bad. There is obviously a fundamental truth to this view, but I can attest to the fact that personalities, especially those of government leaders, can and do count. They may not override the system of governance, but they do affect the tenor of bilateral relations. When leaders get along well with one another, as Mulroney did with Reagan and Bush, they converse frankly and frequently. Their priorities become priorities for others. Their officials, to a great degree, take their cue from this rapport and act accordingly. They try harder to get solutions. Access, if not influence, for Canada's ambassador in Washington is determined in similar fashion, not to score points as much as to gain a reasonable hearing. When the relationship is sour or cool, as it was between Trudeau and Nixon or Trudeau and Reagan, the opposite is true. Access then is by the book – nothing more, nothing less.

Access is the lifeblood of diplomacy. It is determined by relevance, by capability, and by the ability to deliver when it counts. You can get attention, as Trudeau did, by mounting a peace mission, treating the United States, not as an ally, but as a superpower in need of education, but you become relevant by seeking to influence American policy as an ally and trying to turn that influence to Canada's advantage. It is not easy doing the latter, especially when the former is much more popular on the home front.

Unquestionably, Pierre Trudeau had a global outlook which, on many occasions, clashed with the views that prevailed in Washington. It was more than a matter of different personalities. Trudeau's priorities reflected his own attitudes or interests on global affairs. There was less of a direct link to Canadian interests. His focus on the North-South dialogue and on disarmament was unquestionably noble in the broadest sense, but it was seen in some quarters, especially in Washington, as dilettant-ish, if not provocative. His distaste for NATO and his dalliances with Castro were regarded even more skeptically. None of these questions had much relevance to Canadian interests, but they gave the veneer of "distinctive" Canadian involvement on global issues and appealed to a Canadian desire to be seen to be "doing good things" and being at variance to US preferences. (Jean Chrétien's penchant for Africa in the final years of his leadership had some vestiges of the Trudeau approach but little of the panache.) Trudeau's general lack of interest in economic issues diminished his capacity to drive an agenda that served Canadian interests and probably reinforced his ambivalence towards the United States.

A posture of "safe distance" has obvious popular appeal in Canada, as demonstrated by both Pierre Trudeau and Jean Chrétien. When he called on George Bush senior in 1991 as Canada's leader of the Opposition, Mr Chrétien stated, "Friendship is friendship, but business is business." This, he said, best expressed his approach to this relationship. He did not elaborate then or since. He also declared firmly at that time that he had no desire to go fishing with the US president. Instead, as it turned out, he chose golf!

Brian Mulroney saw Washington as the apex of global power, as well as the capital of greatest significance to Canadian interests. He cultivated close relationships with many in the administration and Congress, and his foreign policy priorities consistently focused on relations with the United States. He was convinced this approach would ultimately serve Canadian interests and also enable Canada to exercise some influence on global issues in which the United States' role was paramount. His success on free trade and acid rain has been unmatched by either his predecessor or his successors. Whether he was successful in the global context may well be a matter of judgment and less easy to quantify, but his involvement at G7 meetings, on East-West issues, and in the Gulf War coalition were extensions of this fundamental predilection. His actions on South Africa, on Star Wars, on Haiti, and on global environmental issues demonstrated that he could also differ sharply with the United States without jeopardizing the fundamental chemistry and commitment of his approach to the relationship. However, Mr Mulroney's achievements were undermined by perceptions in Canada that he was "too close" to the Americans. Tony Blair fell under similar criticism at home for his support of President Bush after 9/11, but he at least had the advantage of an ocean of distance. Conversely, Mr Trudeau's "crusades" for peace or in support of developing countries were celebrated on the home front even though little of substance accrued from them.

Prime Minister Mulroney placed a premium on good relations with the United States and would acknowledge that he had the scars to prove it. He did not, as some would, equate civility or good neighbourliness with subservience. By working to resolve bilateral irritants, Mulroney did not diminish Canada's "distinct voice" on foreign policy issues. Rather, by improving the tone and substance of our bilateral relationship, he actually established a basis for access and influence on global issues which few, if any, Canadian prime ministers have matched. The significance of his influence is a matter of record in the memoirs of George Bush senior.

Ultimately, the measure of foreign policy is relevance and influence. To be relevant, you must be engaged. To be influential, you need to establish a basis of trust with your counterpart anchored more by tangible commitment than by simple rhetoric. During the Mulroney years, Canada was relevant and influential in Washington. That did not make the task of ambassador easy by any means. But we were engaged consistently and constructively with the United States on bilateral and multilateral issues of the day, and the record speaks for itself.

Much has been written about the need to raise the profile of Canada's ambassador in Washington, including suggestions that the individual be given cabinet status or broader responsibilities for the operations of Canada's consulates general in the United States. Neither would be beneficial. The ambassador's "profile" depends primarily on the priority our relations command in Washington, on the chemistry between the leaders of the two countries, and on the confidence the prime minister has in the ambassador. Cabinet status or enhanced authority would not substitute for any of these factors, and in any event, status in Ottawa does not in itself convey status in Washington. Cabinet status might, in fact, complicate rather than strengthen the ambassador's position. There would, for instance, be the potential for overt conflict with Canada's foreign minister and with other ministers who have a direct stake in the relationship. Because the ambassador represents the whole government, he or she is better able to perform this function without cabinet status, provided it is apparent to all in Ottawa and Washington that the ambassador enjoys the full confidence of the prime minister.

I am less adamant that the position be filled only by "professional" public servants. While this practice has certainly been the custom and one which, I believe, has served Canada well, it is entirely possible that a prominent "outsider" known and trusted by the prime minister, could do the job. It would, of course, politicize and therefore "taint" the appointment somewhat, but the potential benefit might well outweigh the risk.

The overriding factor determining whether or not the ambassador will play an effective role for Canada is primarily the attitude and priority the current government attaches to the relationship. If neglect or differentiation is the order of the day, as it has been for so much of the past decade, no individual can establish a profile that commands respect or attention in Washington.

American global priorities today are very clear: the war on terrorism and homeland security are paramount. The threat of nuclear proliferation and concerns about rogue states and the Middle East are crucially important as extensions of American preoccupations with global security. Relations with Russia and China are next on the list because each represent a balance between opportunity and risk. All other issues and relationships are decidedly secondary.

Knowing this focus, Canada can decide whether and how to deal with the United States on global issues. Our shared stewardship of North America should make homeland security a joint responsibility of similar prominence. Recognizing this responsibility does not mean we will be co-opted, but it does open up opportunities for us to play a constructive supporting role, one with the potential for broader dividends if we play it with care and discretion. One thing is certain: if we choose not to be involved, the United States will act in its own self-interest and possibly in a manner that will impact negatively on tangible Canadian interests. More generally, we can choose at any time to stand on principle and publicly oppose US positions on current issues, presuming, of course, that this stance serves some higher purpose for Canadian interests and has more than narrow political appeal in Canada.

Trying to straddle a position somewhere in between is what we have been doing in recent years. Whether we envy or resent American dominance, we do share similar views and concerns on most issues. If we want to influence the direction of US thinking without overreaching or holding inflated expectations, we are better placed than most to gain a hearing. But talk alone does not carry much weight in Washington. Ultimately, Canada, like any other ally or neighbour, will be judged more by what it does than what it says. The choice is ours to make.

The end of the Cold War and the rise of terrorism are affecting Canada-US relations in essentially divergent ways. With the end of the Soviet Union, the glue that held the Western alliance together has dried out. European members are increasingly turning inward, and the expanding European Union is becoming their dominant focus. Former Soviet satellites have been eager to join both NATO and the EU, more from fear of the past than from concern for the future, but European integration is their priority as well. Canada's place is becoming even more ambivalent, as are attitudes more generally in Canada about the necessity for any form of military capability other than peacekeeping, let alone alliance solidarity. Following 9/11, the United States deemed itself to be in a new global war but with an enemy as difficult to find as to defeat. All of this, I suggest, is creating new priorities in Washington and less relevance for Canada. A gradual and gentle drifting apart became an abrupt and, for the Americans, unexpected rupture over Iraq.

The fact that France and Germany drew most of the American venom provided a relief of sorts but did not alter Canada's position of increasing irrelevance. Nonetheless, the decision was very popular on the home front, particularly in Quebec. The Cold War reflex response no longer worked, and the terrorist threat did not have the same meaning for Canada as for Americans. Our long border may still be more or less undefended. but it is becoming more clearly marked as perceptions and concerns about the challenges we face continue to diverge. The logic of greater economic integration and the centrality of the United States to our economic well-being are compelling, but as the global landscape shifts, along with Washington's global priorities, there is scope for greater divergence of outlook and attitude. Finding the right balance for managing our most vital relationship should be a top priority for any Canadian leader.

THIRTEEN

Looking Back

My career at External Affairs spanned nearly thirty years and ranged from the most trivial assignments to the most critical. Unquestionably, the free trade negotiations represented the single most important policy initiative of my career. The success of that negotiation was pivotal to Brian Mulroney's re-election in 1988 and to much of the growth of the Canadian economy into the twenty-first century. The challenge itself, the risks involved, and the strong sense of achievement provided great impetus for the choices I subsequently made and for the way I acted in other capacities. The experience was invaluable and left an indelible mark on my character.

As for the verdict on the agreement, there does not seem to be much doubt that the FTA and its successor, NAFTA, have generated more trade and more wealth for all participants. Some of the most severe critics eventually became champions of these agreements. We had wanted more-open and more-secure access to our most important market. What we got was not perfect,* but it did put our trading relationship with the United States on a sounder footing and, as with all trade-liberalizing actions, it generated improved productivity in the Canadian economy. It was, of course, a compromise, as is the case with any negotiation, a combination of give and take by both sides, but with a mutually acceptable result. The FTA provided the impetus for more trade liberalization generally and an improved basis for resolving disputes, which subsequent trade negotiations, regional and global, have sought to emulate.

What we obtained must be measured against what existed before and, more importantly perhaps, by what we had to pay to get it. By creating a binational dispute settlement mechanism to oversee judgments

---

* Ambassador Gotlieb cautioned us consistently and correctly "not to let the best be the enemy of the good."

by our respective trade tribunals, Canada and the United States established a unique appeal body. For us, this meant a check against arbitrary or capricious rulings by US trade officials. It was a partial victory: we did not get a set of rules to address subsidies and competition that would have allowed an exemption from US trade remedy. That proved to be a "bridge too far" for the negotiations. Nevertheless, I doubt whether Canada would have been prepared to pay the political and economic price for a total exemption. It would have required, among other things, a common subsidy regime, one that would have imposed more onerous restrictions on Canada than on the United States, especially given our disproportionate dependence on trade. The Americans have rarely complained about the "threat" of Canadian trade remedies. In the end, we paid very little for what we obtained. But even so, we obtained, both symbolically and substantively, a greater degree of certainty than we had before. That for me was the litmus test of success for the agreement as a whole.

The Free Trade Agreement triggered substantial increases in bilateral trade, but the largest increases in Canadian exports came from value-added products. The agreement was subsequently expanded into NAFTA, and aspects of its general dispute settlement provisions were eventually emulated in the WTO agreement. All of this demonstrates convincingly just how valuable the initiative was. The political capital and risk was substantial, especially for Canada's prime minister. I believe that the positive results for the Canadian economy will stand as his strongest legacy.

My back-to-back assignments in the PMO and as ambassador in Washington were certainly the high points of my career and were as exhilarating for me personally as they were demanding. Simply by surviving as chief of staff in the PMO and concluding a major bilateral negotiation, I realized that it would be possible to tackle something beyond the foreign service. I went to Washington with that very much in mind. I was tempted, briefly, to consider a more overt political career somewhat in the manner that took Mike Pearson and Mitchell Sharp into politics after years of senior public service. Like Pearson and Sharp, I was deficient in French – my second language being Japanese – but it was more of a handicap in the 1990s than in the 1960s. It also provided a good excuse at the time.

Instead, I joined Bell Canada Enterprises in January 1993 as executive vice-president (international) and soon became chairman and chief executive officer of its international investment arm, Bell Canada International. When I explained to BCE's chairman, Red Wilson, who had recruited me, that I knew very little about either telecommunications or investment, for that matter, his answer was reassuring: "We have twenty thousand engineers at Bell who know more about telecommunications than you and I will ever know. And we have financial expertise as well. I want you to exercise judgment, based on your global experience, about where we should invest, with whom and why." That is precisely what I did until, under new leadership, BCE changed course and decided to divest itself of its international assets.

Once again, I was recruited by Red Wilson to serve as chief executive officer of CAE in the fall of 1999. I knew the company to be one of Canada's major exporters but very little about its core business. Here the challenge was different. The board wanted a change in strategy. CAE was essentially a holding company, a mini BCE, with a highly diversified range of industrial lines of production over and above its core flight-simulation business. After an extensive period of primarily internal consultation, we decided to focus solely on our core technologies (simulation and control systems) but add training solutions to each business to provide greater balance in times of cyclical downturns for equipment and eventually to generate greater value. Despite the ravages of the commercial aerospace market following 11 September 2001, that strategy has taken hold and CAE has been transformed.

With each private sector assignment, I faced a huge challenge. I was moving from a position where knowledge was my strength to one where knowledge was clearly my weakness. In the government, especially my final decade, my views on a given subject or issue, based on years of hands-on experience, were what counted most. My task was to plan, analyze, and recommend. In the PMO, I also had the unique responsibility of implementing policies and decisions on behalf of the government.

In the private sector, I had to rely heavily on skills unrelated to knowledge. But the lessons and the experience of what had worked and what had not worked in government proved very relevant in business as well. The talents that proved most easily transferable were a direct approach to superiors, complemented by a demanding but motivational attitude toward subordinates;* a clear view of what is possible or attainable (otherwise described as focus); a strong sense of communications, for board presentations, messages to shareholders, and so on; analytical skills (an

---

* At my final annual meeting of CAE shareholders, CAE's chairman, Red Wilson, told the gathering that one of our employees had described me as "difficult to please but always inspiring."

ability to separate wheat from chaff); and finally the skill to choose good people and to challenge them to keep challenging their boss. (Those on whom I knew I could depend were given maximum scope for independent action.)

When I look back on thirty years of public service and eleven years in the private sector, what strikes me is the extent to which the whims of fate helped determine choices fundamental to both. Very little seems, in retrospect, to have been predetermined or carefully planned. If my family had not operated a taxi business, I might not have met my wife. If my name did not start with a "B," I might not have been selected to work in the office of our foreign minister. If the Malaysians had moved more quickly on my nomination, I would not have gone to Korea. If I had remained in the Economic Affairs Branch of External instead of the United States Branch in the early 1980s, I would undoubtedly not have been selected by the prime minister as his chief of staff or as ambassador to Washington. If I had not succeeded in these highly varied assignments, my career would undoubtedly have taken detours.

Whether it was the whims of fate or luck or being in the right place at the right time or talent, my External Affairs career gave me a life of tremendous challenge and stimulation. I was supported and inspired by a remarkable cadre of colleagues and by direct involvement at the most senior political level. If I had the choice again, I might have done some things differently or some different things. While I did my share of "moaning and groaning" along with others at External, I certainly have no reason for regret. No two foreign service careers are alike, but I would not trade mine for any other I know.

The values I learned at an early stage – of doing things to the best of my ability, that is, "getting it done" – inspired my effort and commitment to try to serve the best interests of Canada. Whether it was learning Japanese, organizing a G7 Summit, directing the Prime Minister's Office, negotiating a major trade agreement, or representing Canada in our key embassy, this was the driving force for the major moments of my career.

What is evident to me is that I had a career experience that would be possible in few countries other than Canada. Therefore the accident of my being Canadian is probably my most fortunate attribute of all. In most countries, the foreign service is drawn from the elite – families of wealth or prestige or both – while, in others, many diplomatic appointments are political. Canada is, in fact, one of the few where the system of recruitment is completely open and where selection, as well as assignments, is based primarily on merit. Only a very few ambassadorial positions are filled by political appointees. I also had the privilege of crossing over from the purely advisory role of a public servant to the high-adrenalin atmosphere of politics at the top. Taken together, it was a career that was as invigorating as it was rewarding

Index